D0093877

PASTORAL CARE EMERGENCIES

CREATIVE PASTORAL CARE AND COUNSELING SERIES
Howard W. Stone, Editor

BOOKS IN THE SERIES

CREATIVE PASTORAL CARE AND COUNSELING SERIES

PASTORAL CARE EMERGENCIES

DAVID K. SWITZER

FORTRESS PRESS   MINNEAPOLIS

PASTORAL CARE EMERGENCIES

Copyright © 2000 Augsburg Fortress. All rights reserved. Except for brief quotations in critical articles or reviews, no part of this book may be reproduced in any manner without prior written permission from the publisher. Write: Permissions, Augsburg Fortress, Box 1209, Minneapolis, MN 55440.

Scripture quotations from the Revised Standard Version of the Bible are copyright © 1946, 1952, and 1971 by the Division of Christian Education of the National Council of Churches of Christ in the United States of America and are used by permission.

Cover photo copyright © 2000 Tony Stone Images, Inc.

Library of Congress Cataloging-in-Publication Data

Switzer, David K.
    Pastoral care emergencies / David K. Switzer.
        p.   cm.—(Creative pastoral care and counseling series.)
    Includes bibliographical references.
    ISBN 0-8006-3228-1 (alk. paper)
    1. Pastoral counseling. 2. Pastoral medicine.
    BV4012.2.S94 2000
    253.7–dc21   00-27228
                                                    CIP

The paper used in this publication meets the minimum requirements of American National Standard for Information Sciences — Permanence of Paper for Printed Library Materials, ANSI Z329.48-1984.

Manufactured in the U.S.A.   AF 1-3228

CONTENTS

EDITOR'S FOREWORD TO *PASTORAL CARE EMERGENCIES*

I probably experienced more than half of the urgent situations described in *Pastoral Care Emergencies* before I graduated from seminary. Serving part-time in the parish during those years, I faced incest victims, abusive families, the dying and bereaved, as well as teen pregnancy, psychiatric hospitalization, divorce, and more. I wish someone had handed me this book at that time.

Pastoral care is a critical part of ministry that has taken the back seat, of late, as writers have focused on pastoral counseling or pastoral theology. In *Pastoral Care Emergencies*, David Switzer brings it to the fore. He covers a great many of the difficult problems that parish pastors and pastoral care specialists come across in their day-to-day ministry. The book opens with a theological description of the act of caring, which Switzer holds is both an *attitude* and an *act*. This offers a corrective to many recent works that only emphasize the attitude of pastoral care and do not address how that attitude can become action.

Switzer not only discusses what constitutes caring and how pastors and laypersons go about doing it; he deals with a series of specific emergencies that ministers commonly encounter. These include situational crises, care for the physically ill, hospital visitation, caring for the dying and bereaved, and suicide. He also covers a number of family pastoral care emergencies such as divorce, family violence, incest, and having a family member with a psychiatric disorder. He suggests very practical ways to offer pastoral care in these situations. The book concludes with a helpful section on referral in which he not only advises when to refer and how to go about it, but suggests specific referral sources.

I am confident that reading *Pastoral Care Emergencies* will strengthen and enrich your pastoral care, counseling, and general ministry. Switzer brings to his work the wisdom of some forty years of experience as a parish pastor and seminary professor. The scope and quality of the care you offer to others is certain to benefit from his knowledge and sound guidance.

Howard W. Stone

ACKNOWLEDGMENTS

Even though only one author's name appears on this book, it was definitely not a "Lone Ranger" accomplishment. I want to express my sincere appreciation to my good friend Howard Stone for his willingness to read the first edition of *Pastoral Care Emergencies* and for recommending it for publication in the series of which he is coeditor. I then received from him several pages of detailed recommendations for revision. These were extremely helpful and made a better book of it.

I am also grateful to Henry French, my editor at Fortress Press, for his reading of the book and his support for publication. He has been a delight for me to work with by telephone: patient, understanding, and flexible.

This edition would never have been possible, however, had it not been for the competence, commitment, and infinite patience of Ann Ralston, secretary to the faculty of Perkins School of Theology, Southern Methodist University. Her uncomplaining grappling with pages and fragments of pages that must often have seemed to be a constantly changing and never-ending puzzle has been an amazing accomplishment. Her eyes picked up my errors and incomprehensible sentences and have made this a more readable book.

Because the diskette of the original manuscript was no longer available, and because the publisher requires this, I want to thank Southern Methodist University for providing the support services for the scanning of the manuscript pages onto a diskette. I want to thank the real human beings, Ian Aberle and Tony Cuevas, who were so pleasantly cooperative as well as efficient in getting this tedious task done.

Finally, my spouse, Theresa McConnell, pastoral counselor, social worker, and currently associate minister of a large church, has been a necessary support to me in what has been a pressure-packed several months, which included our moving from Dallas, Texas, to Shreveport, Louisiana. Our daughter, Rachel McConnell-Switzer, has been a constant reminder of what it is that's really important in life: our love for one another. My motivation in the work would have been difficult to sustain without this reminder.

INTRODUCTION
WHAT IS A PASTORAL EMERGENCY?

Being in a position of church leadership, by its very nature, is usually an open invitation to people in the congregation as well as to many people in the larger community. This invitation is to bring for discussion their hurts, pressures, crises, decisions, the great variety of difficult experiences which as human beings they so often need to share with someone they trust. Some persons in these leadership positions in the church are more invitational than others. Due to the ways in which they express openness, caring, trustworthiness, and competence in their other tasks and relationships, they are even more likely to be approached by persons in need.

In addition, regardless of the church position held (pastor, general associate, ordained staff with special areas of responsibility, unordained persons who might be working in Christian education, music, administration, secretarial services, and others), many of these persons in church leadership also have what might be called "subcongregations" of their own: the choir, members of boards and commissions for which they have administrative responsibility, the committee or commission on education, along with church school superintendents and teachers, members of the church school department or class, and various other groups of volunteers. In large congregations, such church leaders are usually closer to their particular constituency than a senior minister/pastor is. So when people within these subcongregations get sick, go to the hospital, are operated on, receive a dreaded diagnosis, die, have serious difficulties in their families, divorce, become shut-ins, it is natural for them or for members of their families to turn for help to that church staff person whom they know best and trust.

Given this broad responsibility and opportunity both to respond and to reach out to persons within the congregation and the community at large, this book is intended for all pastors, ordained and lay, of congregations and subcongregations, as well as for volunteer leaders within the church, such as church school superintendents, church school teachers, lay leaders in various positions of responsibility, and even for those who are not in such positions, yet who might desire to be more helpful to more persons as your expression of Christian service. The need is great.

However, a number of people may raise legitimate questions. "What do I have to offer anyone who's in critical circumstances of some kind? Might I not complicate the situation or make things worse?" We know that because of our personal or organizational relationship with a person or a family or because they've taken the initiative to talk with us, we ought to hear them out, make some response, visit them at home or in the hospital, but we're anxious about it. We're not sure what to say or do. We are aware that the emotional reactions are very strong, and we don't know where all this will take us. In order to provide practical assistance to those who have these very real concerns and who raise these legitimate questions, this book was written.

An initial response to the title of this book, *Pastoral Care Emergencies,* may well be, "Who defines whether a situation is an emergency?" As pastors and other professional church workers or lay leaders, there are two sources of the definition of "pastoral emergency": first, the person or persons in a particular situation, and second, we ourselves. For whom is a situation an emergency: for the other, or for us, or both?

Within months of my receiving my first appointment as a pastor after graduation from seminary (where, by the way, no course in pastoral care was even offered) the doorbell of the parsonage in my rural community rang early one morning. I was just barely up and dressed. I went to the door and there stood a young woman in her robe, her hair in curlers, weeping hysterically. I was immediately in an emergency situation. It was obvious that she needed help of some kind. But there was also no question that regardless of what she was going to tell me, I needed help, too.

She came in, sat down, and began to tell me through her sobs that right after she and her husband had gotten up that morning, he had told her that he was in love with another woman. She couldn't believe it. Reality as she understood it was falling apart, and her experience was that her own mind was going to pieces. She couldn't handle it.

We *both* defined it as an emergency.

On the one hand, there are those occasions when the other person doesn't seem to be aware of any emergency at all, but the pastor is. When I was Minister of Pastoral Care and Counseling in a large congregation, a man made an appointment to see me. Although he wasn't a member of our church, he was dating a woman who was quite active in the congregation and therefore I'd had the opportunity to see him on a number of occasions. We'd spoken to each other, and he seemed pleasant enough. I thought he had probably made the appointment to discuss wedding plans. I was wrong! (Never assume that you know the reason that a person wants to talk with you.) Be ready for anything.

He began by describing a number of concerns which he had, and then he moved to one in particular, which, while legitimate, he began to speak about with some force. I began to be uneasy with his intensity and rising anger as he talked about resistance in the state government to take the action he desired. Adding to my anxiety was the fact that I frankly didn't see any relationship between the government and what he was talking about. He then began to discuss an elaborate plan to force the government to act, and my anxiety level went even higher. By now I had an idea of what was coming, and I didn't like it at all. This time I was correct. He wanted to enlist me in his crusade. I now also knew the sort of person with whom I was dealing.

I sought to deflect him from his request of me, while expressing, hopefully empathetically and I know desperately, my appreciation of his concern and my understanding of his commitment and deep feeling about it. In this case, empathy wasn't enough. He became very hostile about what he perceived (correctly, I'm sure) my refusal to help him.

My own feelings were made much more intense by the fact that he was slightly above average in height and extremely muscular. Even worse, I had a very peculiar office arrangement, which I have never had again since that time. It was long and narrow, my back to the far wall, the desk in front of me, and then two chairs for visitors between my desk and the door. No escape!

I'll never know what took place in the next half hour or so of conversation that led his overt anger to decrease somewhat and his finally making the decision to leave. This was truly *my* emergency, whether my visitor experienced it as such or not.

Technically, an emergency is any situation in which something arises unexpectedly and which needs immediate attention. In our common usage of the word, we also tend to add to that meaning the intensity of feelings that are experienced by the person who is involved. Usually if another person is experiencing a truly critical situation or is facing a crisis, and communicates to us that which from her or his standpoint is an emergency, we're probably going to judge it as something of an emergency for ourselves also. This is not always the case, but whether *we* judge the other's situation to be an emergency, if that person does, then we certainly need to be sure to take the person seriously and to be immediately responsive.

The task of determining what to include in a book on pastoral emergencies is a formidable one. I immediately identified a number of them in my past and present ministry, but I also thought that it might be useful to make an informal survey to see what others might say. The survey made no attempt to select a population that would be adequately representative of all clergy and other church workers. However, it did include a substantial number of persons: black and white, male and female, most ordained but a few not, a range of education from seminary graduates to a few who had not even completed high school, years of experience to those relatively new to the ministry. The questionnaire asked them to make two lists, one in order of frequency and the other in order of intensity of what they judged to be pastoral emergencies in their ministry. For the most part, there were no surprises.

The cluster of items around death (dying, suicide, life-threatening illness, accidents and operations, and bereavement) were at the top of the lists in both frequency and intensity. Related to this cluster and over-lapping it were all hospital emergencies.

The group of situations rated second in both frequency and inten-sity had to do with marriage and family conflict, parent-child relation-ships, and divorce. Third in line was the visitation of the physically ill (excluding the terminally ill, which was in the first cluster) and of those facing and recovering from surgery in the hospital. Next in order was the working with persons who are alcoholic or who are abusing other drugs, and with members of their families.

Many other situations were referred to. Once again I was impressed with the deep involvement in every possible aspect of human life on the part of clergy and other church workers. Increasingly the church is hav-ing to respond to those persons who have just lost jobs or farms or busi-nesses, the longtime unemployed, the financial problems of persons and families and even whole communities where there is unemployment, persons and families who are evicted from their homes, the poor and the hungry. Church workers minister to the elderly, shut-ins, families where a person is being taken to a nursing home. Various types of physical abuse are coming more and more to the attention of representatives of the church, including rape and other types of physical assault inside of and outside of the family. Some pastors spoke of the need to follow up these persons for a long period of time after the particular event.

Also included as pastoral emergencies were conflict and hurt feel-ings among members of the congregation, something which all church staff members face and have some responsibility for. Many of these situ-ations have the potential for real explosions and damage, but there also are significant opportunities for growth within the Christian life of indi-viduals and of the congregation itself.

All of these areas of human conflict, distress, and extremity warrant examination. It's obvious, however, that they can't all be dealt with in a brief introductory book. The most useful approach seems to me to look first at our Christian motivation for caring, what caring really involves, and ourselves as persons who care. Second, it's critical that we try to get clearly in mind precisely how we are to listen and then to respond to people with words, regardless of the situation in which they find them-selves. In other words, what are the minimum absolutely fundamental ingredients of the most facilitative responses we can make? Third, the most frequent and emotionally stressful situations in which we'll probably be called upon to engage ourselves with persons, those situations which for the most part were named by the people in the survey, will be considered in some detail.

Since we all know that there are certain sorts of persons for whom we can't possibly be the primary helper and certain kinds of situations which are too complex for us to be able to deal with alone, it's important that we be able to identify these and know something about how to direct these persons to someone else who is better trained and/or has more time than we. Finally, a brief and selective set of readings covering a number of these other topics will be given so you may pursue those that seem most relevant to you in your situation.

1

WHAT DOES IT MEAN
TO SAY THAT WE CARE?

Regardless of the precise way in which we conceptualize and talk about our motivation for entering and continuing in our ministry in the church, how much emphasis we place on God's initiative and our response to God's call, whether we phrase the central direction of what we are doing in terms of serving God, almost all of us are also quite aware of our sincere desire to be helpful to persons.

There are two sets of questions to raise in response to this declaration, however. The first of these is, "How is it that our response to God is also understood as a commitment to serving persons? How do we see ourselves as Christian helpers, and why? Why *do* we care?"

A second response to our statement concerning our desire to be helpful to persons ought to lead us to sit up and take notice. There is a set of questions that we must answer as honestly as we can. "We *want* to be helpful, but are we really? To what extent? How much? To what percentage of people with whom we come in contact? To the extent that we are, what are the ingredients of our helpfulness? In instances when we are not helpful, why not? What is it that we need in order to be most helpful to the greatest number of people the largest percentage of the time?"

In the next chapter, we'll be discussing a concept and an approach to a caring ministry which deals with this second set of questions. This chapter, however, will attempt to address the issue of how it is that our response to God is also understood as a commitment to serving persons. Why do Christians care? What does it mean to say that we care?

GOD'S COVENANT OF CARING

My first response to the question of why we care is quite commonplace, even self-evident.

It all begins with the total history of the coming into being of the Jewish people and their covenant with God, God's initiative in promising to make of them a great nation and their promise to be God's people, to be obedient to God. This covenant was reflected in their cohesiveness as a people, their group commitment, their sense of relation to one another. This in turn was demonstrated in their worship of God, the dramatic acts celebrating both their covenant with God and their relationship with one another. The covenant was also the source of their moral laws, principles governing their behavior toward one another. Gradually, God's reality broke into their awareness that God was One and that the One God was the Lord of all people, not just of the Jews themselves. However, as we all know, the Old Testament is not just an account of their loyalty to God, but it also contains the many descriptions of occasions of their breaking the covenant by their disobedience.

At a time when, as a result of their being conquered by another nation and their own nation ceasing to exist as a viable political unit in 586 B.C., one prophet, whose writings we find in Isaiah 40–55, presented the picture of a small group of Jews who would remain loyal to God in the midst of their defeat, their exile, their trials, their suffering. Those who remained faithful to their covenant with God even at this time were conceived of as being God's suffering servant in restoring the relationship between God and the rest of God's people. It was their faithfulness that God would use in bringing them into being once again as a whole people. This vivid and moving description of the suffering servant was not the only way in which the Jewish people came to conceive of God's future dramatic acts in history to restore them as a people through a specially chosen agent, God's Messiah, nor was it necessarily the most predominant one, but it was there as a part of their tradition, their faith.

Into this people and this faith Jesus was born. The New Testament writers make it clear that Jesus was remembered as one who sought and did the will of God. His obedience led him to the proclamation of the coming kingdom of God, what many scholars think to be the unifying theme of Jesus' whole life. His obedience to God and his looking to the coming kingdom led him to a series of very concrete acts which ministered to the physical, emotional, and spiritual needs of persons while he was also developing around him a community of faith.

The early Christian church, those of Jesus' own generation and the generation to follow, were also a community of faith, faith in the same God that the Jews had known. Now, however, they were unable to conceive of God and God's activity, God's will and purpose, apart from the life and ministry of Jesus. If we think of the word *Christ*, the anointed one, as meaning the person who performs the acts of God in the midst of human events, and Jesus as being the one who performs this function of God in human history in a definitive, decisive, and irreplaceable way, then the word *incarnation* takes on a clearer meaning. It's operationally defined.

Jesus, in obedience to the will of God, was the ministering servant of God, the physical body, the activity of Christ. After Jesus' death, the disciples were brought back into community by their experience of the continued life of Christ in their midst, that is, their memory of Jesus and the immediate presence of the Holy Spirit as one inseparable experience.

They came to be known as the church, and they understood their existence in the world as directed toward performing the same function as Jesus himself. That is, in a literal sense, they, the church, also became the physical body of Christ. Their purpose in being as a community was to seek and do the will of God, in their quality of life with one another in the world revealing the loving, suffering, redeeming God to the world. They proclaimed and began to act out the life of the coming kingdom of God. This function has clearly been shown in the ministry of Jesus as he had revealed God, indeed, had brought or conveyed to God by persons by his accepting the role of suffering servant, meeting the needs of the total person, existing on behalf of persons.

Without a doubt, the early church saw the healing of human ills as being a primary emphasis within their total reason for being since they depicted Jesus' servanthood so frequently in these terms. While the healing of persons was portrayed very clearly in all the gospels, it is done very dramatically in Mark, where in chapters 1–10 only chapter 4 has no reference to healing. In others there are a variety of pictures: several detailed descriptions of particular persons being healed, or general statements such as, "And he healed many persons." Sometimes it would be the other person's initiative to which Jesus responded. On other occasions it would be his initiative in turning aside from other activities to meet an immediate need which he perceived. He used different words and actions. Different types of disorders were healed. The personal ministry to individuals in a variety of kinds of distress, not only healing, but responding to those in grief, forgiving those who seemed to be caught in a trap of self-depreciating and self-negating behavior: all of this must have been clearly understood by the early church as being in harmony with and supportive of the proclamation of the kingdom of God and a part of the caring for one another that was to be characteristic of the life of the kingdom.

The words of Isaiah, which were used as Jesus' initiatory declaration at the beginning of his public ministry as reported in Luke 4:16-21, seem then to be central to the *church*'s self-understanding and its acting out of its faith:

> The Spirit of the Lord is upon me, because he has anointed me to preach good news to the poor. He has sent me to proclaim release to the captives and recovering of sight to the blind, to set at liberty those who are oppressed, to proclaim the acceptable year of the Lord.

This is the way in which Jesus understood his mission in obedience to God. This is God's purpose for the church. This mission is literally who we are. It's our reason for being.

What all of this is saying, then, is that inherent in the coming into being of the church is its concern for persons, for the alleviation of their sufferings, for their health and wholeness, and we today as the church of Jesus Christ are called upon to perform our ministry in these areas with the same dedication and vigor, and we are called upon to do it with competence. What we refer to as pastoral care in the church, our concrete acts of caring for one another, is one important way of acting out the ministry of Jesus in obedience to God and the world today, a way of giving our lives for one another, of being servants. This is why we care. The church is by definition, as a result of God's initiative in caring for us, the caring community.

WHAT DOES IT MEAN TO CARE?

To this point we have discussed our motivation and our purpose in caring as they are drawn from our faith. But what does it mean to care? In some of the groups I often found myself in, the word is used frequently. For example, I asked students at the beginning of many courses to list their three major strengths which they see as contributing to what they say they want to do as ministers. Almost all of them say as a way of communicating one of their strengths, "I'm a caring person," or "I genuinely care about people." Unfortunately, though, the caring to which they're referring has usually been difficult for many of these people to define or describe in any clear-cut concrete way when asked to do so. It seems as if it's just a sense that we have of ourselves or a feeling of ours, something that we can just exude, with the faith that this is supposed to carry some mysterious powers in helping others.

What is caring, anyway? It's obviously not just a Christian word. One person who has sought to elaborate a definition of human caring and its meaning for human life from a purely secular point of view is Mayeroff (1971). By secular, I mean that he makes no reference to any religious experience or religious writings whatsoever. What he does do is to analyze basic human experience itself. The result of that analysis seems to me to be entirely applicable to pastoral care, as well as to other forms of caring within and by the community of faith, how we conduct ourselves in all our relationships with one another, in our preaching, educational practices, business and program planning meetings, what activities we choose to carry out in the church and community and how we go about executing these.

Mayeroff states:

> To care for another person, in the most significant sense, is to help (that person) grow and actualize himself [or herself]. . . . [It] is the

antithesis of simply using the other person to satisfy one's own needs. The meaning of caring ... is not to be confused with such meanings as wishing (another person) well, liking, ... or simply having an interest in what happens to another. Also, it is not an isolated feeling or a momentary relationship, nor is it simply a matter of wanting to care for some person. Caring, as helping another grow and actualize himself [or herself], is a process, a way of relating to someone that involves development. ... (P. 1)

As I understand this definition as he elaborates it in more detail, Mayeroff is saying that caring is both a persistent *attitude* toward persons and concrete *acts*. Caring and being cared for are essential for truly *human* life in the world, and our own caring for others has the impact of helping us find our place in the world's scheme of things. Caring is both an organizing and a unifying force in the life of the person who is caring, thus a contribution to the growth and actualization of the one who cares as well as to that of the one being cared for.

In order to care for another in these terms, he says, we experience the other

as an extension of myself and at the same time as something [Shouldn't he have said *someone?*] separate from me that I respect in [her or his] own right. ... Instead of trying to dominate and possess the other, I want [him or her] to grow in [his or her] own right, or ... to be [himself or herself], and I feel the other's growth as bound up with my own sense of well-being. (Pp. 3–4).

Mayeroff states the fundamental principle of caring quite clearly, and this is something which I believe that we need to take *very* seriously and use as a test of our own words and behavior as Christians as we respond to the needs of others.

In helping the other to grow I do not impose my own direction; rather, I allow the direction of the other's growth to guide what I do, to help determine how I am to respond and what is relevant to such response. I appreciate the other as independent in [his or her] own right with needs that are to be respected. ... (P. 5)

There are several things to note about such a statement which I hold to be absolutely essential for caring, and which, as a Christian reading the documents of the early church, I understand to be Jesus' attitude and behavior toward people. To respect the other person's unique needs, that particular individual's potential, and to allow and encourage the other person's freedom in decision making does not imply that we are value-less ourselves, or that we should pretend to be, or that we must never share our values and convictions and experiences and faith with another. In fact, it's absolutely essential that we never lose touch with who it is that we genuinely are as Christian persons as we engage with another in caring for that person. But as a result of valuing *our* values, being aware of needing to have *our* needs met, cherishing and exercising *our* freedom, true caring must mean encouraging the growth of just such experiences in the other.

Preaching and worship, Christian education, evangelism, other programming in the church, our involvement with others in pastoral situations, regardless of the differing forms and specific purposes, are all essentially witnessing, the sharing of experience in an attitude and with acts of love. It is a contradiction in intent and goals if we are coercive or manipulative. Therefore, to seek to impose our own goals, purposes, values, programs, faith, to manipulate or to coerce, however subtly and smoothly, is a failure to trust the basic process of human development within relationships, and, more importantly, the failure to trust the power of the Holy Spirit in human life. We cannot trick people or lead people by the nose into personal growth and change, into significant decisions in their lives, into growth in Christian faith, or into the kingdom itself. The *attempt* to do so is not Christian or even human caring.

After all, the process of caring itself as an attitude and relationship as well as concrete facilitating words and acts inevitably produces the greatest potential for the growth of the other person's capacity to care: to care properly for oneself and for persons and causes beyond oneself. No one ever grows without becoming freer, more self-determining, choosing his or her own values and ideals and commitments grounded in his or her own actual experience.

But it is important for us to be aware constantly that *we,* as those who are caring for the other, are a significant *part* of *that* person's experience, and our total set of experiences are a vital part of who we are. Therefore, sharing ourselves in an open and honest way with the other is an essential part of the process of caring. The effectiveness of such sharing is, of course, dependent upon sensitive timing and upon a form which does not seek to impose upon the other.

The Ingredients of Caring

Mayeroff lists several major ingredients of caring which flesh out the definition which he has so well begun (pp. 9–20).

In presenting these elements of caring I have made a change in the heading of one of his categories and the particular ordering of them, have summarized his points, making some modifications in his wording, and have added brief exegesis and exposition at some points.

1. Knowledge: an understanding of the other person's needs and the competence to respond constructively to them. Good intentions and loving feelings do not guarantee either understanding or competence.

2. The capacity for self-evaluation: the ability to look critically at our own behavior in relationship to the other person. Have we helped? If so, what was helpful? If not, what was missing in our response? This type of self-evaluation is absolutely necessary for our ability to maintain or to modify our behavior in order to be of the greatest help to the other.

3. Patience: staying with the person as she or he is enabled to grow at her or his own time and pace. This patience refers not only to time but also to space, whatever combination is necessary of being physically with the other, speaking or listening, sitting with the other and sharing in the silence, or of actually physically withdrawing in order to allow for the other person's process of assimilation of thoughts and feelings.

4. Trust: trust in the process, the relationship, the other person's possibilities (and for us as Christians —though Mayeroff makes no reference to it at all—trust in the power of the Holy Spirit). Trust also involves not overdoing for another, not overprotecting the other.

5. Honesty: seeing oneself and the other as we actually are and not as we would *like* to present ourselves or the other as we would like for that person to be. In the moment of helping, it is critical for us to be able to see both ourselves and the other only as we actually are, neither more nor less.

6. Humility: never allowing ourselves to think that we know all there is to know about the other person or ourselves or how to help in this particular instance, the recognition of our own limitations and our need to be alert and open to learning more about ourselves and the other.

7. Hope: in regard to what will happen to and for the other person as a result of our caring,

> hope is not an expression of the insufficiency of the present in comparison with the sufficiency of a hoped for future; it is rather an expression of the plenitude of the present, a present alive with a sense of the possible. . . . it is hope for the realization of the other through my caring. (P. 19)

8. Courage: a necessary prerequisite for the hope just described. There is a risk involved in investing ourselves as we do in caring for

another without knowing the outcome. We always lay down some part our lives for the other in the helping process. Courage is going into the unknown with another. We don't know what will happen to the other person, what he or she will decide to do, what he or she will become, not even what changes will occur to us ourselves.

These are some of the significant elements of human caring. They can be identified from a close and sensitive observation of our own experience and the experience of others. They can be noted and described completely without explicit reference to the Christian faith, although in the context of presenting Mayeroff's definition, I've made several such references. However, when we look at this concept of caring and we place it in the context of the previous brief review of the Scripture, we see that caring is *pastoral* when it is not merely one person's caring for another, as Mayeroff has described, but when such caring is *an expression of the whole life and purpose of the Christian community.* Just as Jesus' caring was intertwined with his proclamation of the kingdom of God and was a foretaste of the life of the kingdom, so is the caring of the community of faith today. Pastoral caring is defined by the whole event of Jesus' life, death, and resurrection, culminating in the coming into being of the church, with its mission understood in the words of Isaiah as recorded in Luke 4:18-19. Thus, a pastor is any person who is specifically designated by any means as being representative of the church. The person who is ordained is obviously set aside in a special way by the community of faith so that the person's vocation is to serve and represent the church on a full-time basis and to be the usual administrator of its sacraments. But, as has been pointed out earlier, nonordained professional church workers (deacons, diaconal ministers, certified directors of Christian education, music, etc.) also serve and represent the community of faith. In addition, other laypersons may, for longer or shorter periods of time, be asked to represent the church in particular types of services. The word *pastoral* is appropriate to them also when they are performing these designated functions.

Caring: *Agape* and Empathy

In order to complete (for the purposes of this book) a definition of *why* we care and what it means to care, I'd like to try to link the etymological origin of our present word *care* with *agape*, love, as we find it used in the New Testament, and also with *empathy*. According to the *Oxford Dictionary*, the word *care* comes from the Old Gothic word *kara*. As a noun it meant something like mental suffering, grief, a burdened state of mind, or a matter or object of concern. In its verb form, it meant to sorrow or grieve, to be troubled about. That seems to convey that caring is somehow to suffer or grieve with someone, to carry a burden for or along with the person, to be troubled alongside another.

The noun and verb forms of *agape* in its non-New Testament usage conveyed the meaning of love, kindness, generous or spontaneous goodness. Its New Testament usage came to mean primarily, though not exclusively, benevolence to one's neighbors, which was manifested in concrete actions. (Some scholars tell us that the word *philia* seems in a number of places in the New Testament to contain within it the meaning of *agape*—Furnish, 1972, pp. 134, 231.) *Agape* love means something like "action for the well-being of another, regardless of feeling or the nature of the relationship." In acting for the well-being of your neighbor or your enemy, you may not necessarily become friends or feel affection.

We see, therefore, that caring and *agape* love were not identical in their original root meanings, but for the Christian they are clearly linked, both scripturally and dynamically. John 21:15-17 portrays Jesus as asking Simon Peter three times, "Do you love me?" Peter responds each time, "Of course. You know that I love you." (In this interchange, both of the Greek words for love are used at different points.) Each time Jesus directs, "Then feed, or take care of, my sheep." The total message seems to be, "If you truly know my love for you, then you will love me, and then you will obey my commandments. You will love one another; you will feed my sheep." You will become literally a pastor, the word *pastor* meaning originally to feed and later expanded to mean take care of a flock. *Agape* and caring for God's people are inseparably connected in the New Testament.

Dynamically that which links caring and *agape* seems to be empathy. What does it mean to care? To care means that to some extent we see ourselves in another person. There is *no one* with whom we don't have some point of identification. It's not just, "There but for the grace of God go I," but usually much closer to the truth, "There go I!" This point of contact with another human being allows us the possibility of viewing the world, events, life from the perspective of that person. Without the capacity to understand another person and that person's world as if we were in some sense that person, without entering into the life and world of another, we can't truly care and act most effectively for that person's well-being. I certainly don't mean to imply that in entering into another's world and trying to view what goes on from that person's point of view we lose our own identity and perspective, nor do I mean that we somehow should be able to have the same reactions as the other person as we are taking her or his perspective. It does mean increased knowledge, understanding, genuine compassion, patience, trust, humility, hope, courage, as some of these were defined earlier. To be empathetic, to understand another person in this way, also offers some concrete guidelines as to how to respond most helpfully and competently with words to the other person and with other actions on behalf of the other. Caring as "suffering with" becomes *agape:* effective, concrete acts that assist the growth and actualization of the other.

Care, empathy, and *agape* love are like one another in two other ways. First, I've already pointed out that one of the goals of caring is that the other person experience an increase in his or her own ability to care. Empathy, too, as a characteristic of many human beings, is itself both a primary means and a major goal of particular forms of a helping process. Likewise, *agape,* an attitude toward others which expresses itself in concrete acts on their behalf, is a power which has the tendency to produce a like response in the other. "We love, because God first loved us" (I John 4:19).

Second, it isn't sufficient merely to *feel* caring or to *want* to care, to *be* empathetic, to *have* loving feelings or *wish* that we did. All of these require, in order to complete their definitions and to be effective in assisting the growth of another, their open expression in words and often in other acts, words and acts appropriate to the condition and situation of this particular person or group of persons at this particular time. The need of the helping person is not merely a certain attitude and certain feelings, but *competence in the behaviors of helping.*

So, pastoral care is the type of caring which we've defined as an expression of the life of the Christian community, or of a person or persons who are representative of the community, when it is acting out God's purpose in the life, death, and resurrection of Jesus in and for the world. Pastoral caring is one clear expression of *agape* love, the attitude toward others on our part which is representative of the "being-for-others" of God as God is known in Jesus Christ.

There is one final thing that this response to God's grace as we know it in Christ compels me to say at this point. I am quite aware that this book is intended to deal with our responses to people in situations of intense human need, pastoral emergencies. These pastoral responses are essential to the internal life of the church and to the church's witness to the world, our servanthood in the name of the suffering servant, but I definitely *do not* want to be misunderstood as affirming that pastoral care in emergency and other situations is the only, or even in many instances, the most important or appropriate form of the church's servanthood. Not at all! Pastoral care is not the only way in which healing is brought about. There are many sources of separation, many forms of alienation, many varieties of brokenness within the human family: between the church and the world, between nations and between races, between individual persons and within persons. There are many different forms and causes of suffering. There are literally huge multitudes of people in the world whose suffering and personal and social deprivation arise from the personal, social, political, and economic restrictions which are forced upon them by the structures of society, by the greed and fear of some of those in positions of wealth and power and privilege who wish to maintain their positions at any cost. There are large numbers of people who are pushed into an existence on the fringe of the mainstream of their society by those either in the majority or who as a minority control the power. Therefore *agape* love, caring as Christians, not only leads us to visit the sick and dying, minister to the bereaved, support the emotionally disturbed, help the alcoholic and abusers of other drugs, counsel persons and couples and families in distress, but also thrusts us into the midst of a variety of actions necessary to reduce the prejudice and discrimination and tendencies toward oppression *within* us and *around* us, even in the organization of our whole society and even of our church itself.

SUMMARY

This chapter has sought to clarify and to elaborate in detail the source of the church's motivation for trying to respond helpfully to persons and families and other groups in their extremities of life as well as on occasions of less pressing need. Those of us who are in places of designated leadership in the church may rather naturally as human beings seek out or respond to those persons in such situations. In addition, however, as Christians we're also:

1. being obedient in feeding Christ's lambs, being servants as Jesus was a servant, as God called him and calls us to be. Thus we're literally participating in the life of Christ himself as we suffer with those who suffer, weep with those who weep, rejoice with those who rejoice, sharing our time and energies and sensitivity and skills and faith;

2. making most possible the openness of the other person or persons to growth in faith, growing in faith ourselves in the process; and

3. contributing to the edifying, the building up of the body of Christ, equipping it for fuller and more effective service and witness to Christ in the world.

REFERENCES

Milton Mayeroff, *On Caring* (New York: Harper & Row, 1971).
Victor Paul Furnish, *The Love Command in the New Testament* (Nashville: Abingdon Press, 1972).

2

THE CARER AND THE CARING:
WHO ARE WE AND
HOW DO WE GO ABOUT IT?

In introducing the preceding chapter, we indicated that most of us working in positions of leadership in the church understand ourselves as genuinely wanting to be helpful to other persons. That chapter went on to examine our motivations from the point of view of the Bible, what it means to be the church, and then to define in more detail what it means to care for others.

Now we turn to a second set of questions which were raised in the introduction to that chapter. We want to be caring, to be helpful. But are we? Are there certain guidelines and procedures which can be shown to be more effective than others in talking with persons about their concerns and to have a higher probability of assisting them in their self-awareness, their awareness of the issues, and decision making? The answer, fortunately, is yes. We're not left entirely with "feelings of caring" and then "doing what comes naturally." Both the "feelings" and "what's natural" for us are quite unreliable guides for the relevant words and other behaviors which are most helpful in facilitating the emotional and spiritual growth of persons who are in various kinds of need.

Reactions of theological students and clergy and other staff persons and laypeople to this last statement run along a continuum. Toward one end are those who agree. They are the sincere but hesitant helpers. They have anxiety about visiting hospitals, talking with the dying, ministering to persons who have just experienced the death of someone close to them, counseling with a couple who are fighting with each other, continuing the conversation with someone who has just told them that he or she is a homosexual person. Their anxiety is explained by them very succinctly: "I wouldn't know what to say. I'm afraid I'll say the wrong thing." Their first statement is often quite accurate. There are numerous expressions, often with high emotional intensity, of people under duress (panic-stricken, furious, depressed, suicidal, etc.) which are difficult enough for a well-trained and experienced person to respond to in highly facilitative ways. All of us have found ourselves at a loss for words at times. Unfortunately, in our own anxiety in those moments, we may attempt to force something out in order to break the silence and take care of our own anxiety. Therefore, it's only by sheer coincidence that we come up with something which also speaks effectively to the needs of the other person right at this moment.

At the other end of the continuum are those who reply to the statement concerning the inadequacy of the "doing what comes naturally" as a primary guideline for our helping. "What's wrong with just being *me* in the situation? After all, I *do* care, and all I need to do is 'be there' for the other person. My caring will just naturally communicate itself to the other, and this in and of itself will carry healing power." A brief description of a course in "Pastoral Counseling" offered to clergy included the statement: "Much of what you do as a pastoral counselor you do 'right' *intuitively* [emphasis mine] because you love and care for the persons you are called upon to help."

Well, yes and no! The genuine caring is critical, of course. There's no substitute for it. Most people who care do communicate it in a number of ways to many people. There is something to "being there" with another. But when we consider ourselves as the human beings we are, products of our own families of origin, what we were taught was right and wrong, *how* we were taught these values, the losses we've experienced and how we've attempted to adapt to them, the power of our own emotional life, the hidden inner conflicts that we all have, and at the same time consider the variety of situations and issues and powerful conflicts and emotions which different types of people may discuss with us, what I, as the person *I* am, may then do *naturally* or *intuitively* may simply miss or even reject the most immediate pressing needs of the other person.

Remember that Christian caring is not the same thing as a *feeling*, nor is it *only* an attitude. It is also, and essentially, concrete action designed to meet a person's need. A story which Jesus told stated that when the Samaritan saw a man lying wounded by the side of the road, "he had compassion. . . ." But the story didn't stop there. It went on: "and *he went to him* and bound up his wounds . . ." (Luke 10:33). Christian caring means *acting* appropriately to meet the needs of the person, and doing so as competently as we can.

THE PERSONHOOD OF THE PASTOR

Our caring (attitude and *behavior*) is always limited by the nature and intensity of our own needs and our repressed feelings and conflicts. Therefore, the course description referred to above does helpfully go on to say, "You will need to understand yourself better if you are going to help the other person. . . ."

The unfortunate trap that we're all in is that until we ourselves are forced to reevaluate our own inner being, either by the pressure of being in a training program in pastoral care or counseling, or by some dissatisfaction with our lives that leads us into psychotherapy, or by some extremely traumatic event which shakes the very foundations of our being, most of us believe that we *do* understand ourselves quite well. I did for many years, years of "successful" ministry, doing a great deal of pastoral care and counseling, only to begin to discover bit by bit, slowly, to my own dismay and finally shock, that there were vast areas of my unconscious life that I had not known at all. These had been profoundly affecting many aspects of my behavior in a handicapping way.

Without some type of pressure or pain, most of us ordinarily are not too open to investigating our own inner life and questioning the meaning of our behavior sufficiently to grow significantly as persons ourselves and in the of quality our relationships. Therefore, we fail to improve the degree of our helpfulness to many people in different conditions and sets of circumstances. Yet because we know that we really do care (feeling and/or attitude), and because people seek us out to talk or because they respond to our initiative, we have a tendency to "trust our intuition." We believe that we're doing just fine in helping the other, when, in reality, very often we're not.

A woman came to see me when I was pastor on a large church staff. She regularly attended worship services. She began by talking about her intractable depression. Over several sessions a description of a number of her compulsive rituals began to unfold. These centered on the need for cleanliness and the avoidance of germs. Certainly by this time, perceptive readers will recognize that most pastors and laypeople would be in over their heads in seeking to be of significant help to this woman. (She was, by the way, seeing a physician and was taking anti-depressants.) I'd had some training in counseling by then and she and I had established a good working relationship in the sessions. She was talking more and more freely and I genuinely cared (feeling and attitude) for her, and I'm sure that she realized that. I knew that this was a very difficult condition to deal with and that I had limitations, but as it turned out, I just didn't know what they were. So we continued. But before too long (perhaps eight to ten sessions), things began to close down in our conversations. Nothing new was happening. After improving in some ways, there was no further change. I began to be frustrated, but sought to deny it. I consulted with a psychiatrist (proper procedure) and got some new insights into what might be going on in the woman (*not* in myself). A session or two later, we were sitting in painful silence. Her depression had increased. She had stopped talking. If I couldn't "mirror" what she had said, what could I do? I didn't know. Finally, she said, "There's no use in our going on. You're not doing anything to help me." I tried to respond to this. She got angry and told of her frustration. I tried to respond to that. She got up and walked out. She never came back.

Some of us are very clever in discovering some flaw in the other person which leads to their refusing help from us, not wanting to talk with us, or not "improving" when they do talk with us. At times we may be accurate in our discernment. But we must never overlook the possibility that we're not being caring *in a way that is effective*. I'm now very clear that in the instance of this woman, my own repressed feelings of anger, my "sense" that I was being empathetic when in fact I was not, and my lack of knowledge of what else even to try to do *beyond* empathy, combined, were *realistically* quite frustrating to her, angering and hindering her.

My extremely painful experience of my failing this woman sets our agenda both for this chapter and all of our future caring for persons. Let me illustrate this two-point agenda in my own revision of the "Pastoral Counseling" course description referred to a few paragraphs earlier.

If you love and care for the person you are called upon to help, *some* (note the change from "much") of what you do as a pastoral counselor you do "right" intuitively. However, your intuition can be educated and made more accurately perceptive by understanding yourself better, and your loving and caring can be made more effective by learning how to respond more helpfully in different types of situations with different people in a more consistent manner.

There are definitely some ways of responding to people in conversation that are much more facilitative than others. My experience has led me to the conclusion that most people's intuition does not automatically produce those responses. Our task, if we wish to care *effectively*, is to increase continually in two kinds of knowledge: knowledge of ourselves as human beings and knowledge of what to say and do in a variety of situations. Who we are as human beings who care for others affects significantly what we are open to learning about procedures of helping and our capacity to act on that knowledge. Our own total being, conscious and unconscious, and our knowledge of helping procedures are in constant interaction with one another, either limiting or supporting the other.

For example, even though the Samaritan "had compassion" and knew what the beaten man needed, and was aware that he was capable of doing it, if he had been the sort of person who faints at the sight of blood, his compassion and knowledge would have been useless. A lot of us can faint, so to speak, at the sight and sound of various kinds of emotional "blood."

It's a fact. Unconscious needs, feelings, and conflicts initiate, inhibit, and shape our behavior, including what we do and don't hear and our selection of words in response. To the extent that we can become increasingly aware of what's actually taking place inside of us and can recognize that our behavior is beginning to be particularly influenced by our inner drives, the more capable we become in relating to others in terms of *their* needs which they are now expressing to us rather than in behaviors (including words) which are subtly (and sometimes not so subtly) expressing *our own* needs.

In order to care in pastoral emergencies, we need to be able to stay with the person who is expressing very strong emotions without trying to take those feelings away from the person by denying them or minimizing them in any way. We need to be the type of person who can hang in there with someone who is extremely confused without attempting to impose upon her or him what we perceive to be *our* clarity. It's essential that we be able to allow, even assist, their experiencing of their feelings, whatever they are, their pain and anguish. Our helping task with persons requires that we facilitate their expressions of guilt and fear and anger at whatever level of intensity they have them.

If we need always to feel safe and secure and clear, then it's very natural and easy for us to impose our set of defenses against anxiety and insecurity and confusion on the other.

If we're afraid of our own anger or that of other persons, we'll tend not to hear many of the other person's angry statements, or we'll diminish the intensity of their anger by the way we respond, or we'll change the subject.

If we feel uncomfortable with certain aspects of our own sexuality, we may feel very anxious and repelled when someone is discussing her or his sexual difficulties or become unbelievably self-conscious, flustered, and tongue-tied if a person expresses his or her sexual attraction to us.

If our needs in a particular troublesome area are sufficiently strong and we are attempting to facilitate the other's exploration and/or decision making in the same or a similar area, then we are in a position of possible hurt to ourselves as well as to the other. If our need to be needed is greater than our motivation to care for another, then we will find ourselves in the unfortunate situation in which we as designated helpers are actually manipulating, albeit unconsciously, the other person for our own presumed benefit. Again, we both may be hurt.

We could go on in even more detail, but you've gotten the point. Another important part of this issue is, of course, that we can't wait until we're "perfectly" adjusted, "perfectly" emotionally healthy, "totally" insightful concerning our own inner being (whatever any of these would look like were they even possible) before we are called upon to respond to a person in need or before we take the initiative to go to that person with our genuine caring and with the intent and even the capacity to be helpful. At the moment, we can engage ourselves only as the persons we are. We shall be helpful to many as we learn how to offer ourselves more effectively; we shall hopefully learn from our successes and failures; and we shall also hopefully learn to withdraw from some situations, putting the person in need in touch with other helpers. We can then seek out help for ourselves when we realize that something in our own personal life has interfered with our caring effectively for this particular person in this particular instance.

HOW CAN WE BE HELPFUL?

The Facilitative Conditions of the Helping Relationship

So here we are, just before our next occasion of being a pastor to someone who is confused, hurt, despondent, afraid, suffering, facing a major decision. What is it that the other person needs? The experience of being understood, being valued as a human being by another person, an increasing ability to think clearly, receiving and being able to reflect upon the discrepancies in their lives in a corrective way, increasing intimacy in relationships, that is, the opportunity to share with another one's most personal thoughts and feelings, including those which are a part of this particular relationship, even those which we view as making us vulnerable.

We can probably recognize the value to ourselves of these elements of human life and relationship, those which are already a source of satisfaction and comfort and meaning and human competence to us and those which we would like to experience more fully. These elements of human experience also suggest an outline of conversations which we have with distressed persons and even guide much of what we say and don't say. These "facilitative conditions" of all helping relationships which depend primarily on our talking with one another are identified, substantiated by research, and systematically developed by Carkhuff (1969) and have been presented in detailed form in the context of an outline of the entire counseling procedure by Egan (1990) and others.

Empathy. The underlying power of such a helping process begins with and always involves our persistent attempt to understand what it is that the other person has just said about herself or himself and to check out with that person whether we've understood accurately and completely or not. It's very important that we not misunderstand this point. In the midst of conversation with a troubled person, we are not trying to understand the *whole* of that person at any one time or of that person's "problems," but merely the experiences, feelings and their intensity, thoughts, opinions, perceptions, interpretations of events, to the extent that these have just been expressed in the *immediately* preceding statement or statements. Obviously, fuller understanding comes only with the accumulation of many of these conversational exchanges, and usually with many conversations.

Neither is the purpose of the process to listen and to encourage talking on the part of other persons and to ask questions so that *we* may understand *them* and their situation so we may then tell them what the solution is. Rather, the purpose is to demonstrate our understanding of what they *just said* so consistently that *they* are empowered to look at themselves more accurately, more fully, more deeply, and begin to understand *themselves* in such a way that the issues before them become clearer, the alternatives for their thinking and acting may be more reliably chosen by them, and so that they experience being supported in these decisions by us.

Think of your own experiences when you've had a personal matter of great importance to you, perhaps something quite sensitive. You've finally decided to tell a family member or a close friend about it, but when you do, you get a blank stare or a response that doesn't seem to grasp at all what you've been sharing or how serious it is to you. It's extremely frustrating. It tends to close us off from further conversation.

For example:

> "My spouse and I just haven't been able to agree how to handle the situation with our sixteen-year-old daughter. She's driving us crazy with her sneaking out and meeting boys we don't even know. We know she drinks with them, and Lord knows what else is going on. I've been anxious and mad at her and not knowing what to do myself, and now she seems to be driving a wedge between my spouse and me. It's just awful."

> *Response #1:*
> "Oh, I wouldn't worry too much about it. You all have been good parents and your daughter will come around. A lot of kids go through this."

This illustration isn't just drawn out of thin air. It's happened. Imagine yourself in the position of the speaker: your daughter, whom you love and care for, your spouse with whom you've had a good life, and now it's all in turmoil. You're hurt, sometimes angry, terribly worried about your child and your relationship with your spouse, frustrated in your struggle to bring order into chaos and closeness instead of separation. It's not easy to tell someone about it. But you need help. Listen to yourself saying something like this, try to feel what it's like. And then the person with whom you are sharing your distress responds in the words of Response #1.

Now how do you feel? Do you want to go on and try to explore the situation and your feelings further and share them with this person? Probably not. You are even more frustrated. The respondent gives no sign of having heard what you are saying about the relationship between you and your spouse, about how distraught you are, what your specific feelings might be. You are not being understood.

Contrast that with the following:

Response #2
"You are really anxious about your daughter and don't know what to do to change the situation. But you're also terribly concerned about what's happening to the relationship between you and your spouse.

Now on the printed page this response may seem to lack spontaneity and feeling and power. It's what many ministers have reacted to in our workshops by calling it "too clinical," by which they mean impersonal, a cool, detached observer "parroting" words. They would rather do just what comes naturally to caring persons like themselves. They want to give the person some assurance that things are not as bad as they seem, to comfort, to support, to give a person some hope, to help a person have faith. But when I ask them, "How? *How* do you *give* someone hope? *How* do you comfort or support them? *How* do you stimulate another's faith?" they either can't say or they come out with words more or less like response #1, or they just don't say anything and wait for the distressed person to say something else, or give some kind of direct advice as to how to handle the situation or ask a series of questions to "get" more information. While there are times for explicit words of reassurance, prayer, nodding in silence, asking an informational question, or suggesting for one's consideration some course of action (not the same thing as advice), the prior need of a person, chronologically and in terms of importance, is always to be understood.

Certainly the words of response #2 are not the only helpful ones. They're not necessarily the best ones to communicate an understanding of what this particular confused and hurt person is describing, but they *do* show understanding. In *being understood,* we *gain* understanding. We experience being comforted, having hope, moving into a condition and relationship where faith has the greatest possibility of being stimulated. We don't *give* faith, hope, assurance, and comfort to people. We can only seek to provide the condition within which the other person is most likely to experience one or more of them. This condition is best brought about when we understand accurately what the person has just expressed, state our understanding accurately in words (perhaps supported by non-verbal means which are natural to us). The other person grows in the experience of being increasingly understood, thus becoming more capable of looking at herself or himself in greater depth and detail, and is more likely to continue to share with the helping person.

The beginning point for understanding is listening. Of course! Everyone knows this. But we *don't* all do it all of the time, or even frequently. Truly to understand requires concentration that blocks out external distractions and any wandering of our own minds. A major internal interference with hearing accurately what another person is saying is our self-imposed pressure that we need to have something important to say. So after the first few words from the other, we begin planning our response rather than continuing to listen carefully to everything that is being said. Obviously, whatever we then answer, however "profound" it might be, is based on only a fragment, or several fragments, of what the other person was expressing and only by coincidence will contain the *core* of the *whole message*. Except for coincidence, our response is inaccurate, and the other person realizes that we don't really understand.

The person who coined the expression "active listening" had a point. It means much more than just using our ears. It's full participation of our whole being as the other person is speaking. It involves

1. Intense concentration on the words used and the connections of their meanings with one another;

2. *How* the words are spoken (tone of voice, volume, pauses and pace, tremors of the voice, etc.);

3. Observation of every aspect of the other person's nonverbal behavior (facial expression, reddening around the eyes or up the neck or flushing or whitening of the whole face, what the eyes and hands and legs and feet are doing, tears, posture, etc.) and whether these physical signs seem to be in keeping with what the person is saying or whether they don't seem to fit;

4. Being aware of feelings of ours which are apparently triggered by what the person is talking about or how the person is speaking (*our* anxiety, sadness, anger, guilt, sexual feelings, boredom, etc.), and whether this *present* experience of ours seems to *assist* our understanding of the other person's experience or whether it interferes;

5. Our conscious using of the accumulation of our own past experience to assist our interpretation of the possible meaning, what a particular feeling is like, how persons typically react in certain situations, but our always being aware that it's *our* experience and not *necessarily* what the other is referring to;

6. Being alert to what is not being said in a situation where we would expect a reference to a particular person, a feeling, an event, a particular behavior, etc.;

7. Our imaginative participation in whatever it is the person is describing about his or her inner life, a relationship, an event, attempting insofar as it is possible to *be* that person in that particular part of her or his experience;

8. Finally, putting all of these activities of ours together, seeking to identify the *core* of what the person is expressing at this time.

Now that is *active* listening! We are working extremely hard! It may even sound impossible: all of these activities within a few seconds, or a minute or so. And it *is* impossible if we mean that any human being consistently does this fully and "perfectly" as someone is speaking to us. However, I think we realize that all of us probably do all of these mental and emotional activities at one time or another, whether we are always conscious of them or not, and in any given conversation are in fact somewhat aware of several of them going on at once. Therefore, it seems reasonable that with an awareness that all of these functions are available to us and that they are extremely important, we can train ourselves to be more aware and disciplined in our use of them in our listening to others and seeking to understand them. In addition, there are available periodically in some places workshops and classes and training programs which can assist us in developing more acute awareness and discipline.

Yet even this isn't enough! The understanding which we develop of what the other person has just said helps that person not at all in terms of her or his further self-exploration or self-understanding if we don't *communicate* our understanding accurately to him or her. The power of growth for the other is not in our understanding, but in that person's experience of being understood! This requires that we respond frequently with our *words* of understanding.

A forty-six-year-old man has come in to see his minister. His movements are slower, his voice softer than usual. His face reveals a frown that doesn't change.

Parishioner: (head down, not looking at minister) I have just come from the doctor. I've got cancer . . . in the colon . . . bad! I am so afraid.

Pastor: It's really terrifying to hear those words from the doctor and realize that he's talking about you.

Parishioner: It's unreal. I couldn't believe it. I still don't . . . and yet I do. He was talking about me.

Pastor: It's really confusing, isn't it? The shock and unreality, and yet the fear continuing to break through.

Parishioner: You're right. I feel as though I am out of control, as if I'm going crazy.

Pastor: And the lack of control only adds to the fear.

Parishioner: Yes! I'm afraid of the pain I'm going to have. I'm afraid of dying. I don't want to die. I'm not ready.

Pastor: There seems to be so much of life left for you at your age and you dread being cut off from it, from your work, your family, your job. You dread everything connected with it.

Parishioner: Oh, God, what am I going to do?

(A moment of silence.)

Pastor: There's almost unbearable hurt right now, and fear.

Parishioner: Oh yes! (Deep silence) I'm so grateful I can talk to you about it.

This isn't the end of the conversation, of course, and so far, the minister hasn't said anything particularly profound in this conversation, but has been attentive and communicated his or her understanding of the person and, in a time of great distress, has contributed to the development of the relationship of trust which is so necessary in the helping process. Not only do we communicate in this way our *understanding* of a person, but at the same time we're clearly expressing our *value* of him or her.

Respect. The other person feels more and more like a worthwhile human being as a result of our investing ourselves in the relationship in this way, our obvious attention and energy as we persistently engage in the struggle to see that person's individual experience from her or his point of view. There is no rush to an "easy" or "magical" answer, no attempt to diminish the profound terror or to run away from the engagement at this level of emotional intensity. We truly *respect* a person in this process. The relatively consistent accurate expression of empathy conveys it powerfully to the person, assisting that person to value himself or herself more and more. The need of many persons is not that they not "think of [themselves] more *highly* than [they] ought to think" (Rom. 12:3) but that they not think of themselves more *lowly* than they ought to think. The valuing of the other person is an essential factor in the helping process.

Concreteness. Concreteness is a prerequisite of accurate empathy. The word refers to simplicity and clarity of speaking, asking questions about what expressions or words mean, what feeling or feelings a person is referring to, encouraging the giving of more detail, requesting illustrations. For example (concreteness, you see), we are talking with a person and we notice that the person's face begins to redden. We are aware that she or he is beginning to experience some feeling (unless the room is too hot or the person is beginning to have a fever). But we can't presume to know exactly *what* that feeling is, although often the particulars of our immediately preceding conversation may give some good clues.

If, for example, the person has been talking about an argument in the family and about how mad he or she had been, and then the person's face begins to flush, we might venture, "And you are feeling mad right now?" On the other hand, we could still be wrong. The person might respond, "Oh, not really so much. I'm just embarrassed about laying all of our family's dirty laundry out in front of you."

But if the context of the conversation has had even fewer clues, and the person pauses and the face begins to redden, we might very simply ask, "What are you feeling right now?"

"I am upset."

Is that the end of it? Do we know precisely what the other person is feeling? No, the word *upset* is a *general* or *vague* word. The person is communicating only that she or he is experiencing some feeling, which is what we had already noticed from the change of color in the face. Think of the ways we can be upset: fearful, angry, guilty, sad, embarrassed, etc. We don't yet know how to respond precisely with empathy. So we ask,

"Upset in what way?" or "What do you mean, upset?" or, merely, "Upset?"
"I feel like crying."

We are making some headway. But do we even yet know *absolutely* what the other person's feeling is? Many people feel like crying when they are sad, but they may do so when they feel hurt in other ways, some cry when they're angry, and so on. So we have to pursue the matter further.

"What's the particular feeling you are aware of?"
"I was just remembering when my father died."
(We are still not positive what feeling is being experienced.)
"Would you tell me what that's like for you?"
"I miss him so much."
(Finally):
"You are feeling very sad."

Some readers may think that this illustration is overdrawn. Of course, some people before they are asked will simply say, "I am so sad." Others, after they have said "Upset" when we've asked what they are feeling, and we ask, "Upset in what way?" will answer, "Real sad." But it's not at all unusual for a fairly large number of people to be unacquainted with the easy speaking in concrete and precise ways about their feelings. If we are having a conversation with such a person, it's our responsibility very patiently and persistently to encourage the person to identify and state the feeling in a way very similar to the illustration just used. We cannot communicate *empathy* in an accurate way unless we are sure or almost sure what the feeling is, what the experience is like, what the person is thinking. Often we have to ask, even track it down through several steps, as in the illustration, then express the empathy in our words.

Genuineness. Genuineness refers to the degree of awareness we have of our own feelings and motivations as these factors were discussed in the first section of this chapter. Both our accurate hearing of the other and the accuracy and clarity of our verbal responses are affected by the degree of our self-awareness. Attention and energy given to our own self-protection and cover-up, both conscious and unconscious, take our attention and energy away from the one whom we want to be helping in a time of distress.

Self-disclosure. It's also critical in the pastoral relationship for the other person to know us as the *human beings* we are and not just as the *position we hold:* minister, choir director, church school teacher, lay visitor, etc. In the growing relationship of trust, built on our relatively accurately communicated understanding and our commitment to the relationship, we become increasingly important to the person in need. So at an appropriate time in the relationship and in the particular context of our conversation, it can be very useful to the person to hear us share a feeling, an experience of confusion or pain, our perspective on the issue at hand, our convictions, our faith and its meaning to us. The necessary prior condition is our genuineness, as described earlier, our lack of defensiveness, and our willingness to be open, to be known as a person. It's also crucial that we grow in our ability to judge the other person's readiness to pay attention to us, really to hear, to assess what we share, to assimilate it in a way that may lead to greater insight or decision-making power, or to lay our offering aside if it does not seem to fit for him or her. It's also important for us to be careful in our choice of words, so that we don't seem (1) to be *unduly* calling attention to ourselves rather than continuing to be concerned about the other, (2) to be trying to coerce or manipulate the other into believing what we believe, or (3) to be forcing our advice on her or him.

Self-disclosure is always to be evaluated in the light of the other person's need and the person's readiness to respond in the ways just referred to, and not to be based on our need to disclose ourselves. Self-disclosure is usually most effectively done in a very brief sentence or two and then turned back to the other person.

> "You speak of missing your father a lot after his death. After my father died, I remember the strong urge I had almost daily to go to the phone

and tell him about something that I had experienced, and then suddenly realized I couldn't do that. It was terribly painful."

Such a statement has the impact of strengthening the emotional
closeness of the present relationship between us and the other, contributing to the developing intimacy, of communicating a type of empathy, and of stimulating the person to go into more detail about his or her
experiences.

Confrontation. Yet another facilitative condition of the helping
relationship is the attentiveness of the helper to a variety of inconsistencies or discrepancies which the person may be expressing in words and
behavior. None of us are entirely consistent, nor will we ever be. Yet the
reduction of our inconsistencies is the desire of many of us and is a primary means of personal growth.

So the person engaged in pastoral care listens and looks for discrepancies. Then, at a well-timed point in the process, when the relationship
can stand the potential stress of it, when the other person already has
experienced being understood sufficiently so that he or she trusts the
carer, this helping person, usually using tentative language, points out his
or her perception of the discrepancy.

> "You've told me how concerned you are about the pain you've been
> having in your chest, how awful it is and how afraid you are, yet you
> continue to postpone going to the doctor."

> "You say that you are terribly guilty about having had an affair and that
> you really want to be faithful to your spouse, but also that you don't see
> how you can stop seeing the other person. I wonder if these don't seem
> to you to be in conflict."

Every confrontation, for that is what these responses are, is a type of
crisis for the person, a discrepancy between self-image and behavior, goals
and behavior, faith and behavior, our real feelings and how we would like
to present ourselves, our desire to be honest and our fear of being known.
Yet when this discrepancy becomes known to another, our pastor, for
example, we are anxious. We usually look for a way out. We may deny it all.
Yet the pointing up of our inconsistency has been based *only* upon what
we have actually said and done, and the pastor has merely heard and
observed it, put it together, and said it aloud right to our face. It is our
opportunity for repentance and growth. There is *no* growth without an
honest and courageous and open response to our many discrepancies.

Immediacy. The last of the designated facilitative conditions is
the clear invitation to intimacy itself, called immediacy by Carkhuff,
and divided into two forms by Egan: relationship immediacy and

here-and-now immediacy. Relationship immediacy means that the helping person, when it seems to be useful to the person in need, either initiates or responds openly and directly to the other person's initiating a discussion of the overall relationship between them and how it has developed. For example:

Pastor: I remember how terribly distressed you were when we first began to talk. You realized that you needed help in trying to work things out, yet it seemed so extremely difficult for you to get the details out. You weren't sure you could trust me.

Parishioner: That's really true. I was desperate. But I was so ashamed of what I had done. How could I ever tell you, my *pastor?* What would you think of me?

Pastor: But when you finally did say it, it seemed such a relief.

Parishioner: You'd better believe it! I was scared, and I felt guilty, but when you seemed to understand and helped me clarify things, I knew I could really trust you. That surely did feel good.

Pastor: It felt good to me, too. Actually, we were trusting each other, and we were able to work together so well. I appreciate you for that.

Here-and-now immediacy focuses on what is going on between the persons right at the very moment and what the meaning of it might be. For example:

Pastor: (Following a long silence) I am wondering if you are aware of what has been going on between us during the last few minutes.

Parishioner: What do you mean?

Pastor: Well, what was happening just before I said what I just did.

Parishioner: I don't know. Not much.

Pastor: In a way you're right. Neither one of us had said anything for a while. But are you aware of what was going on in you?

Parishioner: Oh, nothing. I just couldn't think of anything to say.

Pastor: I wonder what the reason for that is, since I think that there is a lot to talk about. What *had* we been talking about just before that?

Parishioner: (Pause) Well, I think that I'd been saying that I really did want to be a better husband and father. (Pause)

Pastor: And?

Parishioner: Oh, yes. Well, (long pause) I think you came down on me pretty hard.

Pastor: What did I say?

Parishioner: Something like that you believed me, but that you didn't see how we could work on it very well as long as I kept having the affair with Joan like I had been doing.

Pastor: And how did you feel when I said that?

Parishioner: (Pause) Put down . . . Disapproved of . . . Like you were going to stop seeing me.

Pastor: What feelings were you having?

Parishioner: Rejected, I guess . . . And a little irritated. I guess I felt like you were telling me how to run my life.

Pastor: You've told me how much you care about Joan and the times you all have together. It means a lot to you. Yet you've also told me that you want a better relationship with your wife and children. And I *do* believe that. But *my* experience is that you can't do both of those at the same time.

Parishioner: (Long pause) I guess I know that. I don't like it, though! . . . I don't know what to do.

Pastor: But in not liking what I said, you felt put down by me, disapproved of, rejected, and mad at me. And you couldn't think of anything to say.

This fragment of a conversation between a minister and a parishioner represents a rather difficult situation. And while the minister needed a certain amount of skill and disciplined persistence, it also took a minister who was a human being with a type of toughness: a commitment to the other person's well-being, the sensitivity to perceive what needed to be said, and the willingness and confidence in oneself and in the God who was in the midst of the process to say it, regardless of how the other person might feel or respond. This interchange illustrates how the minister's initiative to talk about what is going on right now in the midst of their relationship with one another in terms of the relationship itself is a contribution to the other person's capacity for intimacy, to say nothing of a type of action-oriented problem solving.

It should be very clear by now that the "how" of helping in pastoral emergencies as outlined by the facilitative conditions is not just a set of techniques, "skills," as they are often called, or "tools," as all too many people in classes and workshops I've led have unfortunately referred to them (even though I've made dire threats against them if they use such words). Rather, these are truly *conditions* contributed to the pastoral relationship out of the genuine *human being* of the caring person. The conditions reflect who the helping person is. Is valuing or respecting another human being a technique? Is our genuineness (self-awareness) a tool? Are a basic openness to another and the capacity for intimacy merely skills? By no means! We can't *do* them if we are *not* them.

This rather lengthy discussion of the responsibility of the pastoral carer to be this quality of person emphasizes the overarching importance of these facilitative conditions in *all* pastoral care. This does *not* mean, however, that all eight of them must be a part of *every* conversation we have with a person. Certainly our respect for persons is always necessary, as are empathy and concreteness and whatever degree of self-awareness is possible, but the other conditions may or may not be present in a *particular* conversation. It would be ludicrous and even counterproductive if we were to try to drag all of them into every encounter in an artificial way.

Nevertheless, our awareness of the necessity of these facilitative conditions in the helping relationship, our alertness in introducing them at appropriate times, and, to be sure, some amount of verbal skill are all prerequisites for the improvement of our capacity to be useful to persons in time of their intense need.

The Means of Grace

The means of grace are not tools either, yet they are very much a part of the helping process in pastoral emergencies. Some means of grace are more formalized in the life of the church: participation in congregational worship, prayer and devotional activities, reading the Bible and listening to its being read, the designated sacraments. Yet we realize that these don't bind and limit God. God offers divine grace at all times, in *all* situations of human life.

For example, a pastoral relationship based on the facilitative conditions that have just been discussed, producing a relationship of increasing trust, in which insight is stimulated and decisions for the well-being of the person or persons have the greatest possibility of being made, is very much a means of God's grace.

But in responding to pastoral emergencies, the relationship process can be empowered by our willingness and ability to speak in the language of faith, within the relationship to pray sensitively and meaningfully and to read the Bible with persons, to discuss intelligently (not merely to tell someone) the meaning of certain passages of the Scripture, to administer the appropriate sacraments.

More will be said about various ones of these symbols and activities in the context of discussing particular pastoral emergencies, but it needs to be emphasized here that although any of the means of grace most appropriate to pastoral emergencies (discussion of faith and moral issues and the meaning of the Bible, prayer, reading the Bible, the administration of the sacraments) may carry their own power apart from a well-established relationship of trust between the representative of the community of faith and the person in need, their even greater power seems to be evident when they are a part of a developing relationship.

The pastoral helper must be especially careful that she or he does not use the formalized means of grace as a *substitute* for relationship, for conversation which can lead to the development of the relationship, as a way of avoiding threatening and difficult topics, of protecting oneself against the vulnerability of intimacy.

CONCLUSION

The quality of the person who represents Christ and the congregation in times of crisis and distress, the ability of that person to provide the facilitative conditions of all meaningful relationships, the willingness and competence of the person in offering the means of grace, all combine to provide to those in human situations of emergency the greatest possibility of transformation and growth.

REFERENCES

Robert Carkhuff, *Helping and Human Relations* (2 vols.) (New York: Holt, Rinehart and Winston, 1969).

Gerard Egan, *The Skilled Helper* (4th ed.) (Monterrey, Calif.: Brooks/Cole, 1990).

RECOMMENDED READING

The Personhood of the Pastor

Herbert Anderson, *The Family and Pastoral Care* (Philadelphia: Fortress Press, 1984), chapter 8, "The Helper's Own Family of Origin."

Carrie Dearing, *Taking Care: Monitoring Power Dynamics and Relational Boundaries in Pastoral Care and Counseling* (Nashville: Abingdon Press, 1995).

Barry K. Estadt, Melvin C. Blanchett, and John R. Compton, eds., *Pastoral Counseling* (Englewood Cliffs, N.J.: Prentice Hall, 1991). Barry K. Estadt, "Profile of a Pastoral Counselor."

John Patton, *Pastoral Care in Context: An Introduction to Pastoral Care* (Louisville: Westminster/John Knox, 1993), Part Two: "The Carer As Person, Learner, and Teacher."

Karl A. Schultz, *The Art and Vocation of Caring for People with Pain* (Mahwah, N.J.: Paulist Press, 1993), pp. 5–8, 51–60.

David K. Switzer, *Pastor, Preacher, Person* (Nashville: Abingdon Press, 1979), chapter 1, "The Minister: Person, Pastor, Professional."

The Means of Grace

William E. Hulme, *Pastoral Care and Counseling* (Minneapolis: Augsburg Publishing House, 1981), chapters 5–7.

Wayne E. Oates, *The Bible in Pastoral Care* (Philadelphia: Westminster Press, 1953).

William B. Oglesby, *Biblical Themes for Pastoral Care* (Nashville: Abingdon Press, 1980).

David K. Switzer, *Pastor, Preacher, Person* (Nashville: Abingdon Press, 1979), chapter 5, "The Word in Scripture and Relationship: The Use of the Bible in Pastoral Care."

3

RESPONDING TO PERSONS' NEEDS IN SITUATIONAL CRISES

One important thing to note about both the *most* common of the pastoral emergencies and many other situations which the clergy in the survey referred to as emergencies but which they encountered with much less frequency is that practically all of them are what may be classified as situational crises.

The ministers reported that they were called when

A family was evicted from their home;
A home was broken into and the person assaulted;
Persons were victims of other crimes;
A family lost their farm;
A crop they were depending on to make debt payments failed;
A man was dismissed from a job because of the economic slump;
A woman left her husband;
A man was beating his wife;
A mother had physically abused her baby;
A thirteen-year-old daughter had run away;
A parishioner was arrested;
and many more.

WHAT IS A SITUATIONAL CRISIS?

In all of these instances, as with physical illness and accident and death, something happened. An event took place in a person's or a family's life which was experienced as a serious threat.

Beverly, a young married woman with two children, was also a graduate student, preparing herself for work to which she was quite committed. She was an excellent student, applied herself diligently, and, in a sense, was proving herself to herself and others through her achievement. Before she had enrolled in graduate school, she and her husband had talked over her plans and had agreed that she should pursue them. This couple was active in a church.

One morning, about 9 o'clock, the minister's phone rang. He picked it up, and heard Beverly's voice trying to say something through her crying. It was something about not being able to finish her paper for a course and not being able to take a final exam, having cut her hand, going to the doctor. There were clues as to what was happening but at this point it was still somewhat incoherent.

After a few minutes, she was somewhat calmer. The day before, she had accidentally pushed her hand through a window and had cut it fairly badly. She had called her husband at work and he rushed home and took her to the doctor. Several stitches were required to close the wound. It would be a number of days before she could either write or type. Unfortunately, during that time was the due date for her term paper on which she had already done a lot of work and a final exam in another course was scheduled. She saw her full semester's work being lost; she saw herself failing the courses. There wasn't anything she could do. She began to cry again.

The minister was sensible enough to know that it was probable that several things could be done. He was also sensible enough not just to say that on the phone at this point and thereby communicate that he wasn't taking her distress seriously. So after about ten minutes, he asked if it would be possible for him to come by for a visit after lunch and they could talk about it further.

When he arrived, they reviewed in more detail the events which she had related on the phone, with her reexpression of her perception that she couldn't complete her courses and that she would be a failure. She had been feeling out of control, having one spell of crying right after another. Further conversation brought out how important it was for her to do well and that to fail was really to lose a significant part of herself which she was building up. In addition, as she had tried to discuss all this with her husband the night before, she had sensed that in spite of what he had agreed to earlier about supporting her schooling, he seemed impatient with her, not to be taking her present situation seriously, and stated that he had commented about how much better everything had seemed when she hadn't been in school. She felt let down, unsupported. The one whom she could usually count on when she needed a listening ear and understanding and help didn't seem to be responding in a way that was helpful at this time.

So, not only was there her first sense of panic about her courses, but her usual source of strength didn't seem to be available to her. The pastor understood that both of these issues needed to be handled, but separately from one another. In her own experience, she hadn't separated them into two events. Much of the feeling which she had as a result of talking with her husband had now been merged into her first response to believing that she was not going to be able to complete two of her courses. In the merger of the feelings of two events, the impact on her had reached overwhelming proportions and she felt out of control.

The minister reminded her that there was a procedure for requesting extensions of time both on term papers and on whole courses. Then reframing, or reinterpreting, took place. If she got the formal extensions these were not considered to be failures as far as the school was concerned, but merely common considerations when there were legitimate reasons that a person wasn't able to complete the work at the original specified time. She certainly had a good reason. Perhaps she could begin to see the situation in these terms, too. In the midst of her strong emotional reaction, based on her first interpretation, her good mind hadn't considered this simple process. The minister suggested that she request these extensions just as soon as they got through talking and that she let him know how it turned out.

About an hour after he returned to the church, he received a call from Beverly. Her voice was back to normal. She had talked to the dean's office and the extensions had been granted. She felt very relieved. The minister expressed his pleasure that she had made the arrangements and was feeling good about them, but reminded her that there was still another unresolved issue, the need to talk with her husband. She was more reluctant about this. Why not just leave things as they were? He was a good person; they had a good marriage; he would see her through school. The minister recognized that just telling the husband the good news of the extensions and letting it go at that was one option, but raised the question of whether she felt entirely comfortable with that decision. How had she really felt about him during and after the conversation the night before? She had felt let down, unsupported, misunderstood, quite disappointed, and, after a bit of work on the minister's part, admitted to being somewhat irritated. The minister asked her to imagine the scene of her raising with her husband that evening their conversation of the night before. In her imagination she was anxious, but couldn't see any really negative consequences. The minister then asked her to imagine what a positive outcome of the conversation might be. Beverly then began to lean toward talking with her husband about the matter and the minister supported her in that. He also asked her to give him a call in the next day or two to let him know how she was.

She called the next day and reported that she had told her husband how hurt and unsupported she had felt in their earlier conversation and that in reflection she realized that she had been quite irritated with him about it. He then admitted to having responded to her more out of his own irritation with the whole situation and the actual inconvenience that it had caused him without fully taking into account how bad she had felt than he had with understanding of what she was experiencing. Certainly her being in school had had its impact on him and realistically complicated his life somewhat, but he had no intention of going back on his word to support her venture. The air was cleared. Not only was her crisis resolved, but some things were better in her marriage.

Most of the pastoral care and counseling which is done within the community of faith, whether by clergy, other church staff, designated lay pastoral visitors, or friend to friend, is with persons in situational crises or someone who is in one of the precrisis stages. Whatever has taken place in the person's life which is disturbing may often come up in the context of merely a casual conversation, or a person may have called the minister or some other member of the church staff or some group leader within the church or may have come by specifically to talk about the matter. Or, we may have heard about something having taken place and called the person or gone by to visit. There are really none of us, I believe, who haven't had someone begin to talk with us about some troubling situation in his or her life. Most of the time it's about something that has happened fairly recently, often about changes in some personal relationship or some type of loss. That which has taken place is seen by the person as being anxiety-producing, sad, angering, difficult to deal with. She or he is not sure about what to do, or can't see anything to do. Depending upon where a person is in the precrisis stages or within the crisis, the person will be from mildly to deeply disturbed, uncertain to frantic, still fairly rationally weighing options to severely distraught and unable to see any options at all, in or out of control.

Everyone has been helpful to a number of persons in terms of intervening helpfully to divert that person from moving into crisis or to assist another in resolving the crisis. However, that which is most useful to us in helping the person is to be able to determine very clearly relatively early in conversation whether what the person is talking about is a situational crisis in contrast with much longer-standing troublesome personality characteristics and/or conflicted relationships. While Christian caring calls us to listen and respond to persons who wish to talk about these complex and longer-standing problems and their deep-seated feelings, and while such responsiveness may be experienced by the other as supportive and communicating our love and the love of God, we'll usually not be able to help the person in effective decision making and change.

So, what is a situational crisis? Review the illustration given. Beverly was intelligent, well-adjusted, in a good marriage, had many friends, and was functioning very actively in her church and extremely competently in graduate school. No problems. But remember also that all of us are human, have common human needs, some of which (these differ from person to person) may be very strong. We've learned to meet even these strong needs relatively well. The ways in which we do so with our behaviors of thinking, feeling, and acting also differ from person to person. The strength of these particular needs within a given person's life can also be considered that person's points of vulnerability, and the methods which they've learned to meet those needs also vary in terms of degree of effectiveness. All of us have times when, for different reasons, these particular needs are not well met, when our usual methods of meeting them begin to break down. We feel anxious in reaction to the growing intensity of the needs, and the anxiety increases rapidly when the ways that usually work to get them met are not working. Beverly could not meet her own standards of competence when she realized that she couldn't complete her work on time, even though rationally no one could fail to understand the circumstances. Then when she went to her primary source of support, her husband, she failed to get from him what she had learned to expect. She moved quickly then into a situational crisis, but even in the midst of it was able to remember that she could call the minister and perhaps get help.

Think of other possible examples of being cut off from significant sources of need fulfillment:

> Think about what being in the hospital does to the usual effective ways of our needs being met.

> Think about the death of a parent, spouse, child, other close family member, or friend, and being cut off from the meaningful contacts with that other person.

> Think about losing one's job of ten, twenty, forty years, losing one's income, losing daily contact with friends of years' standing, and what all of this does to the adequate meeting of our needs.

All of this isn't difficult to understand, because we've all experienced not getting strong needs met any longer and then trying to recover from the setback. It involves pain, time, struggle.

Figure 1 shows the chronological progression of the development of a situational crisis. There is an identifiable event (or the anticipation of an event), which precedes by only a short period of time (a few minutes or hours or days) the onset of the feelings and/or behaviors that are disturbing and dysfunctional. If the event has preceded the onset of the distressing feelings and/or behavior by much longer than this, the person may not be experiencing a situational crisis.

Many of these events involve a loss or threatened loss of some kind. Probably most of them would be experienced in a negative way by most persons. Yet people are different and can't all be expected to react in the same manner to what appear to be similar events.

A child is physically handicapped. The family discovers that a new surgical procedure and its follow-up physical therapy can give him a normal life. Even better for them, since the family is quite poor, the

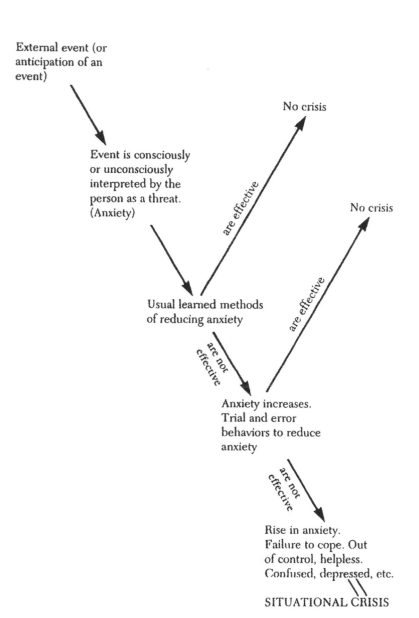

External event (or
anticipation of an
event)

No crisis

Event is consciously
or unconsciously
interpreted by the
person as a threat.
(Anxiety)

are effective

No crisis

Usual learned methods
of reducing anxiety

are effective

are not effective

Anxiety increases.
Trial and error
behaviors to reduce
anxiety

are not effective

Rise in anxiety.
Failure to cope. Out
of control, helpless.
Confused, depressed, etc.

SITUATIONAL CRISIS

The Development of a Situational Crisis
Figure 1

whole process will not cost them anything. But the child will have to be taken to a city about two hundred miles away for a period of perhaps three to four months. Neither the father nor the mother is in a position to stay in that city during the time the child is in the hospital. There are other children and the need to continue work. As the father and other members of the family begin to talk and make plans for the child to go, the mother

1. Responds with joyful anticipation to the new life being offered her child;

2. Becomes more and more depressed.

In the actual situation, Response #2 is what occurred. What a strange reaction this seems to be. Wouldn't most mothers be grateful for such an opportunity and look forward to the child's being able to do more of the things children ordinarily do and to grow up physically strong and active?

But what if the mother has had little identity of her own as a person, has overinvested herself in taking care of the child, has received the praise of her family and others for her dedication to him, feels as if she needs the child with her every day to make her own life complete? This all need not be conscious on her part, but it may accurately describe her emotional condition and how she gets very important needs met in relationship to her child in his present condition. So unconsciously she experiences the threat to her own well-being in her anticipation of being separated from him for several months and his not needing her in the future precisely as he does now. She becomes depressed.

This situation clearly illustrates that it's not the event itself which *causes* the crisis. A critical factor is also how a person interprets the event or anticipated event from the point of view of that person's conscious *and* unconscious needs, whether the event is or is not viewed as a threat to one's sense of one's own self. Yet a third interacting factor is how well or poorly a person has learned to deal with intense anxiety when it arises in one's life, the number and types of resources that are available to a person, and the person's flexibility in utilizing various resources. Even though there are individual differences between us in regard to all of these factors, we have one thing in common. We can, and do, *all* experience situational crises under certain circumstances. No one of us is totally invulnerable.

Figure 1 presents these three forces in their chronological order. A person is not in crisis because of the event, or even because the event is seen as a threat and the person begins to experience anxiety. This is the frequent, almost daily experience of large numbers of us. But we've also all learned certain ways to deny, reduce, avoid, or, for a certain period of time, tolerate a certain level of anxiety. So, even *with* anxiety, we undertake the job, talk to the person who is involved in the situation in which we feel anxiety, go listen to music or play tennis or exercise in some way, discuss the situation and our feelings with someone else, try to change some situations which look as if they might be changed, etc. Most of the time one or more of these work and our anxiety is reduced. We change the situation, or for other reasons it changes after a period of time which is still within the time frame of our ability to tolerate anxiety. Our intensity of feelings lessens and we get a new perspective from talking with someone. As a result, our tension is reduced and therefore we ourselves can see the situation differently. We have been anxious, but we have not been in a situational crisis.

But when these methods don't work, we begin to feel worse quickly. We do some other things which we hope will help, and, after a couple of failures, suddenly something we do has some effect on the situation or on another person or on ourselves. We don't experience the intensity of the threat any longer. There is no crisis even though we were panicky for a short period of time.

But when nothing works, all of our attempts to cope fail, we have the experience of not being able to do anything else that can be effective. So there is the sense of loss of control, an extremely high level of anxiety, a great deal of confusion, perhaps a rapid move into depression, repressed anger, our interpretation that it's all now hopeless, or any number of other behaviors that are automatic attempts to deal with high anxiety. There may be withdrawal and apathy, or a hyperactivity which uses some of the energy of anxiety and gives us the sense of doing something but really does not do anything that is truly functional, or rather severe distortions in our thinking patterns.

A situational crisis looks and feels bad. There is no question about it.

A person moves quickly into a situational crisis and usually moves fairly quickly out of it. Being a state of heightened emotion, there are varying degrees of regression. This means a greater sense of helplessness. But it also means a greater responsiveness to help from others. Most crises are resolved within hours, days, or a few weeks just as a result of the presence of the usual sorts of influences in people's ordinary environment: a parent, a child, a spouse, a neighbor, other friends, coupled with their own internal resources. They don't go to a psychiatrist or even to a minister. Yet, as I have already indicated, persons in situational crises do come to ministers and other church staff and officials and make up the largest proportion of pastoral care within a congregation. The congregation, its ordained clergy and its lay staff, other congregational leaders, individual friends, groups within the congregation to which a person belongs, corporate worship itself, are all important resources to people in crisis.

Quick and sensitive intervention by people in the community of faith will assist in a more rapid and positive resolution of the crisis. This will usually take place in no longer than approximately six weeks. Often it will be less. The anxiety diminishes to its usual level, depression lifts, the person is thinking with her or his usual level of clarity and is functioning well in her or his work and in other responsibilities. In addition, the person has probably learned some important things from the experience.

Unfortunately, in some instances, after six weeks or a little longer, if a person has few resources or has not used them, if no outside helper has been involved, these positive changes may not come about. Perhaps some of the severity of the symptoms has diminished, but they are still there. The person seems to be locked into a state of anxiety or depression, confusion, a lack of decisiveness, relative helplessness, nonfunctioning or a low level of functioning. These persons may still improve with proper help, but the critical transitional period during which change comes about most quickly and easily is passed. The person is no longer technically in a situational crisis and now needs a well-trained professional counselor and a longer period of time to feel better and be at their precrisis level of competence.

Exceptions to the "approximately six weeks" guidelines are those situational crises of grief following a severe loss of a person by death, divorce, or some other radical means.

Persons may be judged to be in a situational crisis (other than the situations of grief just mentioned) when their disturbance has begun not more than about six weeks before, and when an external event which can be logically connected with the particular symptoms of the disturbance precedes the onset of the symptoms by no more than a few days (or occasionally somewhat longer). These time periods aren't absolute and rigid, but they do tend to cover most cases.

In these instances, persons who are aware of the nature of situational crises and know something of the goals and procedures of crisis counseling can be very helpful in assisting the upset individual in resolving his or her crisis within a relatively short period of time: hours, days, a few weeks.

When no precipitating event can be found, the disturbing feelings and/or behaviors are either not the result of situational crisis or there exists some complicating factor which is preventing the discovery of a triggering event. In these instances, it's important for the helping person to put the disturbed person in touch with an experienced professional in the field of counseling.

HOW DO WE HELP?

The following outline of the crisis counseling process has already appeared in this same form (Switzer, 1993, pp. 132–61; 1986, pp. 65–89). After a great deal of thought based on continued involvement with a large number of people who are in situational crisis, I see no reason to change the way in which this procedure is presented. However, since the other two publications give such great detail, I'll follow this outline here with only very little comment and hope that the reader will go to one of the other publications.*

Contact	*Focus*	*Cope*
1. Establish the relationship.	5. Explore the present situation.	7. Inventory problem-solving resources.
2. Identify the presenting problem and the precipitating event.	6. Identify the threat.	8. Assist in decision making.
3. Assist catharsis.		9. Emphasize relationships with others.
4. Build hopeful expectation.		10. Summarize new learning.

All of the facilitative conditions of the helping relationship and other resources for pastoral care presented in chapter 2 are relevant here. The establishing of the relationship as described in that chapter and which is necessary in crisis counseling is brought about through the combination of the attitude of respect, the personal characteristic of genuineness, and the accurate communication of empathy, assisted by concreteness. Even if we've known the person well prior to the time of this crisis, in the present condition he or she is a somewhat different person and therefore a somewhat new quality of relationship needs to be established. There is no substitute for the verbal communication of empathy.

This process, of course, facilitates open emotional expression, contributes to the building of hope, and very often in and of itself clarifies the presenting problem and reveals the precipitating event. Therefore, it can be seen that the four headings under "Contact" aren't entirely different steps which follow chronologically in this exact manner. They're all

---

* The outline in this exact form is presented here with the permission of Abingdon Press.

taking place at the same time. If, however, the person, in the telling of his or her distress doesn't clearly specify an event which can be understood by both that person and the helper as being the precipitant, it is our responsibility to initiate the search. This needs to be done in the very first conversation in order to determine whether the person is in situational crisis or not, and therefore whether we're going to be the primary one assisting the person through the difficulty or whether we need to get that person to someone who is more capable of dealing with longer-term and more complex problems.

Therefore, if no precipitating event has been clearly identified in the conversation within ten minutes or so, we ask the two critical questions:

1. When did you first notice your beginning to feel this way (or have these experiences, or notice that something was wrong)?

Some people can almost immediately pin the time down with considerable accuracy. Others will need our patient, persistent questioning in order to do so. Once the beginning point of the change is established, then we ask

2. Can you think of anything that happened in your life shortly before that time which was different in any way (or which had some impact on you, or which disturbed you in any way)?

Again, some people will quickly be stimulated to remember a particular event, while others will need detailed guiding through the hours and days prior to their beginning to feel bad, perhaps including our needing to ask concretely about various aspects of their work situation, their family life, other important relationships, etc.

The purpose of the second section, "Focus," is to go into sufficient detail about the person's reactions to the precipitating event so as to be able to clarify the reason that this particular person at this particular time responded to this particular event with the intensity of threat which issued in the particular feelings and behaviors which the person is experiencing, that is, *this* crisis.

The final section all has to do with problem solving: identifying internal resources which have been hidden by the person's intense feelings and confusion and sense of helplessness, identifying external resources (other persons, church groups, other support groups, agencies, etc.) which are relevant to this person's needs.

On the basis of these needs and the available resources, we then look at what the person needs to do in order to help herself or himself, assisting that person's decision as to what is especially relevant to his or her situation and what to do first, second, etc. Remember Beverly. On her own she did think to call her minister. But prior to that time she had not thought of calling the graduate school dean's office and she hadn't thought of the potential value of talking over the whole situation with her husband. For her, these two additional conversations were all that she needed. Other persons in other situations might need to make more decisions and take more action.

There's not a simple and smooth progress during the crisis counseling process. There may be some regressions on the part of the person in crisis. Issues talked about once may need to be talked about again. Sometimes it's crucial that a person take some action even before all of the initial exploration has taken place.

In helping persons through crisis, it's more useful to talk with them more frequently (two or three or more times a week face-to-face and perhaps a phone call or two). Also for effective intervention, the focus of the conversations must be only on the present crisis. It is not helpful (in fact, it's a trap that can prevent progress) to spend time with them talking about experiences of theirs much earlier in their lives or other current issues and relationships unless these can be clearly identified as having some impact upon this present crisis, its onset, and its resolution.

An additional scheme which will be quite helpful to clergy and lay caregivers in bringing into focus what they will more often do with persons in crisis than the more complete process outlined above is what Slaikeu (Slaikeu, 1984, pp. 85–94, 103) has referred to as "psychological first aid," or "first order intervention." This process refers to the *immediate* response to the person or persons in crisis by whoever happens actually to be there or to be most available. The goals of psychological first aid are to (1) provide support, (2) reduce lethality (or other physical harm in instances of violence or suicidal or homicidal feelings), and (3) provide linkage to helping resources. The process, all of which can usually be reasonably accomplished in this one contact, includes (1) making psychological contact (establishing the relationship as stated above), (2) exploring dimensions of the problem (*immediate* past, present, and *immediate* future), (3) examining possible solutions (literally, what to do *next*, not long-range solutions), and (4) helping the person(s) take concrete action. Slaikeu also makes the distinction between helper behaviors which are facilitative (where the person in crisis, after discussion with the caregiver, is capable of taking responsibility for her or his next behavior) and those which are directive (where, again after discussion, the person in crisis is not capable of the action called for and the helper takes the action, or they take the action together, and/or other persons are called in to be involved in the immediate helping process).

The last part of the process is (5) follow-up. Thorough understanding of the details of this procedure will be invaluable to the pastoral helper. (See also Slaikeu, chapter 10, "Crisis Intervention by Clergy.")

The procedures listed and briefly discussed here are useful to consider in all situations where someone is possibly in a situational crisis, but are not to be followed slavishly and rigidly. When a person is in the hospital, critically ill, facing a serious operation, when there's been the death of a family member, it's obvious what the precipitating event is. In a five- to seven-minute hospital call, we can't go down a checklist of the ten "steps." In grief, it's totally unrealistic to push for resolution in approximately six weeks. If it's not a formal counseling situation, we may have combinations of either shorter or longer conversations. But many of the elements of the process can still be useful to keep in mind even in these instances.

CONCLUSION

Much detail has not been included in this discussion of pastoral response to persons in situational crises. This is merely an introduction. Persons who are going to be involved fairly frequently with pastoral counseling, pastoral oversight for any group or groups within a congregation, or lay caregiving really need to read one or more of the resources listed in the References and Recommended Reading sections.

REFERENCES

Karl A. Slaikeu, *Crisis Intervention: A Handbook for Practice and Research* (Boston: Allyn and Bacon, 1984).

David K. Switzer, "Crisis Intervention and Problem Solving," in Robert J. Wicks, Richard D. Parsons, Donald B. Capps, eds., *Clinical Handbook of Pastoral Counseling* (Expanded Edition) (Mahwah, N.J.: Paulist Press, 1993), pp. 132–61.

———. *The Minister As Crisis Counselor* (Revised and enlarged) (Nashville: Abingdon Press, 1986).

RECOMMENDED READING

Charles Gerkin, *Crisis Experience in Modern Life* (Nashville: Abingdon Press, 1979).

Karl Slaikeu and Steve Lawhead, *The Phoenix Factor: Surviving and Growing through Personal Crisis* (Boston: Houghton Mifflin, 1985).

Howard W. Stone, *Crisis Counseling* (Minneapolis: Fortress Press, 1993).

Judson J. Swihart and Gerald C. Richardson, *Counseling in Times of Crisis* (Waco, Tex: Word Books, 1987).

4

Visiting the Physically Ill

Visiting the sick has been a part of the life and activity of the church from its very beginning. Our present commitment to such visitation is grounded in Scripture and tradition (Oden, 1983, chapter 16). Understanding this to be the case, it is not surprising to find the clergy in my survey placing hospital visitation as a truly common pastoral function in terms of the great frequency with which they do it. However, considering that life-threatening illness and accidents and operations and ministry to the dying were in another category, we might not have expected that other hospital visitation would have elicited such a large number of responses in terms of the minister's own intensity of feelings.

WHY THE INTENSITY OF FEELINGS IN VISITING THE SICK?

First, when visits are made in the hospital, it's obvious that this place is not our own turf, our own home territory, unless we happen to be the chaplain of this particular hospital and we've been there for a period of time. Someone else is clearly in charge, someone else designs procedures which are foreign to the practice of our vocation and sets the rules for this institution. We see nurses, aides, physicians taking blood, administering medication, adjusting various pieces of equipment attached to the person, asking diagnostic questions, feeling and thumping and always recording items on the person's chart.

What can we do? We say a few things, ask a few questions, listen a bit, read the Bible, pray, all this often interrupted by others doing their own task at the moment or even asking us to step out of the room while they do it. They seem to know what they're doing and why; we who are representing the church are not always so sure about what we are doing and why we are doing it and how it's particularly helpful to the person in this situation.

Second, for many of us, when the sick or injured person asks us certain questions, we seem to lack answers. "I've lived a good life; why is this happening to me?" "Why has God put this burden of suffering on me?" "Why can't I just go ahead and die?" There are numerous other questions. Some of them we become accustomed to hearing, although this may not help us in our response. And periodically very unique sorts of questions are posed. If we see ourselves as the person with the answer, we are lost when we are visiting the sick and the suffering. We feel the pressure of the questions. We sometimes experience ourselves as inadequate for such a situation. We feel very uneasy and are not sure what we should say and do that would be of most value to the other person.

Third, we see the attack that has been made on the physical body of the person we visit: the debilitation, the wasting away, the place where a leg once was, bruises and lacerations and swelling, the face distorted with pain, and we smell the unfamiliar and unpleasant odors of the hospital, of the sickness, of the incontinence. As human beings we feel for the person who is sick or injured, but we also fear for ourselves as we identify with her or him. We see ourselves in the bed and we are frightened. In addition, we may sometimes be reminded of close members of our families (a parent, a child, a spouse) who has suffered or even died in a hospital.

In visiting the sick and suffering, those facing critical operations, those who have been suddenly hurt and maimed by an accident, we may try to protect ourselves by being unfeeling, but then many of us rebel inwardly against that response because we want to be feeling people, and we know also that we can't minister effectively without engaging ourselves emotionally with those in intense need of our relationship with them.

There may be other reasons for certain pastors to have a high intensity of feeling in regard to visiting the sick, which leads them to see any such visitation as a type of emergency for themselves, but the three listed here seem to be the most common ones.

THE HIGH PRIORITY OF VISITING THE SICK

We have already mentioned that visiting the sick has always been part of the life and activity of the church. But what are the reasons that this is the case? Why is it that all of us who are a part of the community of faith also find ourselves responsible for visiting the sick and the injured?

Those of us who are clergy have an immediate and easy answer. We are supposed to. Without even trying to think of any more meaningful reasons, laypersons and ordained clergy together know that this visitation is what clergy are supposed to do. Many, or most, people expect it. In a few places, *everyone* expects it. Some, as we discover, *demand* it. Some are offended when we don't. In certain communities and congregations, none of the rest of our ministry will go well if we don't. Yet all of these "practical" reasons beg the issue. What is the origin of this concern which is expressed in the ways just mentioned? Perhaps if we can understand more clearly the more profound reasons that we visit the physically and mentally ill and the injured, and something of what our presence and words communicate, we can do such visitation with more confidence in our role and function and with less anxiety.

The Church's Mission in Visiting the Sick

First, ministry to the sick is built into the structure and dynamic of the fellowship of faith. Reference has been made in chapter 1 to such a connection between Jesus' proclamation of the kingdom of God, his healing ministry, and the origin of the church. James 5:14 portrays the practice as an expected part of the life of the early church: "Is one of you ill? That person should send for the elders of the congregation to pray over him and anoint him with oil in the name of the Lord." In the church we are to participate in the significant events of the lives of one another: "Rejoice with those who rejoice; weep with those who weep" (Rom. 12:15). In baptism, in marriage (and divorce), in the Sacrament of the Lord's Supper, in all successes and failures, in sickness and in death, the church is not only a fellowship of faith but also a fellowship of suffering, a fellowship of caring in terms of participation in that suffering with the mentally and emotionally ill and injured, the fearful, distressed, bewildered, and hopeless. We declare by being physically present with them, "You're not alone. I care. The community cares. God is here. God cares."

Second, visiting the sick is one way that we respond to and honor Christ: "'I was sick and you visited me,' . . . 'Lord, when did we see you sick . . . and visit you?' . . . 'When you did it to one of these least of these, my brothers (and sisters), you did it to me'" (Matt. 26:36, 39-40). We serve Christ *directly,* Scripture says, by serving others in this way. It is one form of participating in the life of Christ himself the suffering servant; it is one form of *our* servanthood.

Third, a corollary meaning of this passage, it seems to me, is that if we visit Christ in visiting the sick, we not only *serve* Christ, but we may find Christ for ourselves in our relationship with and ministrations to the sick and suffering. It becomes a means of grace for us.

Fourth, when we as persons representative of the body of Christ visit the sick and suffering, we reveal something about the suffering of the Creator who agonizes with the creation and the creatures, the God whom Jesus revealed in the midst of his own suffering and death, the God who used the suffering and death of Jesus to make "him both Lord and Christ" (Acts 2:36), Jesus, whose suffering and death are events with the power to lead us to that very God.

Fifth, in visiting the sick and suffering and communicating through this act the suffering God, we may also communicate something of *how* God cares and supports us in our time of extremity. God participates with us in our suffering (point 4), seeks to draw us closer to God's own self in order to deepen our sensitivity and insight and faith through this suffering which we share with God and God with us. God's participation with us in this way can break down some of the awfulness and pain and loneliness and isolation. This point should not be misinterpreted to mean that God *directly* produces suffering *in order to* bring about a closer relationship with God or to stimulate our personal growth, including the deepening of faith. This viewpoint clashes with my understanding of how God works in human life. But God suffers *with* the distressed, and to the extent that the sufferers become aware of such loving presence, they may make the move toward God in response.

Sixth, faithful and sensitive servanthood, when done *only* to serve Christ by serving others (point 2), is also a form of proclamation (point 4) and offers the condition for the possible increase of faith (point 5). As such, it is an effective form of evangelism. When visiting the sick, however, is done *self-consciously* as an evangelistic activity, it becomes an exploitation of a person's pain and vulnerability. It is only that, *exploitation,* and therefore *not* evangelism, *not* the proclamation of a loving, suffering God.

Seventh, our visitation of the sick, faithfully and competently done, makes its contribution to the healing of a person. What I mean by healing is discussed in the next section.

Finally, visiting the sick is not only a part of the mission of the church in and of itself, but through the healing which does take place in the lives of both visited and visitor in terms of increase in faith, it is a contribution to the edification of the church, the building up of the body of Christ, equipping the saints for the church's more effective carrying out of its whole mission in the world.

PASTORAL VISITATION AND PHYSICAL HEALING

It is necessary to approach the issues of healing from the awareness that we human beings are comprised of many interacting systems which are not exactly identical, all of which are involved in any act of human functioning, any of which may be more or less dysfunctional at any given time, and therefore in need of healing. When a cancer or a damaged heart is causing pain and is threatening our very existence, we would all, under most circumstances, want our physical bodies to be healed, but usually there are other functions of ours which are disturbed as well: our thought processes, our emotions, our spiritual lives. If these are greatly disordered, or if they are clear, strong, and healthy, either way, they have some effect on the body.

Let's look briefly, and therefore in a manner which is inevitably oversimplified, at some of the sources of how we got to be the persons we are. The statement of the renowned psychologist Gardner Murphy is the basis for our understanding:

> The self is not at first "inside"; as the child first learns to know it, it is
> the body. In time, however, . . . the ego is referred "inward." As language

and the system of images develop, the child builds up an "inner world" in contrast to "outer world" (1947, p. 586)

The infant's first self-image is what the infant experiences moment by moment physically. Anxiety as a disturbed state of the whole organism grows out of the periodic feelings of physical discomfort and even pain which are most usually associated with the absence of the caretaking persons (Switzer, 1970, pp. 94–105).

As we develop more and more differentiated and sophisticated mental functions and emotional reactions, there is a way in which many of us begin to experience ourselves as not totally defined by our body (although some number of people *do* define human beings in that way), yet most of us also have difficulty conceiving of ourselves apart from our bodies. The underlying foundation of our human personalities is still to some degree that original self, the body. When our bodies are threatened, attacked, or in the process of debilitation, malfunction, *we,* as a whole, experience being threatened. Certainly there are differences between persons in regard to the occasions and intensities of these reactions and differences within each one of us depending upon the particular physiological threat and how we interpret that threat in regard to the way we now conceive of our whole selves. But whenever we do experience threat to our physical being, that perception of threat is anxiety.

In anxiety, there is regression, an automatic unconscious mental process which takes us back to whatever we have experienced as earlier securities, which protect us from the pain, the fear. Usually, this mental process is not a practical coping mechanism for the problems of mature persons, so for a period of time we are left somewhat helpless and unable to function in our usual ways. Accompanying this particular psychological reaction, if we are sufficiently ill or injured or facing an operation, we place ourselves under (note the use of the word *under*) the care of a physician. If one has to be in bed for a period of time, even at home, there is the withdrawal of meaningful activities, the usual amount of physical contact with one's family and friends, some loss of power over one's own life, as well as whatever physical discomfort or pain there might be. If one is hospitalized, all of the above losses are increased, along with separation even from the physical environment of one's home, with the additional perceived threat to one's body and thus one's self. All of those forces which combine to assist us in the maintenance and growth of our personal identity are either totally withdrawn or diminished. For numerous people these losses include the losses of persons who are part of a community of faith, the worship to which they are accustomed, and the other activities of the community of faith. For many, their faith in God and their participation in the life of the worshiping and serving community is also a part of who they are.

When we, as representatives of the community of faith, visit the sick, we contribute to the person a number of these elements of his or her usual daily life and identity: we make some breakthrough into their sense of isolation and loneliness, bring a reminder of the outside world with some of its activities and symbols and persons into the unfamiliar surroundings and persons and activities of the hospital and into the hospitalized person's own lack of significant activity; we make an important personal contact at the moment, both by our human presence and as a symbol of the faith itself. These symbols may touch unconscious forces in the person's life which may (though not always) bring a sense of calm, peace, comfort, security. Our representativeness of God and the church may in and of itself stimulate the person's faith. In addition, in our personal conversation with the person, as we may read relevant passages of Scripture, have prayer, or administer the relevant sacraments, faith may continue to be stimulated and the person's own sense of identity and wholeness reinforced. The healing of the person is in the process of taking place. There are a variety of ways in which such healing may also influence the physiological system in a positive manner. At times, this may, in fact, contribute to the physical healing or the more rapid physical healing of the person. Of course, such *physical* healing does not always take place, but this result does not mean that no relevant healing has occurred.

Visiting the sick is packed with potential power for growth, healing, and an increase in faith; for actual encounter with God both for the sick and injured and for us, the visitors; for service to the whole church and for support of its total mission in the world. The high priority of this form of ministry becomes clear and compelling.

WHAT WE NEED FOR MEANINGFUL HOSPITAL VISITATION

In order to function most effectively in the hospital setting and with the physically ill and injured, there are particular ways in which we need to be equipped. Of course, all of these assume our faith and our commitment to this responsibility and opportunity.

The Facilitative Conditions of the Helping Relationship

Our first needs have to do with who we are as human beings, which then makes it possible for us to furnish within our relationships with persons the facilitative conditions as these were discussed in chapter 2. They are just as applicable to brief hospital visits as they are to any formal and longer-term psychotherapy or counseling, even though it was within these psychotherapeutic settings that the investigations were made which led to the identification of the conditions. Discussing the theological meaning of suffering, reading the Bible, leading in prayer are not necessarily in direct conflict with these conditions at all, although such religious and devotional practices *may* be at times substituted for the authentic and meaningful relationships which the conditions describe. Obviously, the setting of the sickroom, the length of time of the visit, the interruptions which so frequently take place, and the condition of the patient need to be taken into account in our strategy.

A Theology of Suffering

Throughout Scripture, people are dealing with defeat and sickness and grief and suffering and persecution: at times the whole Jewish people, the whole of the early church; but we read many specific instances of individuals' grappling with these experiences either in their own personal lives or on behalf of a body of the people, such as numerous ones of the Psalms, Job, Isaiah, Jesus, Paul. Why has this happened to me, to us? Why am I being punished, O Lord? What sin have I (or he or she) committed? My God, why have you forsaken me? Is it possible for me to avoid the suffering which seems to be immediately before me? If you cared for me (us), O God, you would not have allowed this to come upon me (us). I've obeyed your commandments; I've tried to serve you faithfully. What can my defeat, illness, accident, etc. mean? Why must I continue to suffer in this way?

These are issues which people struggle with in the Bible, and these are the same questions that are being posed many thousands of times every day in hospitals and homes and nursing homes and emergency rooms and other places.

How do we ourselves cry out when we are sick and severely injured and in terrible pain and infirm with age and are handicapped? Are we ourselves totally without question, anger, despondency, bitterness? How do we avoid it, or resolve it? What does it all mean if God is love, if God is powerful, if we've sought to serve God as best we could with who we are and what we have?

The questions couldn't be posed in this form nor would the issues be as sharply drawn if there were no God. It's all meaningless anyway. This is the way the world and human life is, take it or leave it. We didn't ask for *any* of it, but we're here. So? That's the end of it. There's no comfort in this, and the struggle of the human mind to deal with and accept chance and meaninglessness is no less stressful. There are even theological issues that would need to be dealt with in order to be able to take this position.

But God's role in the world thrusts itself insistently upon a large percentage of the world's population who do in fact believe in God, and certainly upon those who believe in the God of the Old and New Testaments. And it's still a world in which so much is unpredictable and one where somehow we just can't catch on to the scheme of things in regard to the vast amount of all kinds of human physical and emotional suffering.

We visit the sick. They ask, often very explicitly, "Why, why?" "Why does illness like this even exist at all; why do accidents like this happen? Why me? Why now?" How do we respond?

"The answer is that God . . . that you . . ." No, of course not. We don't *tell* people the one and only answer. But we can't engage ourselves effectively with suffering persons, over and over again, or even once, without having grappled as fully and as deeply as we can with the various ways in which the issues are handled in the Bible, by some of the best thinkers in the history of the church, and with what approaches or combinations of approaches have the most meaning to us. Although our purpose in visiting the sick is not to impose our views on another person, or even subtly guide him or her to whatever we've already determined is the "best" position, *the* Christian position, we are limited as pastors if we go with a "blank spot in the brain," our own *nonthinking* about the issues. In fact, we may not even have clearly identified for ourselves the "best Christian answer" which covers all cases. Perhaps there really is no such one. But we have been and are continuing to work at it if we're committed and conscientious pastoral carers.

There are a number of resources to stimulate our thinking. There are, of course, the Bible and the original writings of major thinkers of the church throughout history. There are numerous Bible commentaries dealing with the relevant books or particular passages. For those who have not already become well read in the field of "theodicy," the theology of suffering, I'd recommend your looking at Oden (1983). In his chapter "A Theodicy for Pastoral Practice," he gives a lucid summary of various positions which have been proposed throughout the history of the church, followed by a list of selected historical writings.

A Knowledge of the Bible

If we choose to suggest reading the Bible to a sick person, or if requested to do so, we need to know how to respond, to what passages to turn. Probably the best way to begin is to ask the person if she or he has a passage in mind which is particularly meaningful to him or her. If the person makes a suggestion, it can be very important to read it and then discuss its meaning for the individual. The particular Scripture may be very different from one which we might have had in mind, based on our conversation and prior knowledge of the person. If the person has a particular passage in mind, he or she can usually identify it. "The Twenty-Third Psalm." "Oh, those words of affirmation and comfort in the eighth chapter of Romans (or John 14, etc.)." Fine. We can locate these.

But there can be difficulties with the procedure of asking the other person for a suggestion. What if the person says:

"Read me that story where Elkanah and his family were going to offer their sacrifice to the Lord."

"Who?"

"Elkanah."

"Oh. Uhh . . . where is that located?"

"I don't know. Don't you know?"

You may identify this passage immediately. But I wouldn't have. And I think that probably I'm not the only one. Now, why a sick person would think to ask for this story, I don't really know for sure, although it's a good one in its entirety (1 Sam. 1–3). I just didn't remember the name of Samuel's father. If we don't know 100 percent of the Scripture by memory, and we can't bear to say to a person, "I don't know," then don't ask.

But it *is* important to know as much as possible, both to draw on with flexibility and sensitivity *and* creativity and to respond to others' requests when it is possible to do so. We would all probably do well to have a small book of edited biblical passages which are most likely to be read to the sick. Instead of, or perhaps in addition to this, we probably should make a number of marks in our own Bibles, not only to designate certain passages to read, but also in order to mark verses and sections to omit.

Even in some of the most reassuring and comforting psalms, for example, there are verses which either are not relevant or which are even problematic for the immediate needs of a sick person. For example: Ps. 137:1–4 for a lonely sick person in the hospital. But do you *really* want to read verses 5–9? Or Psalm 135. Do you want to read verses 8–12 to a suffering person?

The Bible is going to be an important resource of words which stimulate faith and through which God can truly act in a person's life right at this time. In order for us to be able to engage ourselves with persons in pastoral emergencies through the words of the Scripture, we have continuing lifelong preparation to make.

THE VISIT

Once assuming our own long-term spiritual growth and Bible study, training in the facilitative conditions, and wrestling theologically with the problem of suffering, as well as our prayer of preparation for this specific person and this specific encounter, when does our professional activity really begin when we visit the sick? Perhaps it begins when we enter the home or hospital, or when we arrive on the particular floor or specific room. At this point, you'll understand that the suggestions which follow are only my perspective, although based on a considerable amount of experience and an awareness of what many other pastors do. Still, the suggestions will be quite incomplete. They can't possibly account for every illness, every hospital, all medical personnel, every sick individual and member of that person's family, and the personality and faith and style of every visitor who represents the community of faith in various parts of the country and in different-sized communities.

Approach to the Patient

Basically, it's a useful part of pastoral visitation to get to know the relevant people: family members of the sick person, hospital staff of various positions and functions, especially the nurses and aides responsible for the area where you will be visiting, the chaplain if there is one, and, when possible, the physician or physicians involved. In a town or small community, this will come naturally and inevitably after a short period of time. Some will be members of your own congregation. In a large city with quite a large number of large hospitals, the truly personal knowing of these people will be somewhat unusual and coincidental, though somewhat less so with hospitals operated by the particular denomination or group of which you yourself are a part. However, it's never out of line, is usually helpful, and sometimes extremely important that you introduce yourself to at least someone available at the nursing station on your first and perhaps even your first few visits to a particular unit.

As a part of this getting acquainted, we will be learning something about this particular hospital's policy in regard to visitation by clergy. Many hospitals prefer that this be done during posted visitation hours. But even these are usually fairly flexible in regard to clergy, if not for other visitors representing the church. Most hospital personnel expect that clergy will come in briefly before an operation in the morning and realize that there will be emergencies outside of regular visiting hours. In addition, other hospitals are quite open, within reason, to clergy's coming whenever they can. It's our responsibility, however, not to presume on our clergy status, and therefore it will assist our ministry in the hospital considerably if we will speak with some responsible official of that institution. Whatever rules they have, it is important for us to make every effort to follow them. When we cannot, and there will be such instances, then we would very definitely check in at the main desk or the chaplain's office or the nursing station and let the person in charge know the circumstances. Nothing turns medical personnel off more than a presumptuous and officious minister. It's also useful to know something about the nature and severity of the person's illness or accident or operation before we see the person. This can usually be obtained from family or friends or someone at the nursing station. What we do with that information may vary, since the patient who is in a life-threatening condition may not yet have been informed of that fact. Usually conveying that type of information and discussing it with the person is the prerogative of the attending physician. On the other hand, we are not to presume that if the situation is not very serious the patient is taking it as lightly as we might be.

Arriving at the room, if the door is open, we are free to step in and see what the situation is. If it is closed, push it open ever so slightly, knock lightly (loudly enough to be heard if the person is awake but softly enough that it wouldn't awaken a sleeping person). Remember, however, and here our knowledge of the person and his or her condition and situation is important, it's not always a crime to awaken a sleeping patient. Sometimes persons will need all the sleep they can get and we don't disturb them; with others, they can sleep anytime and our visit for a few minutes can be very important to them. When in doubt about awakening a person, check back at the nursing station.

Once in the room, move over close to the bed, call the person's name, clarify who you are if there is not immediate apparent recognition (even some people who know you, for various reasons may not recognize you at once), and at least frequently take the person's hand or put your hand on her or his arm. Physical touch can be very reassuring and can communicate caring to many people. Of course, be careful about tubes, needles, bandages, tender places, etc. In other words, don't cause pain or mess up the works.

"What do you say after you say 'hello'?" (Eric Bernes's famous book title is relevant.) I don't know anything particularly profound. There could be a number of quite improper approaches ("They tell me you're going to die, and I just thought I'd better come see you" or something else as obviously gross). A simple "How are you feeling?" is satisfactory or better. Let's look at a few examples taken from verbatims of actual visits. The patient is a sixty-three-year-old woman.

Pastor: Good afternoon, Mrs. J. How are you today?
Mrs. J.: I am fine. That's what's strange. I thought if you had cancer you'd be sick, and I don't feel sick at all.
Pastor: This isn't what you expected.
Mrs. J.: No. The worst thing that happened was that test the other day—that was worse than having a baby. . . .

The patient is an eighteen-year-old woman who entered through the emergency room and was taken to surgery for a tubal pregnancy.

Chaplain: Good morning. I am Chaplain P. I just wanted to come by and visit with you.
Patient: (tentatively) Hello.

Chaplain: How are you feeling?

Patient: I am feeling better now. I had surgery last night. They got through about ten o'clock.

Chaplain: You're looking pretty good to have just finished with that.

Patient: I'm a lot better than I've been for several days. I hadn't slept at all for thirty-six hours before I came in, I was hurting so bad. (Goes then into some detail about difficulties in getting to the hospital.)

Chaplain: That sounds scary.

Patient: It really was. (Continues her story.)

The patient is a sixteen-year-old boy. His sister and mother are both present. The chaplain greets both of them and introduces himself as he enters the room. He then walks to the bed of W., the patient.

Chaplain: How are you doing?

W.: Okay. I'm going to be operated on this morning but it'll be all right. I've got a lot of faith.

Chaplain: Tell me something about your situation. I really don't know much of what's going on.

W.: Well, I've got this bone disease. (Launches into some detail about what's wrong with him.)

Chaplain: W., how are you feeling about your operation?

W.: Well, I'll sure be glad when it's over with. But it's got to be done. I know it's serious, but I think it will be all right.

Note how in each case the simple greeting and question and the following empathy or encouragement to talk brought a response. Most people will begin to talk about their physical condition. They may then begin to say how they feel, or, as you will note in two of the excerpts, the ministers took the initiative to move into the area of the emotions. The procedure is to see where the conversation leads and respond to the other person's cues. Focus on feelings; discover what the person's main concerns are, even if that means asking explicitly about those concerns.

Length of the Visit and Concluding the Visit

Usually, five to ten minutes of such conversation is all that's necessary for a visit that is useful to the person in terms of the purposes of visiting the sick as these were discussed in an earlier section of the chapter. Even a brief visit can be made in an unhurried manner. "Hustling-bustling" care usually is not experienced as genuine care at all. Of course, circumstances may differ from person to person and even visit to visit. Sometimes the visit may be considerably less than five minutes, and occasionally it may need to be longer. When we set out on hospital visits, we need to allow ourselves enough time to be reasonably flexible if necessary. If we stay longer, however, we need to be fairly certain that we can justify the additional time in terms of the real needs of the sick person. Too often, visitors simply don't know how to close off the conversation and leave, even when they realize that the most productive work has already been done and that there are other people to see or that there are other good reasons to leave.

This difficulty can be even more severe when the patient wants us to stay longer and that person seems to have the uncanny ability to hold us in some way. My own insight and "conversion" came one night many years ago. I was a minister in a large congregation. I had spent the day with some amount of church administrative tasks, a few hours of "in-office" pastoral counseling, and several hospital visits right up to dinner-time. Only one visit hadn't been made. I had left it until the last because it was not an emergency and the hospital was the closest to our home. My decision was to go on home, have dinner, and then make the additional hospital visit after the evening meal. A leisurely dinner helped me relax, but it also diminished my desire to go out again. However, I did, even though I was extremely tired. I arrived at the hospital room a little after 8:30. We had what I thought had been a productive visit, focusing on this particular woman's condition (not serious and clearly improving), airing some of her concerns and feelings, followed by my suggestion that we have prayer together. She then started talking again on some "new" issues, some additional needs she hadn't mentioned earlier and a couple of items that she "knew" that I would want to know about. I was polite, patient. Then I began to feel my tiredness, pressure, irritation. I was still polite. I didn't interrupt. I didn't really say firmly that I needed to go. I realized that my angry silent listening was *not* a good ministry to her. Frankly, I have no memory of how I got out of the room (they probably announced over the public-address system that visiting hours were over), but I remember that it was about 9:30: a one-hour visit, at least forty-five minutes of it unnecessary. As I walked out of the hospital and drove home I determined that I was not going to let that happen again. I also redemptively realized that my anger wasn't *all* at the woman; it was also at *myself.* I had been passive and had given control completely over to her. In this condition and situation, we do not serve people well. For my own benefit and the benefit of those whom I visit, I began to function differently.

How? Be attentive, involved, responsive, empathetic, and determine when we need to leave. Then two or three or so minutes before that time, say simply, "I'm going to have to leave in two or three minutes. I wonder if you've had anything on your mind that's important to you and that we haven't talked about yet." If there is, the person raises it, and we may be able to begin to deal with it right then; we *might* decide to stay somewhat longer; we might have a brief conversation and then agree to postpone the fuller discussion for a visit the next day.

When we've clarified this matter, or if the person has nothing else to deal with right at the moment, the issue of Scripture reading and/or prayer is before us. We shall do one or both or neither of these, then say good-bye, walk toward the door, and out of the room.

Praying with Persons

Some people will ask us to read a passage of Scripture. We've discussed earlier something of how we might go about this. Probably even more people will ask us to pray. In order to make the prayer more concrete, thus assisting us in the praying and assisting the other in that person's hearing and responding to the prayer, we ask, "What are the things you would like for me to include in the prayer?" Many people will say one or two or three things, and even if they don't we can pick up on their feelings and concerns as these have been identified in our prior conversation. We then present these to God in our prayer with that person.

A large number of people, however, will not ask us to pray with (or for) them. What then? There seem to me to be only three approaches with regard to praying with people: *never* do it (an abdication of our specific role, our duty and opportunity); *always* do it (experienced by a number of people as an invasion, triggering irritation and resistance and often presenting a barrier to our further ministry); or make our decision on the basis of our best judgment of the person and the situation. The first approach, I believe, is a total error for a representative of the community of faith. Both the second and third approaches will inevitably involve some mistakes. Since that's the case, I opt for number three. Does the person ask for it? Do we know the person well enough to be fairly sure of his or her desire or openness to it? Without prior knowledge of the person, have there been sufficient clues in our conversation: the person' references to her or his own faith or prayer life or church relationship, other language of faith, etc.? And, when in doubt, ask.

We can sometimes be surprised. I was at the church one afternoon and received one of those emergency calls that I always dread. "Have you heard that Ed C. has had a heart attack and has been taken to the hospital a little while ago?" No, I hadn't. I immediately left and arrived at the Coronary Intensive Care Unit. Ed and his wife were members of our congregation and regular worshipers. I knew her very well and him moderately well. He was in an oxygen tent and was obviously very weak. I greeted him, told him how stunned I was to hear about his having to be brought so quickly to the hospital, expressed my concern about him, and said that I realized that it was difficult for him to talk and that he needed to rest and conserve his energy. Therefore, I really didn't expect him to say much of anything, but I just wanted to be with him for a few minutes. (His wife was not in the room.) He smiled faintly and thanked me. I stood by his bed five minutes or so. Then, with perfect confidence (very unusual for me), I asked if he would like for me to have prayer with him before I left. He immediately replied in a stronger voice than before, "No. I take care of that myself." Although I was startled, it actually struck me in a rather positive sort of way and I smiled and said, "Great. Not everybody does, and I thought it was important to ask."

Just about the same time, there was another emergency. Barry was a middle-aged, well-built, physically strong former Marine Corps sergeant, a somewhat gruff-talking man, but very personable and a good human being. He had absolutely nothing to do with the church except his complete approval of his wife's activity in our congregation. I knew him only somewhat more than casually and that was primarily on a social basis. I liked him a great deal. He was hospitalized very suddenly after discovering a critical illness that could be life-threatening. My first visit was the night after he had been admitted to the hospital during the day. He was very responsive to my visit as we talked about the seriousness of his illness and the fear which he felt, but no reference to what his faith was or wasn't. After about fifteen minutes or so, we began to wind down, and my mind was really going, "To pray or not to pray." With considerable uncertainty and somewhat anxious, I said something like, "Barry, I know that you haven't been a part of the church and that earlier you have even been somewhat resistant to talking about it. I don't even know what you believe, but I've been moved by our conversation tonight. I'd like to pray with you and I wonder how you feel about it." His response: "I'd really appreciate that!"

I don't believe anything is ever lost by asking someone whether they would be receptive to having prayer with them unless a person has otherwise made it reasonably clear that he or she doesn't want any part of anything like that. We may get other unexpected answers, though, so we'd just better expect them. These are some things that patients have said to me. "That's your job." "Well, if you really want to." Or even, "If it would make you feel better."

I've spoken earlier of the importance of prayer being most effective as a part of a developing relationship, picking up on the specific needs and concerns of the sick person, but also that it does in fact have power of its own because of its inevitable reminder that God is present and active. Several years ago I had a knee operation in a hospital where I had been acquainted with the chaplain for several years. Contrary to my style, he always referred to himself as Chaplain Tarver, while calling others, including me, by their first name. I had been overanesthetized, and even after a long time in the recovery room was having a difficult time coming out of it in my regular hospital room. I would ease into a bit of consciousness, struggle to try to stay awake, but then quickly begin to lose it. I was completely helpless. Suddenly, somehow I became aware that someone had come into the room. I fought to open my eyes; only one of them opened very slightly for a second. I saw a large figure in the middle of the room some six or eight feet away (not, notice, next to my bed), and the figure seemed to be rocking from side to side. (Now, whether the man was actually doing that or whether this was just my own anesthesia still operating, I don't know.) As my eye caught this unusual scene, I heard a somewhat too loud voice saying very rapidly, "Hello David this is Chaplain Tarver let us pray O Lord . . ." No pauses! I couldn't stay awake. I heard only fragments of the prayer. Then I heard: "Amen I'll see you later." I got the one eye partially open again. He was already moving out of the door. I was in the hospital four more days. He never came back.

The next day I began to think a bit. I could visualize him making out his report for the previous day: "March 18. 328 pastoral visits. Had prayer with every patient visited."

His performance was not a very good model of visiting the sick. Although I was absolutely incapable of conversation the day he came in, he could have said something else to me. He could have walked all the way to the bed. He could have taken my hand. He could have come back to see me! I began to resent the way he did it. But the strange thing is, with all of this, in my state of helplessness and anxiety on that day, the fact that he prayed in my presence, and, I assume, for me, was comforting. God does work in mysterious ways, and through the variety of unusual human vessels which we offer to God for God's service. But there is still no excuse for doing a sloppy job; making mistakes, yes, but a sloppy job, no.

Precisely how we pray for healing is, of course, going to be shaped by our own beliefs. Those who truly believe that God answers the prayers of the faithful person, one who believes that the Holy Spirit has bestowed upon her or him the gift of the power to heal, will pray precisely for the person in those terms in a clear manner with the expectation that it will take place. Yet even these persons know that *physical* healing does not always take place. But there is no lack of clarity in their prayer and their intent.

Others who understand prayer as fundamentally honesty with God about the whole of our lives, may also pray for physical healing, because in fact that's *honestly* what they want. How can we pretend with God that this is not so? But their words may be phrased somewhat differently from the first group. It can be difficult for us at times, those of us who find ourselves here, as I do.

A few years ago, I had been visiting a young man who had a terminal disease. His physician expected him to die and had talked with him about it. Of course, we know that occasionally people with incurable terminal diseases in fact recover and occasionally there is no apparent remainder of the pathology. But when people with such a disease get so close to death, many of us "see" that death. I had prayer with this young man on almost every visit. So on another visit, I asked him what he wanted me to pray for on this occasion. In a voice so weak that I could hardly hear it, he said, "I want to be healed." "Of your physical sickness?" I asked. "Yes!" Of course, he did. And I prayed for that, but I also attempted as best I could to add the words which might help him understand that if death continued to draw closer to him, it didn't mean that God had abandoned him, had given up on him, rejected him, didn't care about him, so that in turn he himself wouldn't abandon God in those last minutes of his life.

It's no easy task that we have, regardless of what our own faith leads us to believe about physical healing. We can only be faithful, honest with ourselves, sensitive to the needs of the person, and with all of the thinking capacity we have and with openness to the Holy Spirit, seek to speak and pray in such a way that the faith of the sick person is nourished and strengthened.

Persons in Coma

Up to this point, I have obviously assumed that the person we are visiting will be able to speak at least to some minimal degree. Of course, there are numerous times when this is not the case. Some people will be alert enough, but with a tube down your throat or with a tracheotomy, you just don't say much. Some people will be quite conscious but so extremely weak that no talking is possible for them. Others will be in a coma. Many of us who visit in Christ's name are more anxious, more self-conscious, more awkward in these circumstances. It's usually even more important that we identify ourselves, take their hand or touch them in some other appropriate way, acknowledge that we understand that they can't speak but that we want to be with them awhile because we care for them, because the church cares for them, and because God cares for them. If it's the case, we can tell them how much we love them. We may stand or sit quietly for a while, continuing to be in physical touch with them. I have heard a physician say that the last of the five senses to leave a person is that of touch and the last sense of touch to leave is that of the pads of the fingers. Touch is extremely important. Realizing, however, that a person apparently in a coma might possibly be able to hear us, we can say some things which can be meaningful to her or him. Someone may have asked about her or him or asked us to convey their love to the person. We may have seen their small child or children and we can communicate that the children are being well taken care of. We may read a Scripture and pray aloud for the person and his or her concerns as we know or presume them to be.

Rituals of Healing

Some denominations and faith groups have brief, formalized sacraments or services of healing, usually including anointing with oil and/or the laying on of hands. Even though such rituals may be substituted for personal relationship and pastoral conversation and thus interfere with the fullest pastoral care, they may also contribute significantly to pastoral visits to the sick. Most of us who have done any amount of visiting the sick have had those occasions when our sensitivity and creativity have reached their limits and we have been at a loss as to what to do or say next. Those of us who have come from traditions that do not include a set service or sacrament of healing have felt even more lost.

I remember hearing well over thirty years ago an experienced ordained minister of a liberal nonliturgical denomination speak of his own situation of extremity when he was visiting a woman who was a member of his congregation. She had been quite faithful, but her husband never attended and had professed to be an atheist. He was devoted to his wife, and he and the minister were friends. After several weeks of illness and numerous visits by the minister to both of them, the wife was now in a coma and very close to death. On this particular day, the minister came into the hospital room, greeted the man, asked about both him and his wife, then went over and stood silently by her side. After a couple of minutes, the husband blurted out in a loud tone, "Well, dammit, why don't you do something?" The minister reported how shocked and helpless he had felt, with the obviousness of his helplessness brought to light by the husband's anxiety and angry exclamation. Desperate, and somehow almost immediately inspired, the minister reached for a glass of water, dipped his finger in it, made the sign of the cross in water on the woman's forehead, and began to say the Lord's Prayer. He was amazed to hear the husband joining in. When they were through, the man said, very quietly, "Thank you."

Hardly the planned ritual of the sacrament or service of anointing with oil, but the doing of this "something" was sufficiently powerful in that moment for the overwhelming dread of a brokenhearted husband who "didn't believe." When our own ordinary words fail to convey power, other traditional symbols may have the power to touch us, move us, even heal us in ways we don't easily understand. Even denominations that have not over the centuries had the tradition of a sacrament or a service of healing are now beginning to develop these and recommend them. We would do well to take these seriously, and even if our own particular denomination doesn't suggest or encourage it, begin to think of some ritual that we ourselves might develop and begin to instruct our congregations about.

Other Ways of Helping

An additional aspect of ministry to the sick is comprised of a variety of concrete tasks which may need to be attended to: taking something from the sick person to someone, picking up something at the person's home to bring to the hospital, conveying messages to certain persons, getting food to the house, having someone at the home to care for the children, whatever. The purpose is to reduce the sense of helplessness and anxiety which the person has by doing what needs to be done and by not doing what the person even from a sickbed might still be able to do for herself or himself. Persons who are otherwise quite assertive often begin to be passive when sick, especially when they are in the unusual environment of the hospital. They are obviously limited in what they can do with regard to many ordinary everyday tasks, but if the church visitor is a helpful resource person, they may still be encouraged to do what they *can* do.

It's especially important that the pastor not get caught in the middle of doing certain things that are *entirely* between the patient and the medical personnel. "Would you talk to the doctor and find out how I am really doing?" "Would you go ask the nurse to bring me a sleeping pill?" "Would you loosen this strap they have around me?" "Would you bring me my medication from home?" The response must always be, "You'll need to talk to the nurse or the doctor about that."

Even so simple a request as to get the person a drink of water isn't that simple, since some persons must not take *any* liquid and the liquid intake of others is being measured. In this case, we can respond that we would be willing to do that, but we will need to check with the nurse first.

None of this is to suggest that for our own understanding of the person and her or his condition, we ourselves would never talk with the doctor or a nurse about the person. Whenever we do, though, we need to realize that many of the medical team will be open and candid with us and helpful to us, while others, for different reasons, might not be willing to give the information. If they do give us medical information or opinions, however, it's not our role to quote them to the patient. There may also be times when we might be present when the patient and doctor or nurse are talking and responsibly enter into the conversation to assist in clarifying the patient's questions and being sure that she or he understands what the medical personnel are saying to the sick or injured person concerning his or her condition or medication or other matters. But we ourselves are never to communicate directly diagnoses or prognoses or evaluation of medication or other treatment procedures.

MINISTRY TO FAMILY MEMBERS

Members of the family, and sometimes close friends, of the ill often have needs of their own to which it is important for us to respond. They frequently have anxiety about the illness or operation or injury or the total family situation which is changed drastically by the condition of the person. The usual pattern of their living is disrupted. Their income may be affected. Especially if the physical disorder is serious and/or if the person is hospitalized or needs special home care for a long period of time, pressures can begin to increase as members of the family attempt to go to work or school, missing on occasion in order to take care of home and children, visit the hospital, or take care of the ill or recuperating person at home. Children may also be anxious about a parent and their emotional needs not being attended to in the usual ways. They can become quite insecure. Persons can easily become physically fatigued and emotionally drained and their relationships with one another may be affected in a negative way. They may even find themselves beginning to resent their family member's being ill, impatient with the normal, though not universal, increase in passivity and sense of helplessness. They may then often feel guilty about this response of theirs. It's not uncommon for them not to have a clear picture of what's going on medically if they've not been at the hospital when the doctor has been there, haven't been able to reach her or him by phone, or simply don't really understand what the physician has said, either because of their own confused state or because the doctor has overloaded the explanation in common medical terms which comprise an unknown language to the family and about which they are hesitant to ask further.

At times when we visit, family members will be present in the room. It is important that we make time to talk directly with the sick or injured person in the presence of the others and directly with family members and their situation and feelings in the presence of the patient. At other times, as in any occasion when we are with more than one other person, our function is to assist them in their expressing themselves openly and clearly to one another in terms of relevant information, their relationship with one another, and their feelings about what is going on, seeking to produce an increase in mutual understanding. We also need to be sensitive to either the sick person's or the family members' need to speak with us alone.

WHEN WE DON'T LIKE EACH OTHER

It's unrealistic to expect that we'll have a good relationship with every person for whom we're supposed to function as pastor. We may have seen them as obstructive and obnoxious on a church board or committee. They may have been openly angry at us, rightly or wrongly, about something we've done or haven't done. They may be chronic complainers. We may have heard that they've been spreading gossip about us. They may not like us for one or more of a variety of reasons and frankly we may not like them. They might resent and oppose us because of what we've said in our sermons and we've been totally unaware of it. If you're a woman who is ordained as a clergyperson, the person with whom you must function as pastor may not really see you as a minister and may even believe that you're doing something wrong by being ordained and functioning in this way. How can we visit people like this? How can we represent Christ and the church to them?

Whoever told us that our life as pastors, whether ordained or lay, would always be easy and pleasant? If we are responsible, we are responsible. Remember that *agape* love, caring, doesn't require that we like the persons involved. We function with these persons in precisely the same way as with others. Prior to our visit, we pray for them and for ourselves and for our relationship and our interaction with one another, that they and we may experience the living God in our visit together. We pray that we may forgive one another if it's a situation that calls for forgiveness. Then we go to them, seeking through our presence, our empathy, our expressed concern, our loving and forthright dealing with any issues between us that may arise explicitly, through the words of Scripture and sensitively worded prayer, to minister faithfully to one of God's children. Remember that human healing includes also the healing of relationships. The healing of relationships involves the healing of our emotional life, and these are both necessary for spiritual healing. In any given circumstance, we may be the ones who are in need of healing.

Occasionally there are other options: another clergy or lay member of the staff or volunteer lay visitor may go to see the person. Many times, however, there is no such possibility. Even if there is, we must not overlook the potential for the additional healing to which we have just referred, including our *own* healing, of course.

OUR BEHAVIOR DURING THE VISIT

As I communicated earlier, everything cannot be said, all bases cannot be covered. Yet there are still a number of important things to remember that somehow or another I've not been able to work into the material up to this point.

Let me first suggest a type of "empathy practice." Remember that empathy involves the attempt to see life through the eyes of the other person, to understand that person in this particular way. Therefore, each time that we prepare to go to visit different persons with different kinds of illness, injuries, those facing different operations, coming out from under anesthesia, etc., let's try to put ourselves in that person's condition and situation, going over in our minds and even in fantasy putting ourselves in that type of physical and emotional condition.

Think of the range and combination of feelings:
• fear
• loneliness
• uncertainty
• anxiety concerning others
• anger
• irritability growing out of anxiety and/or physical pain
• depression or despair
• boredom
• apathy
• sadness

Think of the combination of physical conditions:
• physical pain
• nausea
• lack of mobility, and the resulting overall bodily discomfort
• weakness
• itching terribly and not being able to scratch (Don't dare laugh if
    you've never experienced this!)
• loss of a limb
• thirst, especially when liquids are prohibited

Think of what might be going on in the person's mind:
• disorientation: loss of touch with time, day and night, the outside
    world; distortions of time periods; general confusion.
• paranoid thoughts, usually fairly mild, but often present, and dis-
    turbing:
    What's really my condition? What's this medication for? Why
    do I feel this way after taking it? I didn't know they were going
    to take blood: what are they doing to me? Why hasn't my
    spouse (mother or father, child, etc.) come to see me or come
    today or tonight or . . . whatever? He or she has given up on
    me, doesn't care for me, is abandoning me, etc.
• I wonder how the children *really* are, how it's going at work, etc.

These are only some examples. They are the reason for our regular visitation, for inquiring about physical condition and feelings and listening and responding and representing God and the community of faith in the ways we've discussed in this chapter. They also speak to the relevance of mentioning the day or evening, or the visit yesterday, or the weather outside, or a major current event, or friends or family members who have asked about them; of bringing a church bulletin or newsletter or a tape of last Sunday's service; or doing whatever seems appropriate to the most probable needs of the person.

A number of the physical and emotional conditions also remind us of the increased sensitivity of a majority of hospitalized persons to sound, light, odor, movement.

Therefore, *don't*
- wear perfume or cologne or use scented hairspray
- for a considerable period of time prior to the visit, smoke or come from a place where several people have been smoking
- stand between the person and a strong light
- speak too softly or too loudly
- sit on the bed or hit against the bed
- move the person in taking his or her hand or touching in some other way
- stand or sit where the person can't see you well or has to strain to see you
- joke in an *insensitive* way or be *overly* jovial (appropriate good spirit and good humor are not only appropriate but helpful *at times*)
- talk about your own or other peoples' problems (emotional or relational) and certainly not about your own or other people's illness, operations, etc.
- appear hurried (even if you are in a hurry)
- stay so long as to tire the person
- disagree with the doctor or take sides for or against the hospital and anyone in it
- immediately take personally anger or irritation or abruptness the person might be expressing toward you, or the person's words or other indications that she or he doesn't want the visit (or visit now). (Later realistic reflection upon the person's behavior could prove to be useful. Is it a function of that person's present illness and hospitalization or is there really something between us that needs to be resolved?)
- stand outside the door and speak in a low voice (the person may hear something you don't want him or her to hear, or, if the person can't hear well enough to understand the words, he or she usually will have such suspicion as to interpret our behavior as meaning something negative about him or her or his or her condition.)

CONCLUSION

Concern for the sick and physically handicapped in any way has always been a part of the life of the Christian community, growing out of the ministry of Jesus himself. One of the major contributions that the ordained ministry can make to the life of the congregation is to continue to stimulate that concern and guide the congregation in their concrete ministry to the sick in the church and larger community. In many places, that may very well mean having a formal program of selecting, training, and supervising laypersons who will be regular visitors of the sick in hospitals, homes, nursing homes, and other places. There are numerous sources which describe details of such programs (Detwiler-Zapp and Dixon, 1982; Haugk; Reiner and Wagner, 1984, chapter 6; Stone, 1991; Switzer, 1986, pp. 258–68).

There are times when all of us who are committed to ministry go out to visit the sick and suffering with a sense of liveliness, even though there be accompanying feelings of anxiety. There are also those times when for various reasons we go with reluctance and even a sense of dread. In the latter case, there is no reason to feel guilty or less of a servant, so long as we do go and engage ourselves with those who may have need of us in the ways we have discussed. In these latter instances, it is not at all uncommon that in the midst of the visit or visits that we have approached with resistance and reluctance we begin to realize once again that this work is not only obligation in response to God's command, but opportunity, opportunity not only for the sick but also for us, as we meet God in the relationship with the sick and suffering and as some of those persons themselves make their contributions to us.

REFERENCES

Diane Detwiler-Zapp and William C. Dixon, *Lay Care Giving* (Philadelphia: Fortress Press, 1982).

Kenneth Haugk, "The Stephen Series" (7120 Lindell Blvd., St. Louis, MO 63160).

Gardner Murphy, *Personality* (New York: Harper, 1947).

Thomas C. Oden, *Pastoral Theology* (San Francisco: Harper & Row, 1983).

Lawrence D. Reiner and James T. Wagner, *The Hospital Handbook* (Wilton, Conn.: Morehouse Barlow, 1984).

Howard W. Stone, *The Caring Church: A Guide for Lay Pastoral Care*, 2nd ed., rev. (Minneapolis: Fortress Press, 1991).

David K. Switzer, *The Dynamics of Grief* (Nashville: Abingdon Press, 1970).

———. *The Minister As Crisis Counselor* (Revised and enlarged) (Nashville: Abingdon Press, 1986).

5

Hospital Emergencies

Few phone calls raise greater anxiety in most of us that that which begins, "Can you get right over to the hospital? Bill's suddenly gotten sick. We think it's a heart attack (or a stroke, etc.)." Or "Susan's been in a bad automobile accident (or our little boy has just fallen out of a tree or our little girl has suddenly become unconscious and can hardly breathe)."

Our own hearts begin to pound as we hear words like this, and we feel our own heartbeats and shortness of breath as we are driving to the hospital (or home), wondering what happened, how the person is, what we are going to say and do. These are always "pastoral emergencies" for the representative of the community of faith as well as for the person or persons whom we are going to see in only a few moments.

There is no better way to prepare for our meeting with the persons in the emergency of sudden and/or critical illness and accident than to pray: for each of the persons involved, for doctors and nurses and paramedics, for ourselves as we engage ourselves with them, that God will guide us and them and be active in our relationship with one another. This is a much deeper and more effective preparation at this moment than attempting to figure out ahead of time what we are going to say.

Nevertheless, some guidelines concerning what to say and do can be useful.

Unless we immediately see the family members and/or friends in the emergency room (ER) or intensive care unit (ICU) (in which case we go directly to them), it is extremely important to make our way immediately to the triage desk in the ER or to the nursing station in the ICU, identify ourselves, state who the patient is, ask if they have any information they can give us at this moment, if we may see that person right now, and if they happen to know where family members are.

Our overall effectiveness in these situations is going to be very dependent upon how well we get along with the hospital personnel. Therefore, it is necessary to be sensitive to their situation right at the moment. On many occasions they will be extremely busy, so we may need to wait for at least a brief break in order to say and ask briefly that which has been suggested above. Their first concern has to be the critically ill or injured person, and we need to be careful not to intrude on their duties or even break their concentration. If we misjudge the situation and move in at an inconvenient time, we should not be surprised or offended if someone tells us, sometimes very abruptly and in no uncertain terms, to get out of the way. In fact, we might not even have been physically in the way at all, but we can still move back a bit farther. If where we are standing has interfered with the medical team's movement, then simply say, "I'm sorry," and move away quickly. If there seems to us to be some reason for staying in the area longer, we can usually do so at a discreet distance. Then, if and when the medical activity diminishes, we may ask if we may speak with the person and/or ask to speak with the doctor or one of the nurses briefly. Occasionally, it might be wise for us to leave the area for awhile and check back a bit later. Sensitivity to the tremendous pressure under which members of the medical team usually work and the intense feelings which they themselves often have can help guide us, and they will appreciate our sensitivity.

In the emergency room, it's important for us to tell the injured or ill person that we are there, give our name, state that we are the pastor (or chaplain or other representative of the church) if we are not well acquainted, touch the person appropriately if possible, and, if there is time, express our concern and give a very brief prayer. At times members of the medical team will still be around. We may feel very self-conscious doing all of this with others in our presence, especially if the person seems to be unconscious, but we simply have to go right ahead and do it anyway. At times the medical team will actually be totally surrounding the person and our physical access will be quite limited. Usually we can still let the person know we are there and bide our time until we have the opportunity to move closer for other comments, for touching the person, for prayer, and, when it applies, for the sacrament or service of healing.

Even though some of the emergency medical team may experience a pastor's presence in the ER, or at certain times in the ICU, as an intrusion or bother, most of these persons basically realize that it's important for us to be there for the patient, for the family, and occasionally to some extent for them. There are times when our presence has a calming effect on the person in the critical condition and may then make the medical team's work with the person easier. They also realize that our work with the family, even though it entails some brief interruptions for the medical team, is useful to the family and usually even more efficient for the medical personnel themselves than the often more frequent and less focused communications from this, that, and the other family member.

In addition, there are times, more in the ICU than in an ER, when things are not so rushed and hectic, even in large city hospitals. However, it is important always to check with a nurse about going into a treatment area of the ER or into an ICU room. ICU's almost always have a very or relatively inflexible set of visiting rules, and for very good reason. On the other hand, most clergy or officially designated professional church workers may often visit at other times. It is both courtesy and often medically necessary for us to ask each time, however, and not merely presume that we may walk in and out whenever we wish without any contact with a nurse.

Visits with the injured or critically ill person will always be brief, except in very unusual circumstances. Some patients will be in a coma; others will be unable to speak for other reasons; many will be extremely weak and can speak only very softly and briefly and need to conserve their strength. If we notice any signs of agitation during our visit, it would be very important to draw our visit to a close with some appropriate comment, and, after a *very* brief prayer, leave immediately and report our observations to the nurse in charge.

Otherwise, all that has been described about pastoral visitation of the physically ill in the previous chapter holds true in the visiting of the person in an emergency area or ICU.

The fact is that much more of our attention in these circumstances will be given to family members. Initially, they will usually be in a state of shock, be somewhat confused in their thinking, may have outbreaks of anxiety, weeping, expressions of irritation, repetition of feelings of guilt, and other reactions in various combinations. At this time, the "symbol power" of the representative of the community of faith will, if anything, be even more important than in other circumstances.

Therefore, the approach to them by a pastor will be supported by the pastor's authentic and concrete words. When we see them, we say whatever our genuine reaction is: "I was so shocked to get the call about Bob (or Margaret)." "When I heard what happened, I could hardly believe it. I've been so anxious and so concerned about you all." Whatever words are truly yours in that moment are the words to say.

Next, something more or less like, "How are you doing?" Then respond to whatever they say with empathy.

Then, "Tell me what happened."

I am not sure that the chronological order of these makes much difference. We do want to ask about the person who is sick or injured, about the family members with whom we are speaking, about the concrete events of the situation, and it's usually helpful to the family (and for us) for us to be open and candid about our own feelings in this situation.

However, the situations of emergency of this sort differ sufficiently from other hospitalization that at first it's not usually productive to attempt to spend time asking what feelings the patient and the family are concretely experiencing and then exploring these in great detail. It would be so incongruous as to be ludicrous, if it weren't also so tragic, to attempt to pursue this approach with a person when the medical team is attempting to monitor life-maintaining equipment, sew up wounds, remove shards of glass from a person's eye, etc.

Likewise, family members are hardly in a condition to be very self-reflective and engage patiently and in detail in self-exploration. Rather, "Tell me what happened" as an expression of genuine concern can elicit details of events (the onset of the symptoms, the accident, how various family members responded if they were also involved in the accident, or how they heard about what happened, and what has taken place since then). If more than one family member is present, their stories may be somewhat different, either supplementing or conflicting with one another in detail. One person's statement may remind others of something someone else had forgotten. At this moment, precision and absolute accuracy don't matter. The recounting of all of these details has the effect of breaking through the shock, emphasizing the reality of what has taken place, reducing confusion somewhat, stimulating the expression of feelings which are attached to the various aspects of the event. Our questioning, our occasional empathic responses, the brief expression of our own feelings, taken together, will communicate our caring, assist in developing our human/pastoral relationship with the family members, and help them in the process of reducing the intensity of feelings, gaining some clarity, and supporting one another.

A few people will ask us to pray almost as soon as we arrive. Occasionally we may do that, but I am not sure how to do it well until we have some idea of what is going on. Therefore, to respond "I'd be glad to, but first, tell me what's happened" will both assist the persons in the ways described in the preceding paragraph and also give us information that will enable us to pray for the individuals involved in a much more concrete way.

We may continue to talk, although often we may sit together without much conversation for a fairly long period of time after the prayer. Or we may have prayer as our last act together before we leave.

One important contribution we can make in these emergency situations is that of communicating information to the family. In almost all cases, someone of the medical team will step out occasionally to give the family some news. But they can't do that if all of them are needed for the treatment procedures, which they sometimes are. They are totally taken up with what is medically necessary and it's too much to expect them to be aware of the amount of time that is passing. In the meantime, the family has no information, is anxious, often tends to think the worst, and becomes more and more distraught. We will usually have access to the treatment area at times when family members do not, so we can step into that area, and, if nothing else, determine that treatment activity is still in process. Most of the time, if we'll wait only a minute or a few, we can ask a quick question or two and get a quick answer from someone, and sometimes even more. It's important to the family to have these periodic updates.

When the immediate emergency procedures have been completed, the physician will usually come into the waiting room or family room and explain the person's condition and treatment and what all of that means. Sometimes, of course, this may be done in technical language and the family, often still in shock and in the presence of the physician (Authority), will not raise any questions. It's not out of line and can be helpful if the pastor asks simply, "Are you clear about what the doctor is saying?" followed by, "Do you have any questions (or any further questions) you would like to ask her or him?" Sometimes we may have a question of our own, but we need to be clear that its purpose is to help clarify something for the family or occasionally for the physician. If the information is for ourselves alone, it's better to ask the doctor privately.

Although almost all physicians see this type of family conference as a part of their professional responsibility, there are occasions when they must go directly to another emergency. Therefore, if the minister discovers that the first-order emergency treatment by the physician is completed and he or she has not come out to talk to the family, it is appropriate for the minister to attempt to check out the details of the situation and perhaps ask the head nurse of the treatment process to give at least a preliminary report to the family and make some estimate of the time when the doctor might be available.

Whereas persons are rarely in the ER for more than a few hours, they may be in an ICU for much longer periods of time. The individual's condition may remain critical, and much that the pastor does with the family is based on the seriousness and uncertainty of the situation. Daily or almost daily contacts are a useful part of ministry. If the pastor cannot actually come to the hospital on a certain day, some other representative of the community of faith can come and visit with the family and perhaps the patient. The ordained minister can also telephone a family member in the ICU waiting room or at home.

Persons who begin to recover while in ICU will signal a transitional stage of ministry, part of which has just been discussed in this chapter, and other issues of visiting the sick as these were discussed in chapter 4.

It's apparent that these emergency visits to home or hospital are quite unpredictable in terms of the amount of time that they will involve. Sometimes, by the time the minister arrives, the person will have already been brought into a stable condition and be in the process of either being transferred to a regular hospital room or being discharged to go back home. What has appeared to be life-threatening at the moment has been determined not to be the case. These visits then will be like any visit to the hospital when a person is sick or perhaps only a brief contact as the people are ready to return home. Most of the time, however, the pastor can expect to stay a fairly long period of time with the critically ill or injured person and/or members of the family. It is proper to cancel or postpone most other types of appointments and activities. However, good judgment always has to be used when the pastor considers all of the factors involved in the particular emergency situation and the other sorts of demands upon her or him. We may need after a while to leave the hospital briefly in order to do something else which is truly of a critical nature and then return to the situation and the people involved.

Some persons admitted directly or transferred to an ICU will, of course, die, as they will in emergency rooms or even on the way to the hospital. These situations will be discussed partly in chapter 6 and partly in chapter 7.

6

MINISTRY TO THE DYING

The pastoral visitation of the dying and our pastoral conversations with them offer one of our greatest opportunities for ministry. Yet my own experience and the results of hearing clergy discuss their own time spent with dying persons leads me to the conclusion that it's an occasion of considerable anxiety and lack of confidence in what we are doing. It's obvious that we need something. What is it?

Undoubtedly, we need to know more about dying persons and their needs, the process of dying, how to communicate with them in the most helpful way in whatever particular stage of the process they might be. Correct? Of course. What do *we* need to *do* to help *them?*

Then why is it, do you suppose, that a friend of mine, Dr. Jerry Lewis, a psychiatrist, has entitled an article revealing his experiences and conclusions as a result of being with four friends of his as they were dying, "Dying with Friends"? Why in the world didn't he call the article simply and clearly, "*Being* with Dying Friends"?

We already know the answer, don't we? We've already discussed in an earlier chapter that in order to be competent helpers when the helping takes place in the context of a continually developing personal relationship, we must also be competent human beings. We can't assist people to move beyond barriers in their own lives when we are not aware of those barriers because we are *first* not aware of them in our own lives.

Therefore, the conclusion once again is that the beginning focus in the discussion of the pastoral care of the dying must be on *us:* on *us* as *human beings,* some of whom will grow old and die and some of whom will die before we know anything at all about the latter stages of the aging process. How can it be possible for us to be effective in our relationships with dying persons when the awareness of the reality of our own dying has not been adequately visualized by us, the emotions felt as much as we can, and these relatively well assimilated? How can we expect a dying person to become more realistic about her or his condition when we ourselves are effectively denying our own death?

THE PERSONS WE NEED TO BE

How can we provide Christian ministry which is most powerfully undergirded by close personal emotional relationship when we practice evasion by not visiting the person regularly and frequently, when we enter into collusion with the person and often the family and treat this as "any other hospital (or home) visit" to a sick or injured person or, as Dr. Lewis so perceptively suggests, by a "compulsive lifestyle which focuses on tasks, accomplishments, and productivity [so] as to exclude a broader consideration of life's meaning" (p. 264).

Because so much of what is involved in our ministry with dying persons has to do with life's meaning, how are we going to be capable of being completely present to that person unless we ourselves are in the process of working out the meaning of our own personal lives within the context of the only absolute certainty *of* our lives, our own *death*, and also for *all* of us, should we live so long, our understanding of ourselves as persons with numerous limitations, those who know pain, who suffer, who experience significant losses, who get ill ourselves, and whose inevitable death is a part of our own present being.

Therefore, the awareness of the omnipresence of the "not-yet" of our existence affects the present quality of our lives, the choices of how we live, what we do and how we go about it, *with whom* we relate and *how* we relate to one another, how we talk about the meaning of our lives, and how we engage ourselves as persons with other persons in need. A part of our own maturing as human beings who are involved with the critically ill, the aging, and the dying is the process of experientially bringing into the "now" of our lives that end which is "not-yet." In so doing, we begin to confront, as Dr. Lewis suggests, those defenses against the reality of our own human finitude, characterized most powerfully by our death, which can also limit us in other areas of our present self-knowledge, our personal growth, and our effectiveness in personal relationships. We have the possibility of increasing the depth of our humanity and our human understanding.

A part of our own growth in self-awareness and in effectiveness in working with persons who are dying is the actual visitation of those in that condition, but with the addition of having regular supervisory sessions with some sensitive and experienced person after such visits. It can also serve us well to be a part of a small group of persons who are all involved in visiting the dying and who meet on a regular basis to discuss their experiences.

In addition, I would suggest the following exercise:

> Imagine yourself ill. Be very concrete in regard to some of the symptoms you are having. Get this clearly set in your mind.
>
> Fantasize yourself in the doctor's office, waiting for the doctor to give you the results of the examination. The doctor steps into the room, begins to speak, describes what has been found, and states the nature

of what is considered a terminal disease. Be very concrete in your own mind as you choose for yourself what your terminal disease is. How do you feel? How do you respond?

Now imagine yourself in the hospital several weeks later. You have gotten worse and worse. See yourself there in the hospital bed. You know that you are close to death. You are suffering. Be very specific about the nature of it. See yourself terribly debilitated, having lost a lot of weight. Feel yourself so weak that you can hardly move, can barely speak.

Now you are having your very last thought, drawing your very last breath.

You are dead. Life in the world goes on without you.

Identify the various feelings you have had during this extended fantasy. Note when these feelings occurred. Perhaps you were unable to have any particular feelings at all. Think about that. Note whether you found yourself having to withdraw from the fantasy at different points. What points?

I don't intend by all this to be morbid or to involve you in a process which you experience in that way. If you find yourself becoming preoccupied with death as a result of this fantasy exercise, or if you experienced feelings of panic, or if you were unable to do it at all, be sure to talk with some sensitive counselor about your particular response or responses.

Perhaps it would also be useful for all of us to read, or even memorize, and then allow the following words pass through our minds on a regular basis: "The Lord knows what we are made of; God remembers that we are dust. As for us, our life is like grass. We grow and flourish like a wild flower; then the wind blows on it and it is gone: no one sees it again" (Ps. 103:14-16). This is who we are, each one of us. But the psalmist goes on, and we must not forget to read and repeat to ourselves the continuing words, "But for those who honor the Lord, God's love lasts forever, and God's goodness endures for all generations" (Ps. 103:17).

The first absolutely critical issue, then, in terms of willingness and ability to work helpfully with dying persons is who *we* are as persons. What kind of people can we tolerate? Which ones frighten us, anger us, lead us to feel depressed? These feelings of ours tend to make us very selective of the persons with whom we relate well, frequently, regularly, and effectively, and our behavior of attention or inattention, approach or withdrawal, have an important positive or negative impact upon these persons' lives, and in turn, back upon our own.

WHAT THE PASTOR NEEDS TO KNOW

In addition to our own *being*, with the diminishing need to protect ourselves from dying persons, it's also obviously important for us to know something of the needs of persons who are dying and with whom we relate. It is useful for us to keep in mind that dying is a psycho-social-biological process, and that for many if not most persons it is also a spiritual process. When I use the word *spiritual*, I don't mean something totally apart from the psycho-social-biological process, since that's totally involved. I do mean to say that the person who is going through this process is also considering in some way or another the meaning of one's *having been* in the world, *being* in the world, and now *leaving* the world, and the fact that many of these persons frame these issues one way or another in terms of God. There is a sense in which dying persons move from a first reaction when they become aware of the fact that they are dying, on through a series of other reactions in which there are these psychosocial, emotional, relational, and in some sense, spiritual tasks to be performed, on to whatever their situation may be at the point of death.

Stages of Dying

Most people are now quite familiar with Elisabeth Kübler-Ross's so-called stages of dying (1969). In summary, just to get the scheme before us at this point, it goes like this:

1. Shock and denial—Not me. (It can't be true.)
2. Anger—Why me? (Rage, resentment; envy of those not dying).
3. Bargaining—It's me, (but if you'll . . . then I'll . . .).
4. Depression—It's me. (What's the use?)
5. Acceptance—It's me (and I accept it). (For Kübler-Ross, acceptance involves the beginning of the severing of remaining human ties, withdrawal, quietude.)

Kübler-Ross has made a great contribution to us, the three major ones being the following:

First, she has made our society more aware of dying. She has taken it out of the privacy of the hospital room and has broken the culturally relatively new taboo of talking about it. She has made large numbers of people aware of the needs of dying persons, the contributions which dying persons can make to us who *presumably* will live somewhat longer, and of the need that we all have to prepare for our own dying.

Second, she has presented dying as a process, emphasizing the psychological and social dimensions of it as well as the physiological. She speaks of there being a type of movement within the process and indicates that there *may* be a more or less constructive movement.

Third, she has offered to us as a model of relating to the dying her procedure itself, which pays a great deal of attention to the dying persons, which says to them in a variety of ways that they are important, that they have a contribution to make to us, that they can teach us something, which encourages them to express themselves openly and honestly at length without fear that she would withdraw from them.

Having made this statement of appreciation for Kübler-Ross, it's necessary to go on to say that other observers have not seen these stages as sharply delineated as her outline suggests and as moving beyond the shock and denial in the particular way she describes. Actually, she herself made a few statements in her book indicating that we should not take the stages as she described them too literally and rigidly, but she did not go into any great detail in these qualifying statements, which were almost hidden in the context of other discussions. Quite a number of people have seemed to ignore what she said at those points.

There is no way to exaggerate our indebtedness to Kübler-Ross. However, the fact is that a number of other researchers and workers with the dying have not made precisely the same observations that she has in the sense of finding most of the stages best designated in the terms she uses and moving in the particular order which she suggests. Almost everyone, of course, observes sufficiently similar reactions to be able to speak of shock and denial as a first stage and notes that anger, bargaining, and depression are frequently present.

Schulz and Aderman (1974) have summarized several other investigations. Hinton noted that depression is present throughout, and even increases during, the last two weeks of life. Anxiety has also been observed, also increasing during the last two weeks. He also saw some form of denial operating throughout the process in 60 percent of the patients whom he studied (1963).

Another study (Weisman and Kastenbaum, 1968) separated patients entering the terminal phase into distinguishable groups, both of whom were aware of the reality of their impending death. The first group usually withdrew from daily activities and remained somewhat inactive to the end, the way in which Kübler-Ross described her word acceptance. The second group, however, engaged actively in things about them and even initiated new activities and relationships, responses which Kübler-Ross apparently did not view sufficiently in order to take account of them in her stages. Shneidman wonders whether there is any steady progression of stages at all. He hypothesizes an alternation of acceptance and denial (1974).

Several studies criticize Kübler-Ross's scheme, saying that it is an overgeneralization based on observation and systematization of the data, a procedure which does not account for a number of variable factors. An experimental study by Metzger reached findings that "are not explained by the stage structure" (of Kübler-Ross) (1979–80).

Dr. Lewis's article, which was mentioned earlier, gives a progressive report of his conversations with his dying friends and indicates that toward the end of their lives there seems to be a type of acceptance of death, or at least resignation to the reality of it, sometimes accompanied by a sense of relief. But he goes on to say that these observations should not "be interpreted as evidence of an orderly progression of the so-called stages of dying." All the reactions which are described in various stage theories were noted, but "they appeared in rapid and changing order. . . . The sole commonality was the position of resignation, acceptance, or embracement at the end" (1982, p. 263).

My own observations, which I have never even attempted to systematize, seem to be more in keeping with the variations of different kinds which are noted by many of these other investigators. Certainly, it is useful to think of dying as a complex process through which most people make some emotional, relational, and spiritual movement. The delineation and naming of stages which can account for the greatest number of occasions, however, still remains to be developed.

None of this need suggest that Kübler-Ross did not observe what she said she observed, including her own variations to the major outline of the process, nor that the other persons referred to observed incorrectly. It is to say, however, first, that different people with different personalities and different methods worked with (or merely observed) different populations of patients in different psychosocial settings. Second, we need to be aware that Kübler-Ross's methods themselves were an influential variable in the patient behavior she observed. Her research methods, so to speak, were in fact a rather effective form of psychotherapy. We would expect dying persons who receive such compassionate and sensitive and frequent attention to be involved in a process which is different from that which others not receiving such attention might go through. Therefore, while there does seem to be a process of dying, several factors lead to the conclusion that up to this time no particular set of stages had been satisfactorily identified, and even if they were to be, I believe that we could predict individual variances within them. Third, I believe that there is and always will be a problem with any system which attempts to list stages of any human process which are defined in terms of merely one emotion or one behavior (such as anger, fear, guilt, bargaining) rather than in some more comprehensive terms which can accommodate the complex and interacting elements of human personality. One exception to this statement is something like a stage of shock because it seems to be a valid designation for the initial reaction in a number of different situations.

The Needs of the Dying

Perhaps we ought to say a word about the question of when a person begins to die. There is the old saying that from the time we are born we are all persons who are dying. In a sense, that's true. To say it in this way reinforces an important factor in human life, our mortality. Or, on the other hand, this statement may also be used to deny the reality of how close to death some of us really are at times. There is, in fact, a relativity of the "being alive" part of us and the "dying" part, and at a given time with any person, it may be more of one and less of the other.

As a person grows older, sometimes the "being alive" may actually increase in terms of *quality* of life, but also as we grow older, we move inexorably closer and closer to our physical death, more in the direction of physical dying. Certainly as persons begin to age they are constantly engaged in giving up aspects of their lives which have been meaningful to them.

The whole point I am trying to make here is that what the dying person needs with great urgency and intensity is, on the whole, what we all need at all times. We who work with the elderly and the dying are in a position to use our genuine humanity, our warmth and sensitivity as persons, in the meeting of these needs.

As I have attempted to list these needs which seem to be reflected in some way in all persons who are dying, I have become aware of two things. The first is that the way they are stated doesn't adequately represent the specific set of circumstances of any one particular person. Each person must be known for herself or himself, and that person's *very* specific needs and constellation of needs require our response. Second, many of the different needs as presented in this list overlap, and therefore, both the headings themselves and their particular order might certainly be stated in different ways. Having said this, the following are the fairly common needs of persons who are dying.

Expression of Feelings. Undoubtedly the place to begin is for the person to have the opportunity to express whatever feelings of fear, anger, guilt, sadness, loneliness, or whatever she or he may have; to express grief over the loss of herself or himself, the loss of emotionally significant other people, the loss of meaningful activities; to express concern over problem areas in relationship with significant persons. The need of the dying person is for someone who is willing to take the time to sit and listen, to encourage his or her expression, to struggle to understand, and who is capable of receiving the strong emotions which are involved. Unexpressed feelings, unresolved internal conflict, unresolved issues between people: all of this is unfinished business. None of us is at peace until the unexpressed is expressed, conflicts are in the process of being diminished, and we have done what *we* can do about reconciliation. It's often necessary for another person to give us permission to accept and express our feelings, assist us in working through our conflicts, and be a mediator between us and significant others. "Those patients do best who have been encouraged to express their rage, to cry in preparatory grief, and to express their fears and fantasies to someone who can quietly sit and listen" (Kübler-Ross, p. 119).

The Overcoming of Loneliness. If we can assist a dying person in the expression of feelings, the resolution of conflicts, and whatever reconciliation is necessary and possible, we have also already have helped her or him overcome one of the most awful things about dying, the loneliness. Consider the isolation of knowing that we are dying if we have *no one* to share this with openly: no one to whom to tell our fears, with whom to vent our anger, to confess our guilt, to bring our relationships totally up to date, perhaps even for the first time in our lives. All of this, enclosed just within ourselves! This is an awful isolation. Then there is the dying itself: one of the few significant acts in all life that we can do only by ourselves, for ourselves. We are saved, in some potent meaning of that word, if only one person, or hopefully a few people, will be willing to sit and listen and accept and understand and be *for* us, struggling to participate with us as much as they possibly can.

That One's Life Has Been Meaningful. A third need of every person, of an elderly person, and much more urgently of a dying person, is the conviction that he or she has not lived in vain, that she or he has achieved some important things (within the family, in the community, in work, in the church), that his or her life has had a meaning and a purpose.

Such an experience is necessary for the building or bolstering of self-esteem. As a part of fulfilling this need, the pastoral visitor needs to be able to facilitate dying persons' reminiscences, assist them to talk about their personal past, and be willing to accept without impatience the repetition which is both an inevitable and necessary part of the process of confirming one's place in the world.

To Find Meaning in the Present Moment. Fourth, it is essential that the pastor be able to participate with the dying in their struggle to find meaning in the present process with its increasing debilitation and often pain and its inevitable end. How do they *now* make sense out of their *present* lives *while* they are dying and yet are still alive? While we who represent the community of faith are human beings who have ways of expressing the meaning of *our* lives at the present time, and although we are not prohibited from sharing that meaning with others, we must always remember that even within the religious community, meaning is not only corporate in some sense but is also *intensely* personal. We cannot simply hand our meaning over to another person in the particular verbal form which we use and expect it to become immediately and automatically a vital force in the life of the other. Even less so can we expect such a transfer of meaning to take place when the person with whom we are engaged is not a part of the community of faith. The particularly significant act of ours is our willingness to participate in the others' process with them as they seek to discover the meaning of their dying for themselves.

Our respect for other persons, our valuing of them, is fully expressed only if we can truly allow them, with our participation, to work out and express the meaning of their present experience in their own way, even if it is different from the meaning we might attribute to it. Remember, we're (usually) not the person who is dying right at this time. It also has to be recognized clearly that the way in which we might frame the gospel for ourselves and share it with another person, even when she or he is a person of faith, might not significantly touch the most important concrete issues of that person's life in the process of dying as he or she sees them. Our task and opportunity is to be the facilitator of a *particular* person's discovery in his or her *particular* set of experiences the meaning that may be there for her or him.

Not only do some people explicitly raise the question, "Why must I die (now, like this, etc.)?" but at times we'll hear those who are lingering on ask, "Why must I continue to live? Why can't I just go ahead and die? I'm ready." We don't have the answers to these questions either. Once again, we work with them to help them find some significant response for themselves.

An elderly woman with cancer raised that question with me several times as her pain grew worse and she became weaker and weaker as the weeks went by. "Why do I have to stay alive?" Her daughter and son-in-law were extremely attentive to her and were very appreciative of my regular visits in the hospital. Their faith was stimulated, deepened; they began attending church and later joined the church. They were able to discuss with their mother the details of her funeral, a unique and poignant closeness between them in her last days. Experiencing this process, on one of my last visits before she died, she said, "Now I know why I continued to live. Now I can die." And a few days later she did. My understanding is not necessarily that God *kept* her alive so that her daughter and son-in-law might grow in faith and make their personal commitments and that they might draw closer to one another as a family, but that God worked with us in the situation that *was* to bring about good (Rom. 8:28).

To Continue to Feel Useful. There may be some substantial overlap in what I am trying to express here with the discussion of one's seeking to find meaning in the present moment of the dying process. However, there are some unique factors to stress in highlighting the need to continue to feel one's usefulness in the world. Remember that this was one of the great gifts which Kübler-Ross gave to the people she worked with: the message that "You still have a contribution to make. I value you now."

I have the complete statement of a student in a theological seminary, written several months before he died of cancer. Among the other struggles he referred to, he said,

> The issue that bothered me most was the question of my worth as a human being. I wondered whether people had written me off as being among the dead. I longed for someone to tell me that I was still wanted and needed.

A psychotherapist who was dying of cancer continued to see his patients even as his condition got notably worse. He kept extensive notes of this period of time and in them he recorded that a woman patient told him one day as he was getting much sicker that she had developed a fearful expectation before a particular session that when she arrived for the appointment, he would not be at the office. He continued in his notes: "I felt like yelling, 'But I am not dying. I am hoping for a cure. Don't dispose of me so quickly'" (Kaplan and Rothman, 1986, p. 563). Kaplan, the author of the article in which Dr. Rothman's notes are included, criticizes Rothman for not being fully truthful and open with his patients about the extreme seriousness of his illness. He believes that Rothman was holding on to at least some of his patients beyond the point of therapeutic benefit to them or at least in a way which complicated both their therapy with him and their later beginning therapy with someone else. This may well be true. But Kaplan interprets Rothman's behavior in terms of countertransference. Perhaps this is true also. But it seems to me that there might well be another simpler and more easily understood interpretation. Perhaps Rothman needed to hold on to his patients in order to maintain some hope of his own continued life, to support his denial of the prognosis of his illness. Or perhaps there is yet another interpretation. Perhaps he was experiencing an increasingly urgent need to continue to experience his sense of usefulness in the world by continuing to try to be useful to the persons who were seeing him in therapy. He apparently did make some strategic errors in the way he handled his patients during his last few months, although some of them later reported some significant benefits, too. But it seems to me that the desire to experience oneself as useful is a normal need, which can't be encompassed in the word *countertransference.* This need can be a legitimate expression of a mature person.

What Rothman himself may have missed was that there is more than one way to feel useful and valued.

Some family systems theorists make the distinction between functional roles (those that are useful in accomplishing necessary family behavioral operations) and affectional roles. Many times they overlap, but often they don't. Infants are hardly useful in the accomplishment of households tasks (they *are*, in fact, one of the tasks); they are not time-savers. But they may be very significant in their affectional role and in what these affectional bonds may mean in the richness of family life. Many very elderly people, significantly mentally handicapped people, and others in the family may have little if any functional role, but continue to have meaningful affectional roles.

To these two categories of family roles, I'd like to add the concept of symbolic role, which some family members may possess even in the absence of the functional role and which is not precisely the same as the affectional role: the grandparent or great-grandparent who represents the history, the story, of this family, its continuity with its own past; the small child who represents to the parents their mutual love, their commitment to one another, who symbolizes their creative powers, their future, their contribution to the life of the world.

Even when a dying person is no longer functional in the usual sense, or is in the process of losing functions and is beginning to feel useless, the responsive helping person may meet that person's need by reinforcing his or her affectional value, helping the person identify and affirm her or his symbolic value. A human being's sense of usefulness does not have to be lost.

As one's usefulness either in an affectional and/or symbolic way is brought to light and confirmed, we discover that yet another need is in the process of being met. Observers have discovered that quite a number of dying people feel very guilty about their being sick, their dying, their being a burden to others about them as they understand the time and emotional energy and often money which family members are investing. Easy reassurance is no answer for a powerful feeling of guilt. However, as a person gains a new perspective on himself or herself as a person of worth, one who is loved, one who is still useful to those who relate to her or him, such guilt is dissipated. This particular process of the affirmation of the person which results in the diminishing of this particular guilt is not at all in conflict with the reality that family members and friends very often do begin to find themselves strained by the constant attention they give, fatigued by the difficult emotional visits, and concerned about the financial cost.

The Need to Maintain Some Control over One's Life. In being sick at all we experience some loss of control over ourselves. When we are bedridden, there is even greater loss. When we are hospitalized, it seems as if many other people are taking over the various aspects of our lives: when we wake up, when visitors have to leave, when lights go out, when we take medication, when we *must* eat and when we *cannot* eat, what gets stuck into us where, etc. We are some *thing* that various people do something to and with whenever *they* choose. In the midst of this, there is a great threat of the loss of our own identity, our integrity as persons. In the face of this onslaught, many persons give in to an extreme passivity and regression. Others try to handle it with irritability, punching the button for the nurse frequently, complaining, issuing orders, etc.

When a person is also dying, the last and ultimate sense of control that he or she has seems to be taken away. One frequent way this control is expressed at this time is in the degree of willingness on the part of the dying person to face realistically the seriousness of his or her condition and the willingness to share oneself as a human being with another. Much of what is being said here about ministry to the dying and the needs of dying might lead someone to judge that all the pastor does is to talk realistically with the persons about their dying and what that means. Sometimes this will be the case, but I certainly don't want to leave the impression that this is always or even necessarily most frequently the case. The other person is the one who is dying; therefore, respect for them as persons means respect for their denials and their defenses as they are seeking as best they can to deal with their condition and situation. We are to move at *their* pace, not ours, with the degree of openness *they* desire. Our primary influence is not in our crashing through their defenses as the brave bearers of the objective reality concerning their lives, but with our accurate communication of empathy, our willingness to accept their feelings and share their struggles, tenderly and tentatively responding to their own testing of what it might be like to lower their defenses. Then, with a certain type of toughness, we are called to stay with them if they invite us into the raw and intense emotion of their inner lives.

I was visiting a young woman who had a terminal illness and was hospitalized. She had not responded well to the treatment. In our visits, periodically I would introduce in what I thought was a fairly sensitive way my willingness to talk with her about how she viewed the seriousness of her illness at the present time. Her response was always to suggest that we play one of the several games that she had there at her bedside. So, we played some games. It seemed, and still seems, to me that this was her exercise of control over her own life at that time in the particular way that she needed to do it. To maintain some sense of control is a need of every one of us. We all want that need to be respected.

The Need for Consistent Messages. One of the very most important needs of all of us at all times is some degree of congruity between our own perception of ourselves and some number of other people's perceptions of us. Such a congruity is the way in which we maintain a relatively realistic self-concept, some sense of stability, a lower level of basic anxiety, as well as trust in those for whom it's important for us to trust. Erikson and Hyerstay discuss the stress exerted on dying persons and the negative effect on them of the discrepancies between (1) the persons' awareness of what's happening to their own bodies and the numerous rushed reassurances from others, and (2) these apparent optimistic statements of others and their nonverbal communication of intense anxiety.

The frequent presence of a visitor representing the community of faith who does not feel compelled to make false reassurances out of his or her own anxiety and who is capable of merely receiving and responding to the dying person's expression of his or her own perceptions and feelings can contribute significantly to that person's stability, sense of reality, and ability to continue to trust.

Spiritual Needs. When I use the expression "spiritual needs" here, I am not referring to something completely apart from all of the other needs that I have mentioned up until this time. Spiritual needs are not completely apart from our psycho-social-biological needs because this is the particular kind of being that we are. We know ourselves as thinking, feeling, relational, physical beings. The word *spiritual,* then, picks up the reality of our experience of ourselves in these particular interacting ways but also raises the variety of issues related to the meaning of our being in the world and our leaving the world. The word *spiritual* refers to the fact that large numbers of people frame these issues one way or another in terms of God. Spiritual needs may take the form of the affirmation that God is in all of the process of life, or, for many people, it takes the form of the question of whether there is a God who is in the process of life. The purpose of any pastor is always to help persons grapple with the role of God in their lives in their circumstances of the moment and to contribute as much as possible to the persons' cultivation of their response to God's participation.

Certainly, high among the spiritual needs of the dying person is hope. Kübler-Ross speaks of hope permeating all of the stages of dying as she had proposed them (p. 138): ". . . we found that all our patients maintained a little bit of it and were nourished by it in especially difficult times" (p. 139).

Physicians sometimes refrain from telling patients about the terminal nature of their condition because they don't want to "destroy their hope." When severely ill or injured persons maintain some hope that they'll begin to get better, that a new and effective treatment will be introduced, a frequent observation is that they will be less anxious, calmer, cooperate better with the treatment team. They won't give up. And sometimes, with all of this, they do begin to get better. Who, then, would want to make a frontal attack on a hope of this kind that is cherished by the person? Kübler-Ross speaks of hope of this type as being for some people a "temporary but *needed* denial" (emphasis mine).

But let's not be mistaken about it: the hope that we won't die as a result of our present illness or injury is not the same as *Christian* hope. Christian hope is rooted in faith in the gracious God who is with us and for us now and always. This hope operates whether we die or don't die at this time, whether we hope for a cure or reprieve or do not. "Whether we live, we live to the Lord, or whether we die, we die to the Lord. So then, whether we live or whether we die, we are the Lord's" (Rom. 14:8). It is the hope that answers the question, "Who can separate us from the love of Christ?" There *is* "tribulation" and "distress" and "peril." There are unbelievable "powers" that disrupt and threaten our lives. But hope, anticipation of the future in God's hands, is the outcome of present faith, that *nothing* "will be able to separate us from the love of God in Christ Jesus our Lord" (Rom. 8:33-39).

The Need to Let Go of Life. In the final extremity of dying, when these already-discussed needs are reasonably well met, we must assist by our attitude and behavior the inclination that some number of dying persons have to let go of life. This for most means some amount of the loosening of personal ties, pulling back into themselves, withdrawing from the former level of frequency and intensity of a relationship with friends and family and us. The energy level is decreasing significantly. During the early part of this withdrawing process, a number of dying persons begin by withdrawing from friends and from us as representatives of the community of faith in order that whatever energy they may have may be directed toward significant family members. At this time, dying persons may need our help in feeling that this pulling away is all right, nothing to feel guilty about, as we leave them in peace. To do this requires that we ourselves be willing to accept their lessened need of us, their withdrawing from us, and we, then, must deal with our own feelings of the loss of that person. Otherwise, we will try to cling to them, since we may have needed their need of us, and we end up being very destructive to them in the very process with which we are seeking to help.

MINISTRY TO THE FAMILY OF THE DYING

Actually, some of our most effective work with a dying person is our contribution to the family members. We recognize, of course, the worth and needs of those close to the dying person; it's important that we minister to them just in and of themselves. Yet, as they are ministered to, the impact of this ministry goes on through them to the dying person herself or himself.

The first need of the family is to accept the reality of the situation. We can only be patiently with them as they struggle with their denial and the difficult process of the acceptance of the fact of their family member's dying.

Second, we can assist in facilitating the family's own anticipatory grief. We can help them understand their own personal reactions: their fear, anger, guilt, grief, conflicts, how they differ from one another, and how their reactions affect one another. They have a very difficult process to go through also.

Third, we can help the family understand the dying person more fully: the rising and falling of that person's different feelings, the day-by-day unpredictability of the person's moods and behaviors and levels of energy, her or his irritability, wanting to be taken care of, the person's occasional insistence on special favors, the withdrawal. In such increased understanding this may begin to help them not take personally some of the things which the dying person says or does, although we and they always need to be open to the possibility that some of the behaviors are realistic reflections of the nature of the relationship.

Our helping them understand themselves and one another can also provide a model for them in expressing empathy to one another within the family. Family members have feelings too: not only fear and sorrow, but also feelings which they may feel guilty about, such as being angry at the dying person or wishing that the person would die more quickly.

A part of what is taking place in this particular type of ministry to the family is assisting them in learning how to participate with the person who is dying in working through her or his feelings and in seeking to bring to completion any unfinished business in their own family relationships. Many family members often need assistance in understanding how important it is for them to take the initiative to bring their relationships up to date.

Finally, we may be in a position to play some role in the family's first reactions to the death itself when it comes, including, in some instances, a sense of relief at the death of a person who has become increasingly debilitated, who has been in discomfort or even severe pain, and whose continued life has literally been a strain on the family in a number of ways. Permission can be given to feel fully what they actually feel and express these feelings to one another. We should also not expect that all family members will have the same experience of the dying process and the death itself when it comes. Therefore, different family members may have different feelings with varying intensities and they need to be helped to understand and tolerate these in one another.

THE PASTORAL CARE OF PERSONS WITH AIDS

Certainly everyone has read and heard so much about the Acquired Immunodeficiency Syndrome that we feel supersaturated with the information: the symptoms of the disorder as it progresses, the nature of the human immunodeficiency virus (HIV), how it is and is not transmitted. Since each year's statistics are different from the immediately preceding year, and since medical research and experimentation are progressing at such a pace, almost anything that is written at this time in the fall of 1999 may be out of date by the time the book is published. No "cure" is on the horizon, although it may actually be on its way. Certainly progress is being made in fending off or controlling symptoms and even the possibility of immunization. Some persons with antibodies against HIV in their system seem to be quite healthy for years. Some of them may never get the illness itself. However, once symptoms of the illness appear, some die very quickly; some find their lives threatened, but with periods of some strength and activity between times of critical illness. These ups and downs may last for several years before these persons die from one of the opportunistic diseases. There will likely be for many, if not most, people with AIDS a number of times of emergency, some of these involving their families.

An obvious factor that affects a person who is called upon to represent the church through pastoral visits is an awareness of how the greatest percentage of persons in Europe and North America and in some other areas of the world are currently becoming infected with HIV: male homosexual activity, the intravenous use of drugs, and prostitution and other promiscuous sexual behavior. At this particular point, the percentage of those having AIDS as a result of blood transfusions and infants born of infected mothers is still relatively low compared to these other sources. (For a moving and powerful story of the impact that the discovery of AIDS in family members where the original source was a blood transfusion, read the book by a prominent clergyman, Jimmy Allen, *Burden of a Secret,* and also read of the church's failures to respond to their needs.)

Some persons find themselves unable emotionally to separate who persons are as defined by some specific aspect of their behavior from the present suffering and need of ministry by those persons. We feel as if we ourselves are going to be contaminated in some way by close association with them. Allen discusses this also in his very readable book. Feelings of accusation and even vindictiveness arise. I have heard and read of more than one person who has said, "They've only gotten what they asked for." Striving mightily to keep the thoughts from being concretely in our heads and escaping from our lips, there is still that feeling that "those people" are really worth something less than other persons who are not gay, or drug users, or prostitutes. We *know* that Jesus didn't feel or behave as we do; we *know* that God values us all equally. We also know that we're imperfect Christians, sinners ourselves, saved by grace, this strange mixture of those who want to follow Jesus, to serve our Lord by serving all of God's creatures, *knowing* that God loves all persons just as much as God loves *me*—but not really.

Totally apart from what we believe and feel about homosexual persons, drug users, and prostitutes, can we serve them in the name of Christ when they are in need? Many of us Christian persons need to take a firmer hold on the hand of Jesus and allow him to lead us where he's gone and allow him to place our hands into the hands of those who are struck down by a powerful, debilitating, killing disease, most often with considerable time to think and feel about their own dying. The needs of the person with AIDS are pressing and persistent and cry for Christian compassion expressed in our physical presence with them, our listening to them, our understanding, and our verbal and often other helping responses to them as they attempt to live while they are dying.

Increasingly, we shall discover persons with AIDS in our own congregations, and certainly in our communities. The congregation is under obligation to respond with the offer of Christian ministry. In addition to caring for its own members and those individual persons who come to the attention of the congregation, some Christian groups may be called to offer their pastoral care and counseling services to other community organizations and institutions who are serving in other ways people with AIDS: public clinics, hospitals, specialized counseling centers and programs, residences for persons with AIDS who have no other place to live. Many cities have a program of AIDS Interfaith Network which can be a source of help to us in a number of ways. They, and/or other agencies which are designed to assist persons with AIDS, often have some form of "buddy" program. They train and support volunteers who are paired, one on one or two on one, with a person with AIDS. The volunteer becomes a friend and helper in whatever way possible to the PWA (person with AIDS). A few church congregations officially take on such a program. If you wish to locate the AIDS Interfaith Network closest to you, write AIDS National Interfaith Network, 1400 I Street NW #1220, Washington, DC, telephone 202-842-0010. E-mail: aninken@aol.com.

It is probably the case that, at the time this is being written, the ministry to persons with AIDS and their families is not a frequent pastoral emergency, although it certainly is so for some congregations and clergy. But there is no question but what for at least the next number of years, more and more clergy and congregations are going to be faced with their need to make some response in this situation to these persons. It's not too early for us as individuals and as whole congregations to begin our spiritual growth and our education about persons with AIDS and their families in order that we may adequately represent Christ when the occasions arise. (For a more detailed discussion of ministry to persons with AIDS and their families, see Switzer, 1999, pp. 100–105 and 132–137.)

CONCLUSION

All of what has been said in regard to the needs of the dying person and the needs of the family has been, of course, stated in a generalized summary form. It's self-evident that we respond most helpfully to a dying person as we do any other person, not only in their human commonality but in their human uniqueness, through careful, sensitive, patient responding, eliciting from that other person the expression of that particular person's most intense needs right at this moment and in the particular form which these needs have taken.

In addition, one of the most important things that we do is to give the dying person (as well as members of the family) reason to be able to count on us: to count on our love, to count on our not withdrawing emotionally or physically from them, to count on a certain regularity of our visits, regardless of our occasional or even more frequent resistances to doing so.

REFERENCES

Jimmy Allen, *Burden of a Secret: A Story of Truth and Mercy in the Face of AIDS* (Nashville: Moorings, 1995).

Richard C. Erikson and Bobbie J. Hyerstay, "The Dying Patient and the Double-Bind Hypothesis," *Omega* 5:4 (winter 1974): 287–98.

John Hinton, "The Physical and Mental Distress of Dying," *Quarterly Journal of Medicine* 32 (1963): 1–21.

Alex H. Kaplan and David Rothman, "The Dying Psychotherapist," *American Journal of Psychiatry* 143:5 (May 1986): 561–72.

Elisabeth Kübler-Ross, *On Death and Dying* (New York: Macmillan, 1969).

Jerry M. Lewis, Jr., "Dying with Friends," *American Journal of Psychiatry* 139:3 (March 1982): 261–66.

Ann M. Metzger, "A Q-Methodological Study of the Kübler-Ross Stage Theory," *Omega* 10:4 (1979–80): 291–301.

Richard Schulz and David Alderman, "Clinical Research and the Stages of Dying," *Omega* 5:2 (summer 1974): 137–43.

Edwin Shneidman, *Deaths of Man* (Baltimore: Penguin Press, 1974).

David K. Switzer, *Pastoral Care of Gays, Lesbians, and Their Families* (Minneapolis: Fortress Press, 1999).

Avery D. Weisman and Robert Kastenbaum, "The Psychological Autopsy: A Study of the Terminal Phase of Life," *Community Mental Health* (Monograph #4, 1968).

RECOMMENDED READING

Earl E. Shelp and Ronald H. Sunderland, *AIDS and the Church* (Philadelphia: Westminster Press, 1987).

Ronald H. Sunderland and Earl F. Shelp, *AIDS. A Manual for Pastoral Care* (Philadelphia: Westminster Press, 1987).

————. *Handle with Care:A Handbook for Care Teams Serving People with AIDS* (Nashville: Abingdon Press, 1990).

7

PASTORAL RESPONSE
TO BEREAVEMENT

Up to this point we've discussed the response of the representatives of the community of faith to illness and injury, including that which may be life-threatening, and to those who are dying. We carry our own fears and anxieties into those situations: fears of dealing with death at all, anxieties about what we are going to do and say that might be most helpful to the persons in those situations.

Now, a person has died. We are truly looking death right in the face. How do we feel now? What do we say and do?

I will never forget my first experience with the death of a parishioner. It was in my first pastorate, a rural circuit (four churches). I had just gotten home from a meeting at one of the churches some eight miles away. The phone was ringing as I walked in. I picked it up and the frantic voice of a woman was screaming, "Papa's had a heart attack. We think he's dying." I rushed back on the dirt road to the other community and their home and in ten minutes was being ushered into the bedroom. This was a fairly large family and I was close to all of them. The grandfather-spouse-father had been in the meeting with me only a half hour before. Now he was unconscious on the bed. The doctor was working frantically with him. People kept running in and out of the room, weeping and screaming. One of the daughters grabbed me, literally. "Pray with us that Papa won't die." I thought that Papa had already died, because that's how I had interpreted the few words that the doctor had hurled at me when I first came into the room. However, as three or four family members stood around me, all of us next to the bed, other people continuing to walk in and out and cry, the doctor pounding on the man's chest, I prayed. Don't ask me what I said. I think that my own shock was saving me from absolute panic and disabling confusion in the midst of that scene with my very close friends, including the one who, in fact, was already dead.

Much more experience over decades, supervised training in two hospitals, greater clarity as to others' and my own reactions have combined to reduce my own shock and, I hope, to increase my helpfulness in these situations. Yet the time of death is a powerful event, different from what any imagining of it might be, and I still experience anxiety and wonder at times what I will say or do next.

During the last thirty years or so, a number of small popular and large technical books as well as countless articles have been published on the subject of bereavement, the minister's role and functioning with persons in grief, and the funeral (Jackson, 1957, 1972; Mitchell and Anderson, 1983; Oates, 1997; Parkes, 1972; Spiegel, 1977; Sullender, 1983; Switzer, 1970, 1986, chapter 6). Every ordained person, as well as other church staff and lay visitors who are going to be working frequently with people in grief, owe it to themselves and those for whom they will be caring to read two or three or more of these books.

Because most of them are either available for sale or can usually be found in university and especially theological seminary libraries, this chapter will not go into great detail concerning the nature of the grief reaction, the funeral, and the longer-term ministry to the bereaved. A major focus will be on the *immediate* pastoral response following the death, the time between the death and the funeral, some brief comments about the funeral itself, and merely a summary statement about long-term pastoral care.

THE DYNAMICS AND PROCESS OF GRIEF

The Dynamics

The power of grief seems to be in two primary emotions: anxiety and sorrow.

Anxiety. The anxiety of grief is primarily separation anxiety, derived from the early learning on the part of infants that the absence of the caring persons, separation from them, if long enough, inevitably will produce physical discomfort and even pain. This physiological response very soon becomes an emotional one, with the leaving of the parents or other regular caretakers being experienced as a threat, thus anxiety, insecurity. We now observe an infant crying, not after a period of time when physical discomfort or pain begins, but when a particular person leaves the room. The potent learning is that others are necessary for our psychological as well as physical well-being. We never lose this fundamental human experience. We are pained when we are not in significant relationship with at least some others or when we are separated from those to whom we feel close, very acutely so when we lose by death or some other means someone with whom our lives have been closely intertwined. Elements of moral anxiety, or guilt, and existential anxiety, the fear of our own death and other aspects of our finitude, add to the intensity of the anxiety reaction.

Our own lives are threatened by the death of someone with whom we have a deep and meaningful relationship, especially over a long period of time. We experience their physical death with what might be called a type of psychological death of our own. We feel it at first as our own death inside. We are afraid. The ideas presented in this section are elaborated in substantial detail in an earlier work of mine (1970).

Sorrow. Sorrow is even more consciously experienced and observed by others than is anxiety, yet neither in my own previous book on grief nor in the numerous other books on this subject I am acquainted with is it adequately described. We feel sad. We hurt. We weep. This sorrow is not a form of anxiety, nor is it the result of anxiety. It seems to be the experience of someone's being missing; the hole, the empty space out there; the "once out there" that *isn't* out there any longer, that does not meet my needs and to whom I cannot give; a *wish* for the person who is gone, and the person's not being there, a particularly intense wish and the accompanying emptiness. Sorrow is the unfulfilled wish.

Parkes has written:

Deprivation implies the absence of a necessary person or thing as opposed to the loss of that person or thing. A bereaved person reacts to both loss and deprivation. Deprivation means the absence of those essential supplies that were previously provided by the lost person. . . . [These supplies are the] psychological equivalents of food and drink. People are necessary to people and the loss of a loved person leaves behind a gap. (1972, P. 9)

He is talking about what I have referred to as the hole. In a way, that gap or hole is actually outside of oneself (the other person is not there), but the hole is also experienced inside. It's the inner, dynamic, painful representation of the other person's not being there in external reality.

A number of years ago, I received a letter from a man whom I had never met, followed two weeks later by another letter. His wife of almost thirty years had died some two and a half months before and he had just read *The Dynamics of Grief.* He was sending to me his critique of the book in the light of his own experiences and needs: *very* honest, *very* personal and tender. Some of his experiences did not fit what I had been proposing in my work, but it did seem to fit some of what Parkes was talking about, although at that particular time he had not read Parkes. He's given me permission to quote from these agonizing reflections of his:

Now, living alone . . . , I find myself starving for the rich interpersonal experience which we had with each other. . . . I hunger for an intimate, open interpersonal connection which will replace that feast I had with her. . . . I still hunger for the experience we had in our marriage. . . .

That was from the first letter. He elaborates in more detail in the second:

> Two aspects of my own grief experience seem to be emerging. One is that I shared daily intimacy with her. . . . Another is that I was important to her, brightened *her life,* gave her succor. . . . Now there is no one to whom my presence means so much as it did to her. I am worth less because she is dead. I cry because I am devalued. "Depression" as reported by those who grieve and as understood by psychology is too general a term for describing this phenomenon. Perceiving grief as the emotional response to a devaluation of me and a devaluation of my daily experience is a potentially clear and useful conception.

In addition to saying that sorrow is not a form of anxiety, I want to go on and make clear that sorrow is not the same as depression either, although much of the mood and some of the behaviors look and feel alike. However, depression has as primary distinguishing characteristics a sense of hopelessness and helplessness. Almost everyone following a severe loss experiences sorrow. Some, *not* all of these, also experience depression as a transient reaction within the normal grief process. If a person experiences depression immediately in response to a loss, the sorrow, if it's present at all, is not accessible. This is a truly pathological reaction and we would do well to help the person make contact with a clinical psychologist or a psychiatrist as soon as possible.

Persons in sorrow may certainly experience helplessness about certain aspects of the situation (the death itself, for example), and some of their feelings and behavior seem to be beyond their conscious control at this time. But this is not the same as judging that one is *absolutely* helpless about doing anything at all about oneself and one's present and near-future life situation. The person, even in extremely painful sorrow, is not *ultimately* hopeless.

Other Feelings. An additional factor contributing to the power of grief to disrupt our lives is that feelings other than anxiety, guilt, and sorrow are stimulated. In varying degrees, depending upon the circumstances of the death, the age of the person, our own personalities, and the particular relationship we've had with the person, there can be anger, overt and realistic fears, relief, and the sense of loss of control as these feelings and others arise, conflict with one another, reinforce one another, and seem to have a life of their own which right at the moment we are not able to control. As a result, we become confused and even more frightened. Confusion is increased as some of these feelings may be displaced onto other persons or events. Additional behaviors arise in the attempt to deny, repress, diminish, or escape the anxiety, and we are not always aware of why we are behaving as we are. It's very confusing, and some people feel as if they are literally losing their minds.

The Process

It's important to view grief as a process. A human process implies movement from one condition to another with identifiable differences between the two. There may be regressions, but the movement picks up again in the direction that was first apparent. Within many processes are several identifiable stages: not usually sharply delineated, always overlapping one another as transitions are in progress, certain aspects of a given stage different from person to person, yet with sufficient common characteristics to be called by whatever name is given to that particular stage.

The most useful set of stages of grief in helping me understand where a person might be in the grief process is that of Parkes (1970a, 1970b):

1. *Numbness and denial.* A sense of shock; sometimes seeming to have no feeling at all, as if the loss hadn't occurred. For many persons, five to seven days.

2. *Yearning.* Waves of pain, consciously experienced sorrow, and often other feelings. This stage is characterized by the powerful unconscious operation of the mind to keep the deceased person alive or bring the person back to life; intense longing for that person and preoccupation with thoughts of the other. Many physiological symptoms; confusion. Duration of quite a few weeks or even months.

3. *Disorganization and despair.* A much longer period beginning as the intensity of the feelings and severity of the symptoms of stage 2 diminish considerably, although many or most of them may still be experienced. The person is functioning relatively well, but there is still an aimlessness and something of a "no-future" orientation. May last several months to a year or more.

4. *Reorganization of behavior.* Greatly diminished feelings of the grief, the ability to look at one's future with greater optimism and with concrete planning. A genuine interest in life and relationships.

It's extremely important, however, that all of us who experience grief ourselves and who also share others' grief with them be aware of the wide variety and intensities of feelings and experiences and behaviors of each stage. This awareness will assist us in understanding and facilitating others' understanding of the *normality* of them. When persons shake with anxiety, seem out of control in their sobbing, don't seem to "bounce back" in a few days, are extremely confused and can't make decisions, have thoughts of suicide come into their heads, see or hear the voice of the one who died, they often feel as if there's something really wrong with them and they can become very frightened. Understanding that these *can* be normal experiences under the circumstances of their bereavement can be reassuring and quite relieving. But if feelings of depression, impulses to kill oneself (which always need to be taken seriously; see next chapter), hallucinations, delusional thinking continue, referral to a psychiatrist is called for.

Parkes's conclusion is that it may take as much as a year or more to move well into the final stage. Even though grief is resolved, a person can never be as if the loss had not occurred, may be subject to "anniversary reactions" (the re-feeling of parts of the grief on the anniversary of the death, a birthday, a wedding anniversary, etc.), and even many years later may have the sharpness of the sorrow stimulated by any one of a number of persons, objects, events, movies, or other experiences.

Attig's approach (1996) to constructive grieving, the need to "relearn" the worlds in which we live, is a useful addition to Parkes's stages of the grieving process. He suggests that the grieving person must come

> to terms with the physical world of things, places, and events and our "spiritual place" in the world; the social world of others, including our fellow survivors, the dead, and, in some cases, God; and aspects of ourselves at the centers of our unique experiences of the world (P. 49).

As he elaborates each of these in later chapters, Attig emphasizes the bereaved's active participation in the process in contrast with the idea that a person may just passively allow the "process" to happen, which he believes the usual "stages of grief" schemes seem to suggest. This perception of some of the proposals of stages may well be accurate, as may be his criticism that they are too "generalized" to be helpful in understanding and facilitating the grieving of any one person.

However, I do not believe that this is an accurate characterization of Parkes's scheme. To be sure, Parkes points out the reality of certain unconscious processes that take place within the grieving person and that influence that person's behavior and progress, or lack of progress, through the stages he proposes. Nevertheless, his systematizing of his observations doesn't exclude the reality that the way in which any individual person responds to his or her experiences is a major factor in the outcome of the process.

Worden (1991) adds another useful perspective to the grieving process, while at the same time suggesting major goals and something of an outline of the helping process. He speaks of the needs (he calls them "tasks," a term that may be partially true, but is also too open to misinterpretation) to

> acknowledge the reality of the loss; work through the emotional turmoil; adjust to the environment where the deceased is absent; and loosen ties to the deceased.

Attig makes the very helpful proposal that his "relearning" the several worlds in which the bereaved person lives can be combined with Worden's four tasks, and uses this combination to point out that "We all have some choices as we grieve" (pp. 51–54).

PASTORAL CARE AT THE TIME OF DEATH

The phone rings in the early morning. "Ed died during the night. We're at home. Could you come over?" Or it rings any time with the messages like those we heard in the descriptions in chapter 5: . . . suddenly taken ill . . . been in an accident . . . on the way to the hospital . . . and other words like these. We arrive at the home or hospital; the person has died, or dies while we are there. Or after a long illness or a struggle by a person to recover from an accident and with many visits by us, we get the death message, or occasionally we are called to come quickly and we arrive in time to be with the person and the family when he or she dies.

What do we say? What do we do?

Some words may reflect the conviction of the person who says them and are intended to be meaningful and to convey comfort to someone who has just had a person close to him or her die, but the words miss, they're hollow, even irritate.

I had just finished conducting the funeral for a young man who had died of AIDS. I had known him well since high school and I had visited with him several times during his illness. I was standing alone outside. A woman whom I'd never met before came up to me. She was perceptive enough to realize the personal loss that I myself had experienced and the emotional strain I had been under preparing for and leading the worship, and she commented on that. Her words were very helpful to me. But then she lifted her head upward and went on: "Just remember, He [God, I suppose she meant] always knows best." How could I argue with that? But the words themselves were totally meaningless to me in my condition at that moment. She gave me a gift, then took it away, although she had meant to be helpful and I did appreciate her just speaking to me.

In the summer a few years ago, a bus full of young people returning home from a church camp attempted to cross a low water bridge and was overturned and carried downstream by a river swollen by a sudden downpour. Ten were killed; the sense of shock in their congregation and community can hardly be imagined. As the shock began to wear off, the pain was obviously overwhelming. Theirs was a theological tradition that truly saw God as all-powerful and controlling the events of human life. These were people of deep faith. A psychiatrist who is a committed Christian and active member of another congregation met with some of the survivors and their families and friends. After several adults had indicated that somehow they needed to take God into account in some way in the midst of this tragedy, some saying that it must be God's will, a sixteen-year-old girl expressed herself:

> If I were out there, if I was the one who died, I wouldn't want anyone to say, "Karen's [not her real name] dead. That's what God wanted." I would want someone who would say . . .

She stopped and began to cry. After a moment the psychiatrist replied:

> You stopped. What would you want them to say? It's difficult, isn't it? But you don't want to be erased as being just a part of God's will.

He then asked if anyone else had any thoughts. A church school teacher said:

> We can't take God out of this situation. We know there was some good reason for this. And something good can come from something bad. We just can't know all. He (God) lets us know what he wants us to know.

Karen looked up.

> I guess we're supposed to say that's what's supposed to happen. Don't question it. Just accept it.

The psychiatrist moved over closer to her, and said:

> Well, maybe that's not helping you.

A sixteen-year-old boy sitting next to Karen dropped his eyes and injected, "No, it's not." (Adams, 1987)

The teacher had stated fairly accurately the way in which many if not most of the members of that church, including the youth, would ordinarily express their faith about events. But her words didn't find their target in the lives of this group of shocked and distraught teenagers.

> There's a reason for it.
> Something good can come out of it.
> We can't know everything.
> God lets us know what God wants us to know.

These are all cognitive declarations. The young people knew as they heard them that these words were meaningless to them at this time of their intense need. Their need was to mourn, to cry, to express their anger, fear, bewilderment, to challenge God if they wanted to do so.

An excellent filmstrip, "With His Play Clothes On" (International Order of the Golden Rule) portrays the situation of a real family whose youngest son, twenty-one months old, suddenly became ill during the afternoon. After a few hours, he was continuing to get worse. The parents rushed him to the emergency room of the closest hospital and the medical team began to work on him as soon as they could get a doctor. After two or three hours, a young man came out and directed the parents to the family room. Five or ten minutes later the doctor came in: "I'm sorry. We did everything. Jerry's gone."

Both of the parents just screamed. If you had been there with them, as pastor or Christian friend, what would you have done or said? Think about it a moment before reading further.

The mother continues the narrative:

> ... I guess almost immediately I had a pill in my mouth, and then there was a priest there and we just kept asking, "Father, what are we going to do? What do we do now?"

How would you respond to what the mother has just said to the priest? Think for a moment.

She continues:

> ... he [the priest] tried to explain to us that he could try to feel like we felt, but he ... there was nothing he could say. It was for a reason. I can't remember everything he told us. It was kinda blurry. Uh ... He kept telling us just to go home and be with our boys. Just comfort them. They needed us. And I just couldn't picture going home and telling them.

What would *you* do and say in that situation?

First, these parents do *not* need a theological explanation of *any* kind. They can't hear it; they can't assimilate it; it would be directed to a part of their being which has been made dysfunctional by their overwhelming crisis, their shock, the intensity of their feelings as these feelings periodically broke loose.

Second, they do *not* need anyone to say anything like, "I know how you feel." Of course, we really don't know what the priest did or didn't say along that line, since the parents were in a state of shock. The mother admits that it was all "blurry." Even the way she reported it was not with the precise words that I've just used here. But unfortunately some people do say something like this. *No one* at a moment like that has the right to use these words with a severely distraught person.

Third, even though their other sons do need them, those sons don't need them right now. Attention must be given to *these* two persons, the parents, right here. *Their* needs have to be responded to *first.*

So what do we do? There's no "one right way" with all other ways being wrong. There's no single exact set of words that are always going to fit. However, let's discuss some possibilities.

One or both of them might respond to our taking their hands or putting our arms around them, but the caution in this type of physical touch that we have discussed earlier has to be exercised.

Then, "Let's just sit here in the family room with each other for a few minutes."

"Are there any questions you would like to ask the doctor at this time?"

"Doctor, I am wondering if you could explain as best you can right now what took place."

And, remembering the terrible shock for the parents, their inability to think clearly (and, by the way, the shock and pain of the doctor), "I am wondering if it wouldn't make sense for the three of you to set a time when you could talk for a few minutes tomorrow."

With the doctor still present, if no one has mentioned it yet, "Would you like to go in and see Jerry?" If they do, we go in with them. Most people will weep, many will cry aloud or scream, some few will almost collapse. Some, however, don't do any of these. But we stand with them at this time, often enough, though not always, in silence. We might say at some point whatever is genuine to ourselves that may occur to us.

If they choose not to go in to see the body of the child at this time, we ask the doctor about the procedure from this point on. It's quite possible that in instances like the one described in this filmstrip and in other instances, the doctor will raise the issue of an autopsy. In many places, the law requires it under certain circumstances. Even if not, the physician and/or the hospital may strongly desire it in order to establish the cause of death, which then becomes part of the material for future treatment when similar symptoms are seen.

Some family members are horrified by the thought of it. Such a reaction isn't unnatural. On the other hand, the procedure may be required or be important in other ways, and the pastor can, if necessary, help the physician interpret the importance and/or the reasons for the law and assist the family in expressing their feelings, which so often conflict with their understanding of the reasonableness of doing the autopsy. If the parents need to make the decision, the pastor can help them work with each other in doing so.

At this time, or at least before the parents leave the hospital, they'll probably need to designate the funeral home, sign an authorization for that home to pick up the body, and perhaps sign other papers. Having had the personal experience (in a hospital emergency room) of having several papers rather insistently thrust under my nose when I was extremely distraught, I am aware of how little we often know about what we sign when we are in that condition. A pastor makes a real contribution if she or he goes over the forms with people in shock.

If we've just arrived at the hospital right at or immediately following the death, one effective way to begin with the parents, after whatever greetings, crying, perhaps hugging, would be, "Tell me what happened." Respond with empathy, asking a few questions for more detail and clarity, sharing what are authentically our own feelings with them.

This might take five to ten minutes or much longer, depending on the persons and our relationship with them. They may say something about telling the other sons. If they don't, we may ask, "Have you thought about how you are going to tell your boys? Maybe we could talk about that for a while."

Later, "Is there anyone you would like to call from the hospital before you go home?"

And finally, for this hospital scene, "Would you like for me to drive you home (or follow you home) and be with you when you talk with the boys?" If they do not, let's remember that they can have good reasons for refusing our offer even as they appreciate it. Then, using guidelines we've discussed earlier, we might have prayer with the parents and then set a time for visiting with them the next day. We might also at this time ask if they would like for us to accompany them to the funeral home the next day or perhaps meet them there.

Whether we do or do not accompany them home that night, we do see them as soon as it is convenient for them the next day, either meeting them at the funeral home (if an autopsy is being performed, the body will probably not be there yet) or at their own home. While engaging ourselves with the parents, it's extremely important to do more than merely greet the children and other close family members. We need to allow ourselves sufficient time to have a number of conversations with individuals and family clusters and, at some point, perhaps not the first visit, with the whole family.

In the situation we've been discussing, simply asking the parents how they're doing will usually start the conversation quite well, and our responses are then based upon their statements. Often there will be a review of the accident or illness or the moment of the death itself or their first having heard about the death. Their process of grieving is assisted not only by our communicated empathy with what they're saying, but, if they're not doing so, by our explicitly recounting something of our memory of the person who has died. This may stimulate them to do the same.

In talking with children, the same sort of conversations will be helpful, remembering that they're not to be expected to have the identical feelings as the parents and that their forms of expression will usually be different. Often they won't be able to express themselves as well with words: younger children because of their lack of understanding of death and because of their lack of vocabulary, teenagers because of their difficulty in identifying the exact feelings and probably because a number of them will be self-conscious about talking about how they feel with others (and sometimes especially with a clergyperson). But we do talk with them and help them identify their feelings and express those feelings, including how they feel about seeing their parents grieve.

Family members often have to be encouraged to express their feelings openly in the presence of one another. Some try to hold back because they're self-conscious or because of the misguided idea that they have to protect one another. Speaking about their shock, pain, sadness, anger, etc. and crying in the presence of one another is healthy for everyone involved and potentially strengthening to the whole family.

If visitors from the church stay generally within the guidelines suggested here, including not being afraid to sit silently with people at times, they will perform a helpful ministry with the grief-stricken, will facilitate the grieving process, will be experienced as communicating Christ's compassion, *and* will be saved from "saying the wrong things," hurting people by the compulsion to "explain" events and issue directives:

> "God must have wanted another little angel in heaven" (or, "another flower in the heavenly garden").

> "There's no need to grieve because she is in a better place." (Somehow this nice thought doesn't save someone from the pain of missing a person, but in addition they are now either furious at the person who said it or feel guilty about feeling sad, or both.)

> To a teenage boy: "Well, you're going to have to take your dad's place now."

To a six-year-old girl at her father's funeral: "You're really going to have to take care of your mother now, because if she dies you'll have to go to an orphanage."

At the best misguided, not comforting, and cruel when spoken to children! And yet, we presume, with "good" intent.

I didn't make these up. I've not only heard these but others, often years later from the people who had these sorts of things said to them.

Even when people immediately following a death ask (or cry, or scream) "Why?"

"Why did God let her die?"
"Why didn't God save my child?" etc.,

they're not really at this time requesting a lesson in theology. These words are a cry of anguish, an outburst of anger, a shriek of intolerable pain. We respond to the feelings, not to the literal meaning of the words. Then, the God that didn't save the life of a child or who allowed the mother of three to die can be addressed in prayer as the one who loves us, even as we are confused and hurt and angry. The Christian affirmation can be made in the Scripture and prayers and sermon of the funeral. Then, in the days and weeks following, the persons' anger at God and their pain can be discussed in the light of how they have understood God before this time, how this death has challenged their understanding, what the Scripture reveals about the God who did not save the life of the very young man Jesus even after he had asked to be spared.

Discussion of the Funeral

When visiting a person or family after a death of a close family member, after a while if they haven't specifically said something about the funeral by this time, it's proper, if you're the available clergyperson who's been involved, to raise the question, "Have you done any thinking about the funeral yet?" A word of caution: don't ask the question in any way that communicates your assumption that you'll be officiating at this service or will be the only one involved in it. In fact, we may usually assume so and often be correct. But in the wording of the question it's considerate not to put them under pressure if they have other plans.

There can be reasons that people may sometimes say, "We'd like [or, "have contacted"] Father O'Neill, Brother Edwards, or Ms. Baker to do the funeral." If a clergyperson is new in the community and the former minister has had a close relationship with this family, we simply can expect to hear these words at times. Such action on the part of families in the parish will diminish in time. Or Father O'Neill or the others may be a family member or a longtime family friend even if never the pastor. Sometimes people in grief will do some thoughtless things in this regard. Think about it: "thought-less," without thought. Expect some of that. They're in shock, desperately hurt, confused. They *aren't* thinking well at the time. Both our understanding and our growth in grace which are directed toward the most effective ministry to persons in time of their greatest need can save us from being personally hurt and even resenting them. If we're not truly gracious (literally, "full of grace") at such a moment, we can *act* graciously anyway.

If such a request is made that someone else conduct or assist in the service, we can respond that we'd be happy to get in touch with the person and extend the invitation, since we are the local clergy and others come into our parish to perform such ministry by our invitation. Most people will understand that if they don't already know it. Also, if the bereaved want the other person to "conduct" rather than "assist," we affirm our openness to issuing such an invitation. However, we are certainly within bounds in suggesting that as their pastor, we'd like to have some part in the service, such as leading in the opening Scripture sentences and prayers, by giving a pastoral prayer, by presenting the visiting clergy, participating in some significant but not necessarily the major way.

If the family has *already* contacted the other clergy, then they have been technically "thought-less"; their intent is not to hurt us; they merely haven't "thought." The other clergy (and any one of us is the "other clergy" at times) ethically should have responded by, first, simply talking with them about the death of the person, about that person, and about how the caller and other family members are doing. Some clergy, in principle, never go back to a former parish to conduct funerals, weddings, baptisms, etc.; they need to say this and explain their reasons, hope that the family understands, and give words of support for their present local pastor. If the clergy called by the family knows that he or she cannot come for other reasons, the response is simply to express appreciation for the invitation, state that she or he can't come, and again support the family's relationship with the present parish clergy. If the one called wants to come and can come to participate in the service, it's her or his responsibility to explain to the family that the local parish minister will need to approve and issue the invitation and that she or he will discuss it with that clergyperson when he or she calls.

If we ourselves are going to conduct the funeral and/or give the sermon, we need time to talk in detail with the family about the service. Often, this will need to take place in a second meeting with family members following the person's death, with as many of them together at the same time as possible. I almost always begin something like this: "I'd like to talk with you a while about the funeral. The funeral, of course, is a worship service of the church."

Such a statement is unnecessary for some denominations and faith groups, since everyone understands the funeral as worship. It is *quite* necessary for a large number of us to make such a clear statement, however, because defining the service in these terms provides the guideline for our present discussion of what is to be said and done. We then may immediately continue in the same vein: "Did (the dead person) have any written instructions about the funeral? Did she or he and/or do you have any particular scriptures or hymns or written prayers that have been particularly meaningful and which you might want us to use?" We ourselves in our pastoral care of the persons involved might have learned some things about the person who has died as well as about other members of the family which might lead us to make some suggestions. We offer these for the family's feedback.

If the person who died has left instructions which are at variance with what is meaningful to the bereaved family, or if family members differ significantly from one another, the minister has the task and opportunity of helping the persons identify the issues, express their feelings, think things through, negotiate differences, reach consensus, or make genuine and acceptable compromises. This isn't usually a difficult task, although it calls for our being sensitive and alert, but occasionally it can be a tense situation. We need to prepare ourselves for it.

Worship, of course, in terms of what actually takes place, is different in different faith groups, denominations, and localities. For most Protestants, anyway, a *reasonable* flexibility of what may be included in the worship at a funeral makes sense, so long as it's worship and no single element in the service is truly disruptive. Most of the potential difficulties that can arise in discussion with the family about what they want can be resolved with reasonable flexibility on the part of the clergy and her or his willingness to discuss openly her or his perceptions about how certain suggestions fit or don't fit. Most families are also relatively flexible themselves.

Another important stimulus to discussion is to ask the family what their relationship with the person was like, to share some of their most vivid memories of the person with each other and with us. Even if we've not known the person who died, we can begin to know them through the eyes of this family as they interact with one another in their remembering. In all of this pre-funeral conversation we are getting guidelines for the development of a more meaningful funeral worship service and sermon; the bereaved are being helped in accepting the reality and finality of the physical death of the person they've been close to; their feelings have been stimulated as they've talked concretely about the person and their relationship with her or him; finally, Christian affirmations have been implicit throughout the conversation and are often made explicit in thinking about Scripture and hymns and prayers.

My belief is that the funeral, as worship, should include a sermon. A sermon and a eulogy are different. A sermon works with the meaning of a particular passage of Scripture in a way that is both faithful to its meaning as we best understand it and that is powerfully relevant to a particular human situation today. A eulogy (the Greek meaning "speaking well of") is the act of praising someone, in a funeral, the dead person. Speaking of what is meaningful for us to remember about the person who's died is not only legitimate but can be extremely helpful, as mourning is facilitated, the relationship is in the process of being reshaped in the light of the reality of the person's death, and as we internalize as a part of ourselves what we are hearing about the other at a time of particular openness to such hearing on our part.

But a eulogy should not simply *replace* a sermon in the service of worship. There may be both a eulogy and a sermon. Or, my preference, whether I am conducting the funeral or attending a funeral as a family member or friend, is that the personal references to the dead person and our relationships with him and her be in the form of illustration of the various points which are being made in the sermon, the Christian proclamation.

The Funeral Director

It's important that we and the funeral directors see each other as colleagues who are called upon to work with each other for the well-being of the grief-stricken persons. Every horror story we clergy hear from one another and from families about a particular funeral director (too smooth or fake, manipulative, taking advantage of a family's bereavement in order to sell them a casket and the rest of the service at a price beyond the family's means, inflexibility in regard to how the service should be conducted) can be matched by funeral directors' experiences with clergy who present themselves artificially, who try to manipulate the feelings of the family, who exploit the congregation during the funeral service in the attempt to sell their own particular points of view, or to browbeat people (either crassly or subtly) into a Christian commitment.

The majority of funeral directors are well-trained professionals, concerned and genuine human beings, engaged in a legitimate business which offers a valuable service to people. A few aren't, and the same can be said, of course, about doctors, lawyers, clergy, and any other group of human beings. Even the best of them make some occasional errors, but so do we all. I have personally *never* had any sort of tension in working with a funeral director. We've occasionally had to jockey with each other to set the exact time for the service, and our schedules are important just as theirs are. But that's really just a minor problem to be resolved, and it's always been worked out without too much difficulty.

Some people have experienced some funeral directors as having their own "set ways" of doing things, with the idea that families and ministers just have to go along with it. My own experience is that funeral directors have done things their own way only as a result of default: family and/or clergy have not discussed in detail with the funeral directors the particular forms and procedures which they desire. Since families are usually distraught and confused, the clergy may need to initiate a discussion of the various possible issues concerning the funeral and its procedures with the family, help them reach some decision as to what they want, make relevant suggestions to them for their consideration, and, when necessary, assist them in communicating their instructions to the funeral director. Persistent assertiveness on the part of the *clergy* is occasionally necessary for effective ministry at this point as well as at other times. The funeral director really does want to offer the service that the family understands as best meeting their own needs, and will do so except in the most unusual of circumstances.

CONTINUING PASTORAL CARE OF THE BEREAVED

The grieving process continues for a year or more for many people, according to Parkes. This isn't to mean, however, that reorganization or resolution might not occur several months earlier for some people or take a number of months longer. The point is that pastoral concern needs to be offered to the grief-stricken persons for considerably longer than a single post-funeral call within a week after the service. In some parishes, it may be possible for the one ordained person to visit on a weekly basis over a period of two or three months, then every two or three weeks for another several months. Probably not every bereaved person needs such an amount or extent of time, but some number do. Of course, there are many congregations and communities where the clergy really don't have that much time. In some cases, other persons on the church staff or trained laypersons might be able to carry on this type of pastoral care.

The needs of the bereaved are to express all of their feelings, sometimes over and over again over a period of time, to reaffirm themselves as persons of worth, to break the type of emotional ties with the deceased that can't be realistically maintained now that the person is dead, to experience the resurrection of the deceased within one's own present life, to begin to gain genuine satisfaction in the renewal and deepening of old relationships and the establishing of new relationships, and to work out in a satisfactory way the meaning of the life and death of the deceased and the meaning of one's own life without that person (Switzer, 1970, pp. 195–207).

All of this takes time, reflection, and the stimulation of conversation with sensitive other persons, including persons of faith and some persons who themselves have undergone great loss. People not only need to survive and recover from their grief in some sense, but in a human sense use this time of great pain as an opportunity to grow as persons as they move through the mourning process. They might be able to gain greater insight into themselves, greater sensitivity to and empathy with others, greater strength and resiliency to face other crises, become more capable of dealing with other losses and occasions of stress, develop deeper and more meaningful relationships with others, and, after progressing well in their own grieving, be effective helpers of others who are bereaved. This type of personal growth also properly includes an emphasis on growth in faith. These are the goals which whole congregations need to be aware of in their collective and frequent, if not continuous, ministry to one another in their times of grief. The delineation and possibilities and means of growth within the grief process are detailed in a helpful way by Sullender (1985, pp. 65–215).

It is important that well-trained clergy and other staff keep in as frequent and regular touch as the bereaved seems to need and their own schedules will allow, as I mentioned earlier. Beyond that, however, there are several possibilities for rich ministry to the bereaved, and there are congregations where one or more of these programs are in effect.

Clergy may be the leaders (teachers and discussion and group process facilitators) of grief or bereavement groups. Such groups might not be possible within some very small congregations and especially small congregations located in small communities. However, in a large percentage of congregations and the larger communities within which they exist, there are a number of people at any one time who have experienced recent loss and who may be invited to come together in groups to share their experiences with one another and with leadership which also shares their experiences and makes input concerning the grief process. Clergy and other religious professionals who lead such groups might well have lay coleaders. For the greatest effectiveness, these groups should not have more than ten to twelve participants and most frequently would be limited to four to eight two-hour sessions. Their usual intent is not group therapy in the technical sense, nor to see persons all the way through the grief process to its resolution, but to assist the process somewhere along in Parkes's stage 2 (or 3) and to assist a more effective transition into the next stage. Frequently people develop relationships within these groups that continue after the formal group sessions have been concluded. They continue to be resources to one another in occasional or frequent conversations.

Other congregations, under the leadership of the trained ordained pastor or other professionally competent persons within the congregation or community, may select, train, and supervise individuals or married couples who will become the companions of grief-stricken individuals, couples, or families, sharing with them in their anguish and walking with them through their journey of suffering and growth. Details of the process of selection and training of lay caregivers, including but not limited to caring in bereavement, are found in a number of other places (Haugk; Stone, 1991; Switzer, 1986, pp. 260–68. See References, chapter 4). Such laypersons designated as representatives of of the congregation may be among the first to visit those in grief and visit with them frequently over a period of many months. Even in these cases, however, the ordained clergy are not relieved of their responsibility of at least occasional visits to the bereaved persons during the same period of time.

When those working with the bereaved see little or no apparent changes taking place in those persons, little or no movement through the process after five or six months, the only responsible action to take is for the caregiver(s) to consult with a professional who is truly expert in the dynamics of grief and therapy with the bereaved.

CONCLUSION

This chapter has focused primarily on the response of the clergy and other persons with pastoral responsibility to those who have just experienced the death of someone with whom they have been closely and deeply emotionally involved. This emphasis has been placed in the context of only brief reference to the dynamics of grief, its stages, the funeral, and the longer-term pastoral care of the bereaved. Those who work frequently with those in bereavement need to read several of the detailed foundational books, keep up with newer material in the field, and search out short-term courses or workshops in order to increase their knowledge and improve their skills. Clergy and others who represent the congregation in the pastoral care of the grief-stricken need to be truly expert in this ministry.

REFERENCES

Lorraine Adams, "Teens reluctant to believe death was God's will," *Dallas Morning News,* July 19, p. 26A.

Thomas Attig, *How We Grieve: Relearning the World* (New York: Oxford University Press, 1996).

International Order of the Golden Rule, "With His Play Clothes On" (A Filmstrip). P.O. Box 3586, Springfield IL 62708.

Edgar Jackson, *The Many Faces of Grief* (Nashville: Abingdon Press, 1972).

———. *Understanding Grief* (Nashville: Abingdon Press, 1957).

Kenneth R. Mitchell and Herbert Anderson, *All Our Losses, All Our Griefs* (Philadelphia: Westminster Press, 1983).

Wayne E. Oates, *Grief, Transition, and Loss* (Minneapolis: Fortress Press, 1997).

C. Murray Parkes, *Bereavement: Studies in Adult Grief* (New York: International Universities Press, 1972).

———. "'Seeking' and 'Finding' a Lost Object," *Social Science and Medicine* 4 (1970): 187–201.

———. "The First Year of Bereavement," *Psychiatry* 33 (Nov. 1970b): 444–67.

Yorick Spiegel, *The Grief Process: Analysis and Counseling* (Nashville: Abingdon Press, 1977).

Howard W. Stone, *The Caring Church* (Minneapolis: Fortress Press, 1999).

R. Scott Sullender, *Grief and Growth* (Mahwah, N.J.: Paulist Press, 1985).

———. *Losses in Later Life* (Mahwah, N.J.: Paulist Press, 1989).

David K. Switzer, *The Dynamics of Grief* (Nashville: Abingdon Press, 1970).

———. *The Minister As Crisis Counselor* (Revised and enlarged) (Nashville: Abingdon Press, 1986) chapter 6, "The Minister's Role and Functioning in the Crisis of Grief."

J. William Worden, *Grief Counseling and Grief Therapy: A Handbook for the Mental Health Practitioner* (New York: Springer, 1982).

RECOMMENDED READINGS

David A. Crenshaw, *Bereavement: Counseling the Grieving throughout the Life Cycle* (New York: Crossroad Publishing Company, 1990).

Therese A. Rando, *Grief, Dying, and Death* (Champagne, Ill.: Research Press, 1984), chapters 1–8.

Vamik D. Volkan and Elizabeth Zintl, *Life after Loss: The Lessons of Grief* (New York: Charles Scribner's Sons, 1993).

8

RESPONDING TO SUICIDAL PERSONS AND THEIR FAMILIES

When persons reveal to us that they are thinking about killing themselves, it's an emergency. No doubt about it! For the particular individual, it may be a matter of life or death. For us, as representatives of the community of faith, it's a challenge, which means that a lot of us get very anxious.

How shall we talk to him or her?

How serious is the person?

How close is that person to killing himself or herself? (Is it within a short period of time?)

Do people have a right to do whatever they want to with their lives, or are we called upon to save everybody, regardless?

What about this particular person?

What are we going to do?

I remember the immediate and intense rise in anxiety I felt when I was in my third year as a pastor. My concentration on sermon preparation was broken early one morning by the slamming of the outside door of the church, followed ten seconds later by a young woman bursting through the door of my office. She was disheveled, panting, eyes darting around the room.

I knew the family quite well. The husband, a carpenter, had been out of work for several months, with only occasional short jobs. They had two small children and the mother, the one in my office, was pregnant with a third.

She started talking before she was completely seated. "I was just driving down the freeway. Suddenly I felt overwhelmed by this urge just to speed up and drive off of the overpass just ahead. It was all I could do to hold the car straight. I was terrified. I knew I had to do something, fast. I took the next exit and drove over here to see you."

So there I was. I'd never faced anything like this. I tried to appear calm, though I was at the other end of the continuum. What did I say? I have no idea. Somehow I got her started reviewing her recent life: not taking care of her children well (not being a good mother), having morning sickness, not having enough money, disillusioned about family life. All of this had accumulated and she couldn't face it. She felt absolutely hopeless.

All I could do was to affirm that her life was extremely difficult right now, but we could do something about that. First, we'd find someone to take care of her children that day and the next. I'd talk to her husband about how strongly she felt and ways he could be more supportive. We could offer to them a small short-term no-interest loan.

With these few concrete steps, with her being able to vent her feelings without her feelings being made light of, feeling more relaxed, knowing that she had an ally, she was able to respond positively to what I said next.

I asked, "Do you think now that you can make it until tomorrow morning O.K.?" A firm "Yes."

"Then I'll pick you up tomorrow morning and we'll go to the hospital and you can talk with a psychiatrist and see what else needs to be done."

Not, "Do you want to?" "What do you think about . . . ?" But, "I'll pick you up." And I did.

The next day she felt more hopeful. The following day she was closer to her usual self, although still shaken by her experience. Her husband was more understanding, more attentive, more helpful. She was taking the medication which the psychiatrist prescribed.

The main thing I would now change about what I did would be to drive her home from the church (her husband was there); talk with both of them for awhile; come back within an hour or so, and take her right then to the psychiatric emergency room of a hospital.

Such events don't often happen in a pastor's life, however, but when they do we have to be prepared. In my own survey of clergy, only 1.5 percent mentioned suicidal issues in terms of their frequency. In an older but much more systematic study (Lum, 1974, pp. 189–91), clergy surveyed in one metroplex indicated that in a designated year, 65 percent of them had been involved with only 0–2 suicidal persons, and only 2 percent with 11 or more. Realizing that the median number of years which they had served in the ministry was 20 (one-half had served fewer than 20 and one-half more), 58 percent had counseled with 10 or fewer suicidal persons in their entire ministry. Ten percent had been involved with no suicidal person at all *(to their knowledge)*. Only 12 percent had worked with 20 or more (one or more per year).

In the designated year, only 5 percent had held funerals for three or more persons who had committed suicide, and throughout their entire ministry only 7 percent had held funerals for more than ten persons who had killed themselves.

All of this would seem to make a good case for not including this chapter. But over the years I've grown more knowledgeable, more suspicious, and somewhat more courageous. This combination of characteristics has led me to realize that anytime I'm with a group of several or more people anywhere (including a worship service, a Sunday school class, a church committee or board meeting, *any* formal or informal gathering), there are from one or two to numerous persons who have had suicidal thoughts or feelings, who may be experiencing these at the present time, or who have actually attempted to kill themselves on one or more occasions in the past.

The latest figures (1996) are that there were approximately 61,600 suicides in the United States, up from 30,000 in 1990, with the suicide *rate,* however, decreasing from 12.1 per 100,000 to 11.6 during those years (*Statistical Abstract,* 1998). It is also reasonably estimated that there are some eight to ten attempts for every completed suicide. Certainly there are far more than ten times as many who have had strong suicidal thoughts and feelings and even more who have had fleeting thoughts of killing themselves. How many people, then, are we talking about? A few million, anyway. Their thoughts and feelings reveal a massive amount of human pain, suffering, anguish, sense of failure, hopelessness. A perceptive and knowledgeable pastor can make a significant difference in their lives in terms of lessened pain and can contribute to an increase of satisfaction within a whole family.

Where are all these people? Are they all "out there" somewhere, some *other* place? Not at all! They include some people who are reading these words right now: members of *our* families, our congregations, our church school classes and other church groups, our neighbors and friends. Responding to suicidal persons means responding to all of these. We now realize that we're talking about a phenomenon with various forms and intensities which is fairly common.

The first obstacle to overcome in responding to these persons is our own lack of awareness of their presence among us (and for some, the feeling *within* us), our selective inattention to their messages to us, our denial of their closeness to us. We don't want to deal with such a frightening, such a horrible reality. But if we're called to care in Christ's name, we must open ourselves to this reality, to these persons, because most of them are really like us (or even are us).

Therefore, this chapter is included to reflect that among the common pastoral emergencies are all of this large number of people, chronically distressed or temporarily disturbed, who are waiting for us to recognize the signals of need and to take the initiative to enter into serious conversation with them about the way they perceive their lives and how they really feel.

Among them are a few who are technically psychotic, although they're only a small percentage of the total. There are larger numbers who are chronically or occasionally depressed, who are in grief, who are in other situational crises, who are chronically physically ill, aging, and pained, and seeing no real meaningful life left. And there are others. Hopefully, we're already engaged in caring ministry with all of these, on either an occasional or a regular basis, according to their situation and need. All we need to realize then at this point is that it's quite possible that a fairly large number of these have suicidal thoughts and/or feelings and most of them simply have not been revealing this fact to us.

RESPONDING TO SUICIDAL PERSONS

In order to respond pastorally and effectively to suicidal persons, what do we need? Many references have already been made to the quality of persons we need to be in order to care competently in Christ's name. Surely by now you must believe that the writer of this book has a real hang-up on this issue of our own self-awareness, how to handle our own strong feelings and conflicts, realizing that even with great self-awareness our unconscious continues to influence our helping (and other) relationships, our need for supervision and consultation and sometimes counseling for ourselves. You're correct. I do. My repetitiousness proves it. Here again, with suicide, this is our need, probably even more here than in many other instances.

In addition, in talking with persons who have suicidal feelings, the caring person, in order to be most effective, cannot afford to be a victim of the paralysis of passivity. Only by taking certain initiatives with words and other behavior, and responding clearly and directly to others' initiatives with us, can we possibly be helpful. Even listening, which is so important, is *active*, not passive.

Responding to the Threat of Suicide

Given these personal characteristics, what are the guidelines?

Be Alert. Any time we're talking with anyone, the antenna that picks up the suicide frequency needs to be out, out far enough that we may be fully inclusive in our hearing and capable of observing even the most subtle forms of suicidal communications.

Explicit suicidal language ought to be apparent. In the midst of a serious conversation, a person says, "I've been thinking about killing myself." Other words may be used, but they can be just as clear. Most people, however, don't begin by being this explicit.

Implicit communications can be more difficult, especially for the person not accustomed to paying attention to them, and especially if unconsciously our minds are tuning the words out completely or avoiding the possible suicidal meaning by too quickly attaching another, less threatening, meaning to them.

"I really don't know how much longer I can stand it this way."
"It doesn't seem worth the effort."
"Nothing seems to mean anything anymore."
"Sometimes I don't think anyone would miss me if I were gone."

Of course, many of us have said things like this under certain circumstances without having been thinking about killing ourselves. Therefore, our first response to a person who makes one of these statements isn't, "You're thinking about suicide." However, we can't afford to let statements such as these go by without asking

"What do you mean?"
"Tell me more about what that's like for you."
"What feelings of yours are you expressing when you say this?"

Further conversation will usually clarify the person's meaning as he or she is led further into self-exploration and self-expression by our understanding and our willingness to continue to talk seriously and openly.

Sometimes people veil their thoughts with attempted humor or "meaningless asides."

Parishioner: "Well, after a few more days she won't have to bother with me anymore." (A little laugh.)
Pastor: "What do you mean?"
Parishioner: "Oh, nothing."
Pastor: "But it sounds as if you were talking seriously and saying something about yourself, or your relationship with her, or both."
Parishioner: "Oh no. I was just joking."

By this point, many people would have let the matter drop. He didn't really mean anything by it. He was just joking. And why get caught always trying to make "something significant" out of a joke or something said only casually?

Without continuing to browbeat a person verbally over an extended period of time, there is still sufficient reason to carry the conversation on a bit longer. So we continue,

Pastor: "Well, when you consider that we've been talking about how difficult it's been at times for you and your spouse to work out some of the differences between you, it's really hard for me to hear what you said as not being related to that. What were you aware of feeling when you said that after a few more days she wasn't going to have to bother with you anymore?"

Parishioner: "Oh, I guess I was just frustrated and felt like my wife and I weren't getting anywhere . . . as usual."

The door is now open to pursue in a forthright manner what the man was talking about. His statement might not have been a reflection of his thinking about killing himself. If it wasn't, at least the pastoral helper hasn't allowed him to close off the very important conversation. If, in fact, thoughts of suicide were there, the pastor's tenacity would lead the man to speak of them more openly when originally he seemed unwilling to say anything directly about them.

If a person says something in a joking or casual way, but which could also possibly be interpreted as a reference to suicide, the question can always be raised about the reason the person is joking in this particular way at this particular time.

In addition to verbal clues of suicide, there may also be nonverbal behaviors which need to be explored as to their meaning. A person precipitously quits a job or retires early when there hasn't seemed to be any detailed planning for it. A person loses interest in activities which formerly had been meaningful and even fun. He or she gives away the golf clubs or skis or stamp albums or other collections, etc. A person who has not been interested in guns before buys one. There are numerous others. No one of these, just like the verbal clues, is clear evidence of suicidal thoughts. But any one of them, and especially several of them within a short period of time, *may* be reflective of a person's move toward killing himself or herself.

So train yourself to be suspicious. What does a person mean by this or that statement, by giving up a prized possession, or by some other behavior? Be alert.

Don't Flinch. After hearing either explicit or implicit suicidal language or observing behaviors which may also be the communication of a person's suicidal thoughts, don't flinch from responding in *explicit* language yourself. Be willing to talk openly about their thoughts and feelings, their pain, frustrations, anger, and hopelessness, the details of the situation in which they find themselves.

Two major characteristics of almost all suicidal persons are the sense of being isolated and that no one understands them or is even willing to try to understand them. Just talking openly with most persons without giving our "answers" or superficial and false reassurances at the very least provides the opportunity for the next step for possible change.

There's no danger in our responding with explicit suicidal language when we only picked up a few implicit references. A person will not kill herself or himself because *we* use the words. Quite to the contrary, the danger is in our *unwillingness* to bring the issue of suicide out into the open.

Be Willing to Ask Questions. The importance of the willingness to ask questions has already been implied in the two previous sections. Much of the facilitation of other persons' sharing more and more openly their thoughts and feelings and the details of their situation can be accomplished in forms of response that are not direct questions. The more of that the better.

But there are times when there is no substitute for the proper question. I was talking recently with a teenage boy whose brother had died about a year before. The parents were still having a lot of difficulty with their grief. They were also concerned about this son. He and I had talked for about forty minutes or so, and it seemed to me that he was handling the loss of his brother fairly well, but continued to be somewhat bothered by the persistent grief of his parents. I had been listening and looking very carefully for any signs of depression, hopelessness, suicidal thoughts, but frankly hadn't recognized any. But in grief, and in a grief-ridden set of relationships, it wouldn't be surprising to find someone with suicidal feelings. So, at a time when we seemed to have finished a particular theme in our conversation, I simply asked him in a matter-of-fact way, "Have there been any times when you've thought about killing yourself?" There was no look of surprise or discomfort on his face at all. He paused only very briefly, no more than three or four seconds, as if not expecting the question. Then in a calm manner, he said, "Yes." The issue was out, and we could discuss it. I don't believe he would have taken the initiative to inject into our conversation something like, "And by the way, sometimes I think about killing myself." As it turned out, it seemed as if his thoughts of suicide were not extremely strong, and he also seemed to have a number of very positive things going for him in his life.

Always Take Suicidal Language Seriously. Even if a person is not a real threat to kill himself or herself, the thoughts and feelings are never to be minimized, made light of, treated as a joke or in casual manner. A discussion of the person's internal and external experiences which are related to suicide can be very profitable for that person, even when such thoughts and feelings are only occasional and moderate or less in their intensity. In addition, our taking their communication with absolute seriousness regardless of the way they have expressed themselves is a communication back to them about the degree to which we value them.

Sometimes we hear people say about a person who has cut his or her wrists or taken an overdose of some pills that she or he is "just trying to get attention." Sometimes it will be said that they are "just being manipulative." It seems to me that both of these are very diminishing types of expressions concerning another human being. After all, what's so bad about trying to get attention when we hurt a great deal, when we feel desperate? All of us do it. We happen, of course, to make our bid for attention in different ways. A number of people have learned to be extremely direct: "I'm feeling terribly sad. I really hurt. I need to talk with someone. Would you be willing to talk with me? Would you be willing to try to help me in my situation?" Many people, however, have neither learned to communicate in a direct fashion nor have the self-confidence and assertiveness to do so. Many people use indirect forms of communication. Often these are verbal, but very often, they are non-verbal. A suicide attempt, even if it is not by a highly lethal means, is usually a form of saying, "I hurt desperately. Would you pay attention to me? Would you help me?" To talk directly and seriously with that person about her or his feelings and situation expresses to that person a valuing of him or her that can be extremely meaningful and powerful.

I need to go ahead and note that there are chronic problems other than the intent to kill themselves that some people have which lead them to take overdoses or to cut themselves. These are difficulties that are beyond our capability to help, other than being sure that they begin treatment with a psychiatrist.

Be Capable and Willing to Discuss Issues of Faith. I've never met a person with any background in any community of faith whose suicidal thoughts and feelings and attempts didn't interact in various ways with their beliefs (or their feelings about former beliefs). Our own knowledge of the Bible, our awareness of methods of interpreting its contents and our ability to apply these methods to any given person's present situation, our study of theology and ethics are as essential to the effective helping of these persons as is our ability to listen and to understand and to communicate that understanding. Together, this knowledge and these abilities may contribute to the resolution of the issues disturbing them as they may be assisted to clarify their thoughts and feelings about themselves as suicidal persons in confrontation with God.

Many suicidal persons feel separated from God, as if God doesn't care, as if God is not engaging with them at all. They may be thinking about killing themselves *because* they experience themselves as so sinful, because they experience God's having rejected them. Or, they may feel sinful *because* they're having suicidal thoughts or feelings. Their desire to kill themselves may be intense, but they're being kept alive by their conviction that suicide is condemned in the Bible, that it's the unpardonable sin, that God *can't* forgive it. Or, their suicides may be made easier for them because they dwell on God's loving understanding and forgiveness. Therefore, when they kill themselves, they will not only leave their present pain and what they perceive to be their present hopeless situation, but will immediately be ushered into heaven for eternal bliss.

Does the Bible condemn (or forbid) suicide?

Is suicide a sin, only a sin, always a sin?

If a suicide is a sin, can God forgive it ahead of time because of God's understanding? Or can God forgive it *after a person's death?*

Given that God is loving, understanding, and forgiving, is the promise of heaven all that this may mean to the suicidal person? What do these characteristics and behaviors of God say about possible reasons for that person's continuing life?

If a person is staying alive only because of what the pastor believes is the person's inadequate or false or distorted belief, what's the pastor's Christian ethical responsibility?

Any person involved in caregiving as a representative of the community of faith needs to be well along the way in working out her or his perspective in response to such questions as these. If ever caught in a pinch with someone, though, not really knowing how to respond, it's essential that we know someone else with whom the person can talk in order to try to clarify their questions, work out their feelings toward themselves in the context of their relationship with God, and move toward as responsible decisions as they can make.

Be Able to Make a Relatively Accurate Evaluation of Lethality Potential. Suicidal people aren't equally suicidal. Some people occasionally have the thought come into their minds and move quickly out, or have rare to occasional mild impulses which they rather easily control. At these times, there's no danger that they'll actually kill themselves, although their experiences, as we've already discussed, must be taken seriously and the importance to them of these experiences discussed with someone. At the other extreme are persons who have just about ruled out options other than suicide, whose pain is chronic, or if not chronic, quite severe, who feel hopeless, who are deeply depressed, who are psychotic. All of these have reached the point where, by themselves, they have lost or are about to lose control over the self-destructive urge. They're not *fully* free and responsible to make decisions and choose their behavior at this point. They are immediate dangers to themselves, and they need other people to protect them from themselves, at least for a period of time. There are also many degrees of frequency and intensity of suicidal thoughts and impulses in between these two extremes of the continuum.

How are we to tell? For starters, ask the person directly, "How close are you to killing yourself? How strong are the impulses? Is there anything in your present experience keeping you from killing yourself? Whom do you have, besides me, who knows about how you feel and who can be of support to you?" Most people really do answer honestly, although there are occasional exceptions.

These sorts of questions and others can be set in a framework of nine criteria of evaluation which I'll only list and define or explain *extremely* briefly here. They can and *should* be studied in the greater detail with which they are presented in other places (Farberow, Heilig, and Litman, pp. 7–13; Pretzel, 1972, pp. 96–108; Stone, 1998, pp. 32–38; Switzer, 1986, pp. 211–13).

1. Age and sex. Older people and males kill themselves with a higher frequency than younger people and females, and whites more than blacks.

2. The suicidal plan. The more specific and detailed the plan, the more lethal the means, and the more available the means, the greater the danger. This is the criterion which carries the most weight in the assessment of lethality. If the person hasn't given such details in the conversation, never fail to ask.

3. Contemporary external threatening events and situations: losses, failures, etc. How many, how severe, and how recent?

4. Symptoms. Persons who hear voices telling them to kill themselves, alcoholics and other chemically dependent persons, and especially those who are clinically depressed are more likely to kill themselves. Hopelessness is a major characteristic of depression and that is what leads to suicide.

5. Resources. Available family members and friends, group membership, activities, a knowledge of agencies in the city, even money, versus the absence of these.

6. Lifestyle. Stability versus instability in work, marriage and other significant relationships, place of residence, etc. Prior suicide attempts are usually seen as indicating greater present lethality.

7. Degree of communication. Is the person still talking with and listening to others? A failure to communicate signals danger, as an important inner core of the person is increasingly isolated from others.

8. Reactions of significant others. Are they understanding and willing to be helpful? Do they withdraw? Do they criticize, condemn, or make light of the person?

9. Medical status. Is the person in reasonably good health or is the person chronically, painfully, perhaps terminally ill, or *believe* himself or herself to be terminally ill?

Not included in these areas of investigation but also very important is the fact that some people have intense anger at someone close to them (a family member, spouse, lover, etc.), haven't been able to change whatever they see to be the source of their anger, and are seeking to punish the other person by killing themselves.

The skillful use of these criteria in making accurate evaluations of a person's lethality potential comes only with the detailed learning of them and the accumulation of experience under supervision. But just with the learning of them, giving primary weight to the suicidal plan and usually second weight to symptoms and stress (criterion 3 and 4 above), then erring on the side of evaluating somewhat high rather than low, a helping person can have important guidelines for his or her strategy with a distressed person.

Offer Direct Help. As a matter of fact, direct help has been given if the pastoral carer has been following the procedure as indicated so far. In addition, if it's determined that a person is in a situational crisis, that particular process can be entered into with the probability that change which involves self-understanding, reduction of the intensity of feelings, diminishing of confusion and a sense of helplessness, increased clarity, and responsible decision making will fairly quickly begin to take place.

The other, and major, way of offering direct help is by seeing to it that the person is put in touch with appropriate resources in addition to ourselves: the clergypersons who may be more experienced and skilled than we are, a family member, a psychiatrist, the hospital emergency room, a suicide prevention center, etc. From the very beginning of talking with a person about his or her suicidal thoughts and feelings, and every step along the way, it's critical that we have in our minds, "In order to protect this person's life, in order to assure a more accurate evaluation, in order to help with a particular issue that this person's grappling with, whom does the person need to see in addition to me?"

Whether lay or clergy engaged in pastoral care, we are irresponsible to ourselves and to the other person if we try to handle only by ourselves someone who even possibly is suicidal. We can be of great value directly, but we always need other resources. If we're in any doubt at all, we need to assist the other person's getting an evaluation from a psychotherapeutic professional. Especially if it's clear that the person is even moderately suicidal, it is imperative that some state-licensed health care provider assume the primary responsibility for the person's treatment program.

Using the combination of the other person's pain and the influence of our relationship with him or her, we can usually gain his or her positive response to seeing someone else. Occasionally this may take some persistence on our part, although most frequently the person will understand the importance of taking such action and will do so. If, after a while, the person still refuses, we need to be willing to take such action as having a family member or some other available appropriate person come to where we are and assume responsibility along with us. Laity may under certain circumstances get in touch with the parish clergy to join them in conversation and decision making. If the person is highly lethal, it's essential that the person be in a position of being protected, either by a family member's taking responsibility, or by our actually driving the person to the hospital emergency room or to check in at the hospital.

When a person's life is in danger, the secrecy element of confidentiality is revoked, whether the other person likes it or not. Even if she or he doesn't like it, the person usually will understand our position when we explain it. Obviously, we need to be willing to risk that person's anger toward us in such a situation. It's crucial to remember that confidentiality is not the ultimate value itself. The ultimate value is the well-being of the other person. Most of the time, confidentiality supports that ultimate value, but occasionally not. The threat of suicide is one of these instances.

Responding to the Attempted Suicide

Everything that was said in the chapter on hospital emergencies is relevant when we are called upon to visit someone who has attempted suicide but has not died. Perhaps the only additional thing to be said is the necessity to explore openly with the person issues such as the following, although not always necessarily in this chronological order:

What were you feeling just before you took this action?
What were you thinking just before and as you took this action?
What did you want to happen?
What were your experiences which led you to that point?
What seemed to stand in the way of your calling on someone for help right at that time?
What were your feelings about various family members and other significant persons?
After you had committed the act, did you imagine being rescued? If you did, what do you suppose that meant?
How do you feel about being alive right now?
What would you like to see happen from this point on?
How may I help in this?

Hopefully, the person will be put in touch with a psychiatrist right at this time for continued therapy or perhaps even psychiatric hospitalization. Unfortunately, it's still all too frequent for the physical results of the suicidal act to be treated in the hospital emergency room and the person immediately be released. Therefore, it's important for us to use our influence to put the person in touch with a psychiatrist or other appropriate professional who can make an evaluation and take whatever action may be indicated in regard to medication, hospitalization, and other aspects of a treatment program.

MINISTRY TO THE FAMILY

The Attempted Suicide

The ministry to the family of the person who has attempted suicide is best considered in terms of two time periods. The first block of time is immediately following the discovery of the attempt and during whatever initial physical recovery period is necessary. This usually ranges from a few hours to a few days while the person is in the emergency room and/or hospital for physical treatment or sometimes in bed for a short period of time at home. The second time frame is the longer-term response of the family to the suicidal person.

The Point of Emergency. When we're visiting with a family who has just discovered a family member's suicide attempt, we respond like we do in any hospital emergency, since almost always the person is taken to an emergency room, even if only for a short period of time. It's important to keep in mind, however, the additional intensity of bewilderment, shock and disbelief, guilt, and anger that most family members will be experiencing. There may be self-blame, blaming another family member, anger (in different forms) directed toward the attempter, the diminishing of the seriousness of the attempt, or even denial that it was a suicide attempt.

The sorts of questions and responses that we might use in any other emergencies are appropriate. "What happened?" We then proceed merely to help the people tell their stories, responding with empathy, assisting their understanding of one another, working with them to clarify whatever the physical facts are.

After the Physical Emergency. Some families will rally around the attempter, try to understand, be supportive of medication or hospitalization or other psychiatric treatment, even be open to family therapy sessions themselves. People within families will differ from one another, and family systems will differ from one another. A helping person has to take these differences into account, identify the family's strengths, and point these out to the family in such a way that they can use them to support the attempter and contribute to the whole family's growth.

Some families will be more difficult to deal with. Denial that it was a suicide attempt or a serious suicide attempt may persist, as may self-blame or blame of one another. They may ostracize the attempter. In these situations, usually the most a pastoral helper can do is assist the family to understand that the attempter really does need professional help and that they as a whole family would serve themselves well if they were in touch with the same or a different professional to assist the whole family and help them discover how they might be more helpful to one another.

Bereavement following a Suicide

A family member has actually killed himself or herself. Family reactions will be some combination of those of any grief, as well as the variety of responses which have just been referred to as following a suicide attempt. Research has indicated that most families who have had a member kill himself or herself, in comparison with families where the death has been from other causes, exhibit a higher degree of anger, guilt, and their own suicidal feelings (Stone, 1972, pp. 34, 36, 41–43). There is also the tendency to focus more on the *mode* of the death (suicide) than on the death itself (Schuyler, 1973, pp. 316, 320). Occasionally there may be the experience of relief. The particular set of responses may form a barrier to the full awareness of the *sorrow* of the loss and thus tend to hinder the usual progression of the process of grief. A very persistent denial that death has been by suicide is not uncommon in instances where there is not a clearly stated suicide note or physical evidence which is irrefutable. While different persons from a community of faith may play a very useful role in the support of the survivors of the suicide of a family member by means of their frequent visits and calls, the empathy expressed in conversation, and the acceptance of them communicated by this quality of support, many many families (or individuals within families) often need even more specialized help. Some number of well-trained skilled clergy can do this. Other psychotherapeutic professionals may also need to be of assistance. Many cities have suicide prevention centers where there may be not only counselors available to talk on the phone, but perhaps also some who are available for personal appointments. Some suicide and crisis centers have Survivors of Suicide groups. These groups usually contain only a small number of persons representing family members and friends of several different persons who have killed themselves. They meet together weekly for a specified number of weeks with trained leaders.

Denial that the death was by suicide is a reaction that with many persons may begin to change after a short period of time as they begin to see more clearly and become able to accept the physical and psychological evidence. The diminishing of denial may also be facilitated by numerous conversations with a trained counselor and mutual support within the family as well as support by friends and the community of faith and its representatives. Persons become stronger and the need for denial and other protective mechanisms lessens. It's not wise for us to make a direct attack upon a denial system and attempt to "argue" the denial out of someone. First, it seldom works. Persons tend to become even more defensive. Second, even if denial were to begin to break down under such a direct attack, few of us are capable of dealing with what some of the possible results might be in the lives of those persons for whom it's that important (necessary?) at this time. We also need to keep in mind that persons who have someone close to them commit suicide tend to be at higher risk of suicide themselves.

The issue of their own involvement in a person's suicide is frequently a part of the survivors' struggle. Realistically, in close relationships, our behavior always has an impact on others. Certainly there are ameliorating or aggravating ways of responding to distressed people. What we can't overlook, though, is the distress of those who live with distressed people. They have needs, too. Their needs are often intensified by whatever the behaviors, both overt and covert, of the suicidal person might be. None of us are capable of doing at all times only that which is most constructive. So, yes, the survivors may find flaws in their own behavior in relationship with the person who has now killed himself or herself. All of this can be discussed realistically in the light of a total relationship and all of its interaction. But even beyond this, for the mental health of *all* of us, we need to realize that we don't *cause* other people to behave certain ways. Admittedly, certain forms of interpersonal behavior may have a negative impact on a person, but no one ever *causes* someone to kill himself or herself.

Again, many people who are related to a religious congregation will have their faith challenged by the suicide of a family member. They may have questions about God's involvement or lack of it, the suicide's eternal destiny, or be confused about other issues of faith. If we are to be involved in helping processes with people, we need to study and discuss issues ahead of time so we will be at least somewhat prepared to help people grapple more constructively with the very personal issues of faith which lie before them at a time like this.

CONCLUSION

This chapter has been all too brief. The complex and differing dynamics of suicide which are important for us to understand haven't really been discussed at all. Although theological and ethical issues have been briefly referred to, no detailed discussion of them has taken place.

Throughout the chapter the attempt has been made merely to point to how both laypersons and clergy might respond to different persons with different intensities and frequencies of suicidal thoughts and feelings and to members of their families. This has been only a beginning, a stimulator, to help persons within the community of faith realize how prevalent such thoughts and feelings are, and to give some sense of how to evaluate the persons who have them, and only an introductory approach of how to be of help to them.

REFERENCES

Norman L. Farberow, Samuel M. Heilig, and Robert Litman, *Training Manual for Telephone Evaluation and Emergency Management of Suicidal Persons* (Los Angeles Suicide Prevention Center).

Doman Lum, *Responding to Suicidal Crisis* (Grand Rapids: Eerdmans Publishing Co., 1974).

Paul W. Pretzel, *Understanding and Counseling the Suicidal Person* (Nashville: Abingdon Press, 1972).

Dean Schuyler, "Counseling Suicide Survivors: Issues and Answers," *Omega* 4 (1973).

Statistical Abstract of the United States, United States Department of Commerce, 1998.

Howard W. Stone, *Depression and Hope* (Minneapolis: Fortress Press, 1998).

————. *Suicide and Grief* (Philadelphia: Fortress Press, 1972).

David K. Switzer, *The Minister As Crisis Counselor* (Revised and enlarged) (Nashville: Abingdon Press, 1986), chapter 9, "Intervening in the Suicidal Crisis."

9

MARRIAGE AND FAMILY LIFE: FAMILY SYSTEMS, COUNSELING, DIVORCE

In the Introduction to this book, I mentioned the young married woman who appeared at our rural parsonage door early one morning in robe, curlers, and tears, telling about her husband's affair with another woman. I spoke with her in my living room that morning and with the husband, a high school coach, in the deserted boys' locker room at the school that afternoon, a couple of other times with her in her home, and another time with him in the locker room. It just never occurred to me to talk with them together (conjoint marriage counseling). I'd never heard of such a thing in 1950. The fact that this particular couple also talked with each other, that over the period of about three weeks that I had my conversations with each of them, he stopped seeing the other woman, and that they reconciled and later had an even better relationship with each other, had a great deal more to do with who they were and the resources that they had than it did with my effectiveness as a marriage crisis counselor. Other couples have needed more than this from their pastors. What would that be?

In my second parish, a city church, I received a telephone call from a frantic mother, Mrs. Carter. Her fourteen-year-old daughter, Beth, was driving her crazy. Beth was slipping out of her room at night through the window to be with various older boys, smoking, drinking, and who knows what else. What could be done to stop her from doing this? The mother and daughter had recently been attending worship services, but Beth had shown no interest in our really fine youth group. In brief conversations with them, I had never heard a word about a husband/father. I suggested that she come by the church to talk.

She came to see me that same afternoon. She was terribly distressed and frustrated. There was a husband/father, who seemed, according to her, to function as a family rule-giver but who was otherwise passive and withdrawn in the home. The first most reasonable thing I could I could think of at that time was to see if Mrs. Carter could get Beth to come see me. Somewhat surprisingly to me, Beth called that evening and she and I set up a time to get together.

She was really a fairly responsive young person. She didn't particularly like sneaking out, but she was clearly in a state of rebellion, angry at her parents, and wanted to see the boys she was seeing. She agreed to come back to talk, and we had several conversations. Mrs. Carter also came back a time or two, and made it clear that Mr. Carter didn't want to get involved with any of this at all.

I was curious about this man, so I went by their home one night and met him. The mother and daughter were also present. It was apparent that Mr. Carter wasn't going to be drawn into any conversation at all, much less about his daughter or the family, or at least not in the way I was going about it. (I would handle that evening much differently now.)

I could certainly see the strain and stress and lack of adequate communication in the family, but I didn't know what else to do. Over a few weeks, Beth changed her behavior enough so that the tension was eased somewhat. The mother became somewhat more understanding of her. What I didn't have sufficiently clear in my mind was that no matter how Beth changed her immediate behavior, everyone in the family was being hurt by the way the *whole* family operated, and that inevitably Beth would continue to act out those pressures in some ways that were going to create even more distress.

What did I need?

Based on this reflection of my early experience in ministry and on what I've learned since, I believe that the most useful thing to do in a single chapter is merely to discuss briefly the concept of the family as a system, attempt to make a distinction between an emergency of a person who is also a part of a family and the somewhat narrower definition of family emergency, and make some general suggestions about the need to identify the different levels of functioning of families in order to assist them in problem solving. There are some relevant concepts and practices of conjoint family therapy with which we need to have at least some minimal acquaintance and in which we need to have some skill so that we may function in the most facilitative way with a family unit. Issues related to divorce will conclude the chapter. I also urge the reader to examine some of the books listed under "Recommended Reading."

WHAT'S A FAMILY?

For the purposes of this chapter, I am not going to attempt to deal with all of the complexities of what, or who, a family is in our society today. I am merely going to let you know that as I'm using the words here, I'm referring to two or more people who are living together within one household and who have some type or degree of commitment to and emotional relationship with one another, as well as those family members of whatever generation who have sufficiently frequent contact and significant emotional influence in the life of the family.

So why do people in our culture choose to relate themselves to each other, to live together, to make emotional investments in one another in this way? In other words, what's the purpose of the form of relationship which we call marriage and the family? Even though all of us started out in some kind of family, most people today make some geographical move away from the original home and go through some form of transformation of relationship with the parent or parents, siblings, and others. As older teenagers and adults, the majority of persons begin to seek out someone else to be with. What's the reason or reasons? There are a number of ways of responding accurately to such a question, but whatever else is said or how it's expressed, it boils down to mutual need fulfillment. I need someone to help significantly in meeting my deepest needs as a human being, only one of which is sex. Someone else needs that, too. We usually come together through some variety of somewhat coincidental circumstances and at least begin to have the impression that we're getting important needs met by one another at more or less the same time. We have the sense of loving one another, wanting to be with one another, and therefore, with some level of commitment, we decide that we would like to live with each other. Most of the time, sooner or later, we decide to become officially married, although there is an increase in the number of couples who live together as married who do not go through the formal process, including gays and lesbians.

Part of the excitement and the mystery of close relationships, as well as the source of problems, is that many of our needs are unconscious to us and hidden from the other person. Therefore, there are times of need when I can't communicate openly to the other what that need is and thus the other only by coincidence is able to respond to it. But when the partner doesn't respond to my need, I'm frustrated. I become angry, although I'm not always certain of what it's about. The other person senses the anger and *definitely* doesn't know what it's about. The partner is confused, experiences her or his needs not being met because of whatever *my* angry behavior is. That person is now frustrated, experiences anger, and so it all escalates in a very confusing, frustrated, and frustrating manner, with anger and its resulting behavior increasing every step of the way.

Regardless of the original stimulus and/or source of the needs themselves at this particular time, whether just from within us or as a result of the triggering of needs by some set of external circumstances, frustrated needs within close relationships are inevitable. Whether our needs then get relatively well met and we bounce back from frustration or whether there is a substantial process of escalation as just described depends upon patterns of self-awareness and communication and other forms of behavior that we've learned within our family of origin and which we bring, along with our unconscious needs, into our new relationships, our marriage.

Children are born to or are adopted by couples who interact with one another in these various ways. Just as parents, when they were children, learned ways of relating to one another within their families in the attempt to get their needs met, so do their children. Thus, a system is formed: two or more people trying to get their needs met from the other or others as best they can while attempting to meet those other persons' needs sufficiently well so that they can maintain themselves as a family group, so that they all can continue to get their needs met as well as possible. Both consciously and unconsciously they attempt to relate to each other so they may accomplish this double purpose: maintain the family unit and have individual needs met. Some don't make it. Others are able to develop styles of interaction that are barely satisfactory. Some do better than that. A few do it very well.

The Family As a System

Families aren't just groups of individuals. They are a group of people with ties to one another, who need to get many (and for small children, almost all) of their important needs met within the family group. Therefore, they have a serious investment in maintaining the whole group so they can continue to meet one another's needs. The family is an operational system. What affects one member affects not just other individuals *within* the system, but the whole system itself. Beth could change her "sneaking out" and some of her other behavior, but the longer she lived within that particular system, she would inevitably have to do something that would respond to the terrible tension and lack of mutual need satisfaction between her parents and which would express her anger toward them. She would also be limited to the forms of expression which she had learned within that family. No pastor (or psychotherapist) could "change" her to the parents' satisfaction so long as she continued to live with them. The whole family system needed to change so that all members of the family would be more satisfied with what they were receiving and giving.

Levels of Family Functioning

Just as individuals don't look and act alike, neither do families. As those engaged in pastoral caring, we don't treat all individuals as if they were identical. Neither can we work with all families in the same way and expect to be most helpful to them. We need to be able to make some kind of assessment of the different levels and forms of family functioning in order to guide our strategy with different families.

There are numerous sources of information about family systems from which have been extracted criteria for the evaluation of families and for somewhat different ways of categorizing levels of their functioning.

The one with which I am most familiar and which has been most useful
to me is the comprehensive study still under way by the Timberlawn
Foundation for Psychiatric Education and Research (Beavers, 1977, pp.
42-156; Beavers-Timberlawn Family Evaluation Scale; Lewis et al., 1976;
Lewis and Looney, 1983; Lewis, 1979).

The interaction of family behaviors and the ways in which they can
be categorized for purposes of evaluation are far too complex to be presented here, but perhaps in offering just a taste, you can be stimulated to
read the original sources in more detail.

In order to assess how well or how poorly a family characteristically
operates, it's necessary to look at a variety of attitudes, feelings, and
behaviors:

> The degree to which family members can be distinguished from one
> another;
> The degree to which family members recognize that they need each
> other for the reasonably satisfactory meeting of one another's
> needs;
> The degree to which family members are committed to one another;
> The degree to which family members understand the complexity of
> the sources of their behavior with each other;
> The degree to which family members understand all of their behav-
> ior with one another as a part of an action/reaction process;
> The degree to which family members react significantly with the
> world outside the family and get some important needs met there;
> The degree to which the parents (if there are both husband and wife)
> are capable of meeting one another's adult needs for intimacy,
> support, and companionship;
> The degree to which the parents are capable of maintaining clear dis-
> tinctions between the roles of adults and children in the family,
> share power with one another relatively equally, have affection for
> one another, and work together effectively in the necessary tasks
> that parents need to accomplish;
> The degree to which the parents consider the children's needs and
> desires, receiving the children's input, but maintain a balance of
> power in the family through the creative use of a loving relation-
> ship and usually in a way that is neither crassly coercive nor
> sneakily manipulative;
> The degree to which parents are able to give the children increasing
> freedom as the children, according to their age and experience,
> are capable of assuming greater responsibility;
> The degree to which family members are able to assume responsibil-
> ity for their own thoughts, beliefs, feelings, and behaviors;
> The degree to which family members speak for themselves rather
> than one another;

The degree to which family members are capable of communicating their thoughts and feelings to one another in words as well as in other constructive behaviors;

The degree to which family members are open to the communications of one another;

The degree to which family members encourage initiative by one another;

The degree to which failures by a family member are tolerated;

The degree to which family members seem to have fun with one another, enjoy one another;

The degree to which anger and conflict present is capable of being resolved;

The degree to which family members have and openly express empathy for one another;

The degree to which the whole family works together in family tasks that either need or are useful to be done;

The degree to which the family has a religious faith and/or set of values which guide their behavior and which give meaning to the different experiences of life, including suffering and loss;

The degree to which the family members' description of the way they function corresponds or does not correspond with the way in which a perceptive observer judges their functioning;

The degree to which family members give adequate, clear information to one another about matters important to family relationships and functioning and how they feel about one another.
(Extracted and at times somewhat rephrased from Lewis et al, 1976; Beavers-Timberlawn Family Evaluation Scale; Beavers, 1977)

I believe that apart from research which does in fact substantiate it, common sense also tells us that the greater the degree of these qualities and behaviors, the healthier the development of self-esteem and human competence. With fewer of these characteristics within the family, the more limited the persons will be in certain areas that relate to self-image, quality of personal relationships, adequacy of communication, and the ability to deal with stress. Moving along the continuum to those families who have a very low degree of the qualities and behaviors listed, we can understand that the persons in these families will fail to develop many of the critical elements which contribute to ego-strength, close and lasting personal relationships, a sense of self-worth, and internal and external resources to help them deal effectively with the inevitable problem areas of life.

The ability to assess the strengths and weaknesses of a given family is critical in any pastoral helper's determination of the particular set of responses that she or he might most usefully make to a particular family emergency. In summary, many families handle their own emergencies very well, but can be assisted and supported by visits and phone calls from some concerned representative of the community of faith and by a few concrete acts such as someone's making a few phone calls for them or running a few errands. Others also profit from and appreciate the same sorts of helpful responses, but will probably need more assistance from a pastoral visitor in talking more openly about their feelings with one another and accepting some of the differences which they have from one another in their reactions. Still other families can be most helped by a greater mobilization of help of different kinds from outside the family, more direction in what issues to deal with first and how to go about trying to accomplish what needs to be done, and more changing of certain aspects of their family situation in order to reduce the pressure. For example, in this family there might need to be a brief separation between husband and wife and arrangements made to care for the children, or a teenager or smaller child may need to be taken care of temporarily by someone else, etc.

FAMILY EMERGENCIES

It's difficult to give a precise definition of a family emergency in contrast with an individual emergency of a particular family member. At this point, it's important to make a distinction between what we're calling an *emergency* and what is technically a family situational *crisis,* as situational crisis was defined in chapter 3. You will remember that a situational crisis is when a person's usual capacity to cope is diminished by the intensity of the threat experienced as a result of some specific external event. When that individual is a part of a family, the rest of the family is affected, but most usually they will mobilize their efforts as individuals and as a group to support and help the one in crisis. The *family system* is not necessarily disrupted and their level of functioning diminished. In contrast, a *family* crisis is when the event is a direct threat to the family system *as such* and the family experiences disruption and a decreasing ability to function as a unit (Switzer, 1986, pp. 116, 125–28).

For example, if a child is physically attacked by someone else at school or on the way home, certainly the other members of the family have immediate reactions. They are distressed and angry. Another child in the family may be afraid. But the functioning of the family system may not be disturbed. Physical and emotional attention is given to the hurt child. The pain and anger and fear of the hurt child are a focus of attention. Parents support one another and other children in their feelings. Their ability to decide on some additional course of action isn't hindered. Their usual level of functioning with one another isn't necessarily affected. They still operate as a unit, even though some of their individual reactions may differ. There is a family *emergency*, but the family isn't in *crisis*.

However, if a child in the family is severely beaten by a father who has lost control, the ways in which most families would be relating to and communicating with one another in attempting to solve problems are immediately severely disrupted. The child is traumatized, frightened, confused. Other children may withdraw. An older child or the mother may attack the father or withdraw. The father may leave home. Someone may call the police. The family as *such* is not a constructively functioning unit.

Another contrast would be when a grandparent, who lives at great distance and whom the grandchildren rarely see and whom they hardly know, dies. The father or mother whose parent it is grieves. Family members are affected by this. Pastoral visitation is appropriate. But this *family*'s coping is intact, although the coping ability of one member may be temporarily significantly diminished. But if the grandparent has been living in the home for several years, that person is in fact a part of the nuclear family. Her or his death radically changes the family's *system*. In addition to every individual's experiences of grief, patterns of behavior and channels and forms of communication inevitably change. The family system *as a whole* needs to readjust, assign new roles, establish some new patterns of communication.

A family emergency is any sort of event which happens to the family or any individual or individuals within the family which causes any form of severe deprivation or distress and requires some readjustment, some change in the way family members behave, respond to one another, communicate with each other. This, then, becomes a pastoral emergency for the congregation which in some way understands itself as being responsible to that family.

PASTORAL CONVERSATIONS WITH COUPLES AND FAMILIES

Lay and ordained pastoral counselors are not conjoint marriage and family therapists. To become such a therapist entails extensive study and supervised experience. Even if one had such training, there would very rarely be the time for working with couples and whole family units in the attempt to assist them in resolving long-standing and complex and sometimes truly pathological and psychopathogenic attitudes, styles of communication, and behaviors. However, additional study of family systems issues and at least some of the ways that family therapists function can point us to particular forms of interaction within a family and can suggest to us ways of responding that can be very helpful when we're engaged with more than one person in a family in response to a family emergency.

The function of a family therapist is to help all parts of the family system to get in touch with one another in such a manner that the expression of feelings and other relevant types of information can take place more fully and clearly. The assumption is, somewhat oversimplified in this brief general statement, that as this increasingly takes place, the whole system inevitably changes and the individuals within it change in the direction of meeting one another's needs more fully.

Concretely, then, what does this mean that a marriage or family therapist actually does with people? Or, what can we learn from conjoint family therapy that we can adapt to the particular pastoral conversations we have with family units? First, let's look at a pastoral conversation between one representative of the community of faith and one parishioner: two people. The lines of communication go directly back and forth. One speaks, the other listens; then the second speaks and the first listens.

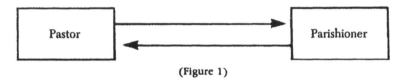

(Figure 1)

Very simple, isn't it? That is, it's relatively simple if we as pastoral carers can provide rather readily the facilitative conditions of all helping relationships as these were discussed earlier. But wait. Some of these conditions themselves indicate that something is missing in our diagram of a one-on-one conversation. We are not just to listen and speak to the other person. We've learned that integral to the helping process is a developing relationship of trust, that an awareness of what's taking place in *our* relationship at any moment is just as critical as *other* relationships a person may be talking about at this time, and that open reference to *our* relationship may sometimes become the topic of exploration.

So if our conversation is only that depicted in the simple diagram above, the pastoral caring can often be very limited. It more properly looks like this:

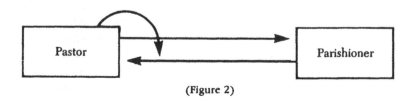

(Figure 2)

We observe not just the other person and attend to her or his verbal story and the other nonverbal communication, we observe the *relationship between* us, and may need to invite the other person to observe this immediate relationship along with us.

It doesn't take a genius to imagine how much more complicated our relational/communication diagram becomes if we're talking with a couple. Adding only one other person, the first thing we might see looks like this:

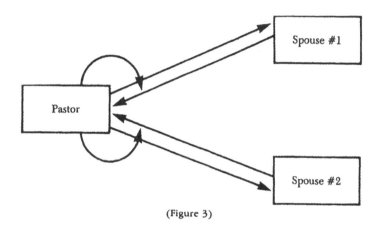

(Figure 3)

However, this scheme doesn't really portray *couple* counseling, but rather serial counseling of first one and then the second individual in the presence of the other spouse, *even* if the content of the conversation has to do with concerns that they both have. Of course, there will be times when we speak to this one and then to that one. In so doing, we'll be modeling for each of them the accurate communication of empathy, concreteness, self-disclosure, loving confrontation, clarity of communication, openness to the expressions of a person and responsiveness to others' statements or questions to us, honest feedback, the sharing of power in relationships, etc.

However, it's also essential that we assist more directly in their own talking and listening to one another in something of the same way. They have a particular relationship and patterns of communicating with each other, and our pastoral task in this form of counseling is to observe their relationship perceptively and to facilitate their talking directly with each other. Thus,

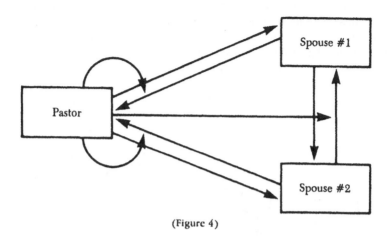

(Figure 4)

Stimulation of discussion directly between the two spouses can be done in a number of ways, at least partially dependent on what has just been said.

What did you understand him to be saying to you?
Did what she said really respond to what you were trying to express?
How did you feel when she/he said that?
Could you tell her what it is you need from her?
Would you say that directly to him?

In the meantime, it is important to remember that each of them is paying attention to how we interact with the other and making judgments about that interaction:

She/he is being more attentive to her than to me.
He/she is teaming up with him against me.
I don't understand why he/she said that to my spouse.

It's important for us to be aware of such possible unexpressed reactions. Therefore, there will be times when we will need to ask that person what she or he is thinking or feeling at the moment.

In this type of process we're helping them to learn to be able to do spontaneously that which will improve their communication with each other and thus their whole relationship, reduce the number of occasions for misunderstanding and conflict, and increase their ability to solve their problems when they arise.

This process is descriptive of what Stewart calls role-relationship counseling for couples (1970). The focus is kept on the couple's present relationship, the immediate clarification of affective and informational communication. The emphasis is on their understanding of their present actual roles and of their role expectations of one another. While not really *simple,* this is a form of marriage counseling (or pastoral care in relatively brief contact and emergencies) which can be most readily learned and which can probably assist significantly the largest percentage of couples with whom clergy and other pastoral carers engage themselves.

This same procedure for the most part can be used with whole families as well as with couples in most pastoral situations. The additional complexity must not be overlooked, however. Just the addition one child into the conversation between the pastor and the parents begins to make a very messy picture:

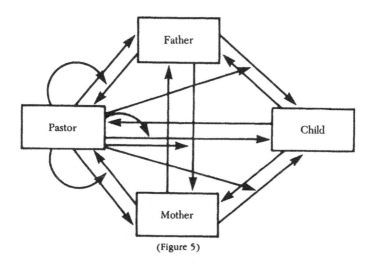

(Figure 5)

Actually, even more lines could be drawn in the diagram as the child observes the interaction between the parents, as one parent observes the interaction between the child and the other parent, etc. Now imagine what it would look like if you added only one other child. This would represent what is a relatively typical family: a mother, a father, and two children. You can begin to see the many interactions that the pastor will need to be observing at the same time and the many different alternatives for intervention that the pastor has at almost any given moment. It does become quite complex.

Nothing will help a person become truly competent in conjoint marriage and family counseling except extensive training by a skilled professional and closely supervised experience. However, what I'm suggesting in this section is that an awareness of the process described here is applicable to very brief pastoral conversations or only a few conversations in marriage and family emergencies. A more thorough and detailed reading and practice in peer training groups can assist clergy and lay caregivers in being much more helpful to couples and families.

DIVORCE

No discussion of marriage and family emergencies would be complete without at least some reference to divorce. Divorce is a tragic reality. Regardless of the theological stance of our particular faith group or denomination, all clergy and lay caregivers are called upon to respond to the needs of persons who are in a deeply troubled marriage, who may be thinking about divorce or annulment or who have already filed, those who have already separated, and those who are recently divorced. How heartbreaking it is that the relationship which was begun, in most cases, with feelings of love and excitement and anticipation and sincere commitment begins after a while to grow dull, to have the joy squeezed out of it by accumulating hidden hostility, the severely disruptive heated arguments, sometimes physical violence, excessive drinking, sexual and other forms of infidelity, the variety of inner experiences and outward behavior which lead to the breakdown of the relationship, consideration of divorce, and divorce itself.

The people who reach this point are certainly not all "bad people." No one is more shattered, more pained, than they. Their behavior in their marriage has been disillusioning, not only concerning whom they thought their partner to be, but also concerning themselves. Most people vacillate between blaming the other and blaming themselves, most of the time being unaware of the source and the nature of the underlying problems which now express themselves in the very obvious feelings and open behaviors. Yet it seems that it is the experienced and expressed feelings and the overt behaviors which get most of the attention, leaving the more important issues relatively untouched.

Divorce and Theology

All of us are aware that different faith groups and denominations differ from one another as to how divorce is to be understood theologically and how divorce and divorced persons are officially viewed and handled in terms of their relationships to the church. It's important not to overlook that there are also differing unofficial responses in any group.

Many of us hold a deep conviction that in Christian faith we've discovered that which at a minimum is a source of guidance and support for us as we seek to make our faith live within our families as well as in our other relationships and activities. To be sure, we're aware that in our lives there is often a gap between our stated beliefs and values and those "below-the-surface" forces which reflect additional and/or conflicting faith and values and which are actually operative in our lives, which initiate, empower, and guide our behaviors. Few of us are without such conflict.

However, it's difficult for any of us to make the move from where we are realistically with our conflicts and inconsistencies to where we would like to be in terms of congruity between our stated faith and our actual lives as spouses, parents, children, without working to develop a statement of our faith which gives some external form to our internal experience, words which describe and communicate as well as continue to help shape our Christian experience. This, of course, is what theology, or more precisely the process of theologizing, is. When our area of concern is marriage and the family, then we work at and speak of the theology of marriage and divorce.

The form in which we phrase our convictions which arise out of our faith has an influence on the way in which we relate to people in troubled marriages, those who are divorcing, and those who are divorced, just as both our unconscious and our conscious attitudes and feelings about marriage and divorce influence our theological statements. It's important in the helping process for us to be just as clear as we possibly can be about what the Bible and our tradition do and do not say. From this increasing clarity we also need to continue to work on making the most honest interpretations that we can that support the ordered life of the Christian community (the "edification of the church") while accounting for and guiding a Christian response to the disordered lives which we human beings always seem capable of producing.

Even though we may disagree with one another about many aspects of interpretation, probably the overwhelming majority of us would agree that the major thrust of the biblical message is that God's primary will in regard to marriage is a committed male/female relationship in which companionship and a variety of physical and spiritual needs are met and in which personal identity is formed and personal growth takes place and that this relationship should continue until it is broken only by death.

In addition, regardless of how we might elaborate it in detail, divorce would always involve human sin. This is hardly surprising, since our sin is involved in all of our relationships. Divorce is failure to follow the perfect will of God. Sin itself cannot be measured. Obviously, the

personal and the social impact of various behaviors of sin differ radically from one another, and in this sense, divorce may cause more pain
and destruction than some other behaviors of sin and less than some
others; it may cause more pain and destruction in some sets of circumstances and may provide opportunities for redemption and reconstruc-
tion in others. This can be judged only in each individual case and after
a period of time.

Therefore, my perspective is that when we are working with persons who are in fact divorcing or who have recently been divorced, we
may be talking with people who have reached the point when mutual
destructiveness seems to have reached the point of no return. Therefore, we must inevitably raise the question of what God's will is for the
person or persons from this point on. It's quite clear that it is not an
easy question to answer. Should a person stay in the marriage, be
destroyed, destroy another, perhaps damage children severely? Our
answers may differ, but we must raise the question of what God's will is
in this particular set of circumstances now that ideal circumstances no
longer exist. After persons have divorced, the question is what the will
of God is for the particular person or persons after divorce. In one set
of terms, it's the same that it's always been: forgiveness of our sins,
renewal of our commitment to God, wholeness and fulfillment in our
lives and relationships, seeking to live the life of the kingdom. How will
a divorcing or divorced person do that? Each one of us is responsible
for working with that person or those persons in the light of all of the
circumstances of their lives and in the light of our particular faith and
tradition, assisting them by all means possible to clarify for themselves
in as conscientious a way as possible what the will of God is for him or
her or them.

The Process of Divorce

Divorce doesn't just happen all at once. It's a process, usually a very long
one. Hunt refers to studies that reveal that over 50 percent of divorcing
persons had seriously considered divorce for one to three years prior to
the granting of the decree (1986, p. 181). A number of books chronicle
the breakdown of marriage, the movement toward divorce, and the
recovery process. Hunt's presentation is especially useful because of its
clarity and its indication of points at which clergy may intervene and
how they might go about responding most effectively.

He lists six stages and three particular points of crisis within the
stages (1986, pp. 181–97).

Stages   Crises

1. The sense on the part of
one or both partners that
something is wrong with the
marriage. Usually no signifi-   1. Making the decision
cant action is initiated.   about divorce. Challenge to
                                       one's self-concept, additional
2. Usually one spouse   tension in relationship with
finds the situation intolerable,   spouse.
may consider divorce, may dis-
cuss his or her feelings with
someone.

3. Any efforts made
toward reconciliation fail and
the decision to divorce
becomes clear. Both spouses   2. Clear-cut decision for
are now aware of the process of   divorce. Beginning of legal
the decision.   procedures. Usually involves
                                       separation.
4. Initiation of legal pro-
ceedings and self-doubt, questioning, numerous other
strong feelings.

5. Granting the final
decree.   3. Post-divorce adjust-
                                       ment. Grief reaction with its
6. Readjustment to being   several stages.
single again.

Occasionally a minister may be called on for help in stage 1, or the minister may, if aware of tension or distress in a marriage, take the initiative to move into a conversation about the relationship with the person or persons involved. Probably, however, a dissatisfied or distressed married person will be more likely to share her (or his, more rarely) feelings with a trusted friend. Such a friend will be most helpful if he or she listens, is empathetic to the feelings, doesn't take sides, and does not give advice, except for the suggestion that the person talk with a sensitive and skilled minister or someone else trained in marriage counseling.

A minister is more likely to become involved in stage 2, but whether stage 1 or stage 2, she or he might consider asking both partners to come together to share their feelings and to attempt to clarify issues and needs. Something of the process outlined within the preceding section, if followed in a perceptive and disciplined manner, can contribute positively to many couples. Some couples may begin the process of genuine reconciliation. If, after three or four sessions together, the minister and/or the couple judge that progress is not being made, referral to a marriage counseling specialist is indicated.

By the time a couple are in stages 3 and 4, a friend or ordained pastor is very likely not going to be able to help them resolve their problems, reach reconciliation, and reconstruct their marriage. Even expert marriage counselors, when it is fairly clear that one or both partners have clearly decided for divorce, will shift into what may more properly be called *divorce* counseling rather than *marriage* counseling. The couple may or may not still be seen together, although very often both partners will be seen individually. Such counselors, including the pastor and laypersons, can help the person or persons to continue to express their feelings, grapple with their sense of failure, support them in their faith, help in reducing the type of bitterness and resentment which too often leads people to want to hurt the other in the divorce proceeding and the post-divorce period. At this time, the most useful task is to assist the persons in disengaging from one another and moving out of their marriage with as little damage as possible to themselves and their children and with the best chance for readjustment. This process can be compared to assisting people in their anticipatory grief, accepting the reality of the loss, and, in the case of divorce, accepting realistically their own share, but not more than their share, of the responsibility for the breakdown of the relationship. Such acceptance is necessary in order for a person to confess, ask for and receive forgiveness, continue to experience being loved by God, and to reconstruct his or her self-esteem, which has usually taken quite a battering for a long period of time.

The period which in divorce may be compared with anticipatory grief corresponds with Hunt's stages 1 through 4. This is the extent of time from the first recognition of something being radically wrong with the relationship and the growing recognition of the inability or unwillingness on the part of one or both of the married couple to work out viable alternatives other than divorce. The crisis at this point involves the alteration of one's life situation and self-concept, occasioned by the anticipation of the loss in the near future of a person with whom there has been significant identification and overlapping lives and concerns.

Weiss, after discussing the strength of attachments, especially those of parent and child and those between spouses, states:

> It is natural that the thought of separation frightens people. Separation means starting over, alone. It means setting off without the partner on whom one has, perhaps for years, relied. It means new vulnerability, and perhaps isolation and loneliness. One cannot anticipate everything it will mean, and this too can be frightening. (1975, P. 25)

To review the divorce process in terms of anticipatory grief, the first reaction, denial and disbelief, is quite common not only for the person who hears a spouse's announcement of the possibility of or the desire for a divorce, but often enough for the person who first realizes that this may be what she or he actually wants. It requires a change of self-concept for many people, a change from a person who never considered divorce a possibility to one who now realizes that he or she may not have made it in this marriage, who may be divorced, who may become single. The inner conflict which they experience fends off a clear decision to talk about or take concrete steps toward the divorce, even in the face of the pain and anguish of the external conflicts in the marriage. The disbelief tends to express itself in the denial of the intensity of the unhappiness, in minimizing the seriousness of the conflicts, and in the repression of feelings. This denial and minimizing also is a barrier to talking with a minister or other counselor about the distress. Eventually, the reality of the severity of the stress and conflict with one's mate may win out and the possibility and perhaps the need of divorce is tested first in thought and then in talking, very often talking first with someone other than the spouse in order to test out what it sounds like, feels like, to one's self, and how another person might respond.

Anger has undoubtedly been experienced throughout at least the relatively recent history of the relationship, usually for a much longer period of time. Therefore, to be aware of that feeling can hardly be spoken of as a new stage in the anticipatory grief of the divorce process. However, it's not uncommon that a new anger at the spouse at putting one in the situation of serious consideration of divorce arises, along with an awareness of anger at oneself for getting into this situation. These angers, like any others, may be displaced onto the children or other members of the family or express themselves in general irritability. This, of course, creates an additional problem.

As in any anticipatory grief, strong wishes for a resolution of the situation in some manner other than divorce continue to force themselves into consciousness, even to the point occasionally of wishing for the death of the other as a rescue both from the situation of the marriage and from the situation of the divorce at the same time, as well as from having to make one's own personal decision. Other hopes of rescue are present: the miraculous change of the other person, or, much less frequently, of oneself so that the other will then respond positively. These wishes arise both from the strength of the attachment itself which still exists and from fears of the future.

The ambivalence is usually very strong. Many couples headed for divorce actually have some temporary truces. These truces may be experienced by them, under the influence of their wishes, as true reconciliations. It's like the dying patient who is doing very badly, but from time to time when we go to the hospital we note that he or she has rallied. The person looks better, seems to have more strength, speaks more clearly, and our minds immediately tell us that he or she is not really going to die. We feel elated. However, the person is still dying.

Depression is also often, but not always, of course, a part of the movement toward the divorce decision or a reaction following the decision. The depression may be a response to the breaking of the attachment to the other, the anticipation of loss, one's own sense of failure and guilt, a deep-seated anger which has found inadequate expression, a sense of helplessness, or some combination of these. This depression is usually fairly transient because it's counterbalanced by other forces, such as the intolerable nature of the present relationship, blame of the other and outbursts of anger at the spouse, and the anticipation of relief which the divorce will afford. While some depression would usually be expected, and expected to be transient, if it persists, the layperson or clergy needs to suggest that the person seek truly professional help.

Up to this point I've been speaking as if only the spouses suffered loss in divorce and therefore had experiences similar to anticipatory grief. This overlooks the deep involvement of children in the home, and, often enough, the parents of the married couple. Usually, they have a much shorter period of anticipatory grief than the couple in distress, because in most instances the couple has been dealing with their divisive issues for a long period of time prior to sharing it with parents and children.

Unfortunately, children too often have no opportunity for anticipatory grief at all as they are told that Daddy is moving out tonight or Mother is leaving tomorrow. This is a crime against the children. While most assuredly for their well-being they must not be brought into the argument or even the negotiations between the parents, they still need to know as soon as possible after a clear-cut divorce decision has been reached so they will have the opportunity to experience and express their own feelings in the anticipation of loss—their sense of fear, rejection, guilt, their anger toward their parents, and hopefully, finally, their acceptance of the inevitable. Only by so doing can they be more prepared emotionally for the actual physical separation and legal divorce when they come. It should be simply and clearly stated to them that the divorce has been decided upon, that it's an issue between the parents and not between the parents and the children, that there is nothing that they (the children) have done that has contributed to this decision, nor is there anything that they (the children) can do to change the decision at this time. Like the dying of another person, they can only feel and express their emotions and try to move to the acceptance of that which is beyond their control. Both of their parents can be helpful to them in that process, including the assurance that both parents continue to love them.

The sense of the reality of divorce tends to dawn gradually for most people. It comes and goes, but usually gets stronger as the legal proceedings are initiated, as the persons physically separate, and as decisions are made about the children and property. But interestingly, a number of people report that the final reality of it struck only when the divorce became final. The death of a relationship seems to be like any other death. With a terminally ill patient, we know that it's coming, we move through the anticipatory grief. Then the person dies. The death is always different from the anticipation of it. The legal decree of divorce is the formal announcement that the patient, that is, the relationship, is dead. For some there may be predominantly relief: perhaps sadness that it had to die, but primarily relief. Or there may be the beginning of the grief process, with sharp stabbing pain, intense fear, a sense of void, which, even if fairly well prepared for, still takes place and has its own particular course. Or frequently, the reaction may be a combination of relief and grief, as it is in response to some deaths.

Whatever the combination of reaction, the post-divorce period itself is a process with certain sorts of stages, just as any other grief also has its stages in the process. Weiss speaks of two phases: transition and recovery (1975, pp. 236–37).

The period of transition is for many a time of disorganization, depression, unmanageable restlessness, and chaotic searching for escape from distress. There may be an obsessive review of the marriage relationship and its events. Moods may alternate between despair and elation. The person may be unable to make or to hold to a decision. Of course, some people feel the relief to such a degree that they are in a state of euphoria. However, they're just as likely as the others to be without stable goals or commitments that can direct their activities. These activities may often be undertaken at a frantic pace. This first part of the period of transition may cover several months. In later months, but still in the period of transition, the individuals are clearer and more decisive in trying to regain their footing, to begin functioning in a more stable manner, and to return order to their lives.

The period of transition usually seems to end for most people some time before the end of the first year after the separation, with eight to ten months being about average.

The second phase, the period of recovering, is then entered. In the first part of this phase, the person has established a relatively coherent pattern of life, but without yet having integrated it firmly enough so that the she or he can withstand new stress in an adequate manner. The person may ordinarily now be functioning as well or even better than before. She or he is less vulnerable to depression, mood swings, and other experiences of instability. There still may be, however, some amount of self-doubt, and there are periods of regression.

However, as time goes by, the integration of a new personal identity, including one's new role or roles in life, takes firm hold, and the person becomes stronger and more resilient. This may take from another one to three years after the period of transition is concluded.

Weiss then goes on to speak of what might even be referred to as a prephase of shock and denial. He speaks of this as being the reaction of only a minority of persons immediately following the granting of a divorce. He states that during this time the people who react this way retain their pre-separation routine and pattern of life as though nothing has happened. They do not feel the intensity of separation anxiety because of their denial. This response, of course, seems to be most prevalent with persons whose separation took them by surprise.

It is important to note that the entire process which Weiss describes may take anywhere from two to four years for complete recovery from the loss which has been brought about by divorce.

There are some ways in which divorce is like the death of someone with whom one has been closely related emotionally. A person who at one time existed for me no longer exists for me. A person who at one time was a part of my life is no longer a part of my life. Yet this doesn't quite state it entirely accurately. In fact, no person is ever immediately free of any important relationship, whether by death or divorce, even if there has been an anticipatory grief process. In addition, there are some differences about the external situations which lead to a death (except by suicide) and to a divorce and some differences in the external situations which follow a death and a divorce. Therefore, there are some necessarily different behaviors and some different intensities of feelings.

One of the main differences is that divorce is clearly intended by one or both of the people, and in death, except death by suicide, it is not. Therefore, the intensity of the anger at the other person (or sometimes other persons) in divorce is usually much greater. Often one's self-blame, guilt, and sense of failure are more intense, and the not unusual fluctuation from one of these reactions to the other is almost unbearably distressing. These experiences become even more disruptive of the person's sense of identity.

A second major difference is that after a death the person is dead and buried, and after a divorce the other person is alive and visible. Often because of children, property, money, sometimes personal desire, that person must be dealt with by phone or even face-to-face. This reality frequently makes some of the necessary tasks very difficult. On the one hand, it makes it more difficult to give up the person. The finality of the separation by death has a greater impact as a counterforce against our strong wishes to maintain things "as they were," with the "as they were" tending to get somewhat idealized as a result of the great pain of loneliness and the practical hardships of the separation. On the other hand, and in some apparent contrast with what I have just said, the anger toward the other person tends to be restimulated by the images of the other's still being "alive and well" when you wish they were dead or at least suffering terribly. This reaction is frequently stimulated by actually seeing the person from time to time. The reaction which I've just recounted describes what I take to be one of the central, if not *the* central, conflicts of many divorces: anger at the other and the wish to reestablish the relationship. The person is lost, but not gone; hated, but still in some ways desired. The fact of the continued life of the other makes the resolution of this conflict more difficult than in the case of an actual death.

Another difference between loss by divorce and by death (again, except by suicide) is the difference in the social attitude of persons toward those whose loss is due to natural or accidental death when compared with their much more ambivalent reactions in the cases of divorce and suicide.

Children of Divorce

The lives of children are obviously disrupted throughout the whole process and in the aftermath of divorce. Their security, self-concept, and behavior are negatively affected by tension between their parents, with or without open arguing or physical violence. The physical separation of the parents, while often providing what seems to be a calmer atmosphere in which to live, always involves many types of readjustment which involve losses and which are threatening. The situations of the divorce where children are involved are too complex to be described here because of the many variations which need to be accounted for, including children's reactions to parents' remarriage and the new adjustments required over the years.

Excellent research has been done and is still in process which deals with all of these issues (Goldstein and Solnit, 1984; Noble and Noble, 1979; Stuart and Abt, 1981; Wallerstein and Kelly, 1980).

Clergy, other church staff, especially those in pastoral care and Christian education, designated lay caregivers, and all laypersons who are so frequently called upon to talk with persons distressed about their marriages, about impending divorce, about their lives as divorced persons, about concerns for their children, need to be prepared to respond to these needs to diminish the individual suffering and the social disruption.

The Church's Response to Issues of Marriage and Divorce

The response of the whole church to unhappy and dysfunctional families and to the problems surrounding divorce includes, but goes beyond, supportive conversation and counseling. Such a response, if it is to have any significant impact, must be comprehensive, visible, and available. It must therefore be interdisciplinary and it must be multidimensional. By multidimensional I mean, first, that it have an influence on society and hopefully reduce the incidence of divorce through the formation and maintenance of better marriages. Second, I mean that it should touch people at different stages of their pre-married, married, and post-divorced lives. It should assist them in different areas of their personal lives: attitude formation, values, decision making, emotional distress, spiritual needs, legal and vocational guidance, etc. Let me merely suggest five levels of such response.

First, the church and the larger community need to give attention to the effective education of children and young people in regard to marriage and human sexuality and to effective premarital counseling by churches, family guidance centers, pastoral counseling centers, and other professionals. Included in this at all levels would be group programs to increase the quantity and quality of communication, especially the communication of feelings between persons.

Second, there needs to be a public campaign to help people become more aware of the early signs of marital distress and to create a public climate which encourages people to seek help at this time in order to prevent the development of more severe marital problems which then possibly could lead to divorce. If people can learn to turn to some outside source of help very early in marital distress, a number of forms of support and guidance may be all that's necessary in order to help them deal with their own relationship in a more constructive way: marriage enrichment programs, couples' communication workshops, couples' growth groups, short-term couple counseling.

Third, there needs to be more, and more competent, marriage counseling for people when serious problems have developed. A much larger percentage of ministers especially need to be operating at a higher level of effectiveness, and community clinics and pastoral counseling centers with sliding fee scales need to be available, even to the point of no fee for those who really can't afford it. Many marriages, even in critical trouble, may be turned around and moved in the direction of greater mutual need fulfillment in this way.

Fourth, there needs to be an increased acceptability and availability of that form of couple and individual counseling which could most accurately be called *divorce* counseling when all other efforts have now indicated that the marriage problems are actually beyond resolution. In the clarification of issues, increased understanding, and more effective communication, a new relationship with one another may in fact occasionally be established. On the other hand, often it may not, and the clarification and understanding and more effective communication may lead to the conclusion that divorce is really the best decision under the circumstances. At this point, then, the issues of divorce and separation become more explicitly faced and come to be the focus of attention: the reduction of dependency upon one another, hostility, guilt; preparation for living alone or as a single parent. This would be analogous to ministry to the person going through anticipatory grief.

Fifth, and somewhat along these latter lines, there needs to be a greater availability of what is referred to as divorce mediation, assisting persons in going through their divorce with the least amount of damage and with the best possible decisions concerning the different areas of their lives that need to be taken care of in a new set of circumstances. (See Coogler, 1978; Haynes, 1981; Slaikeu, Pearson, and Thoennes, 1988.) This process can contribute to the possibility of a better next marriage for the persons involved, and therefore will contribute to the alleviation of further suffering in the future and the overall lowering of the divorce rate.

The final suggestion for dealing with the entire problem is, of course, therapeutic attention to the recently divorced. There is not sufficient help for persons in the grief initiated by the *death* of an emotionally related person, but there is far less available for the divorced. Every minister will always go to a home and to family members where there has been a death, but still relatively few go to people who have been divorced in order to assist them with their grief process and readjustment. We need to begin to realize that a person who has just been divorced really is in grief and at least often needs help beyond that which she or he can get from her or his own inner resources (especially since these usually tend to feel very depleted at such a time) or from the usual family members or friends. In addition to the support of family and friends and clergy, some large number of people need the support of whatever group they have already been a part of. Others need additional groups at this time. At its best, the community of faith can be this for persons in the distressing situation of separation and divorce. Unfortunately, this has not always been the case, with divorced persons no longer fitting into previous couple-oriented groups and emphases and too often experiencing being shunned by many in the congregation. Whole congregations may need to be sensitized to their need for Christian caring for the divorced. Organizationally there may need to be changes. A special lay caregiver may be assigned to keep up with the divorcing and recently divorced person(s) for a substantial period of time. Some congregations have periodic workshops for recently divorced persons, single parents, and the divorced with other specialized concerns.

SUMMARY

The major purpose of this chapter has been to present a simple definition of what a family is, the concept of the family as a system, to define family emergency as distinguished from an individual one, and to introduce just a few procedures which suggest how a pastor might facilitate communication between two or more people with whom she or he might be talking at one time. All of this is intended to provide a basis for understanding the many different forms of family interaction and for possible helpful intervention.

After the discussion of divorce in this chapter, we now move on to a variety of family emergencies in which representatives of the community of faith may take the initiative or be called upon to intervene.

REFERENCES

W. Robert Beavers, *Psychotherapy and Growth: A Family Systems Perspective* (New York: Brunner/Mazel, 1977).

———. *Beavers-Timberlawn Family Evaluation Scale* (Dallas, Tex.: Timberlawn Foundation for Psychiatric Education and Research).

O. J. Coogler, *Structured Mediation in Divorce Settlement* (Lexington: Lexington Books, 1978).

Sonja Goldstein and Albert J. Solnit, *Divorce and Your Child: Practical Suggestions for Parents* (New Haven: Yale University Press, 1984).

John M. Haynes, *Divorce Mediation: A Practical Guide for Therapists and Counselors* (New York: Springer, 1981).

Richard A. Hunt, "The Minister and Divorce Crisis." In David K. Switzer, *The Minister As Crisis Counselor* (Revised and enlarged) (Nashville: Abingdon Press, 1986), pp. 175–202.

Jerry M. Lewis, *How's Your Family? A Guide to Identifying Your Family's Strengths and Weaknesses* (New York: Brunner/Mazel, 1979).

Jerry M. Lewis, and John G. Looney, *The Long Struggle: Well-Functioning Working-Class Black Families* (New York: Brunner/Mazel, 1983).

Jerry M. Lewis, W. Robert Beavers, John T. Gossett, and Virginia Austin Phillips, *No Single Thread: Psychological Health in Family Systems* (New York: Brunner/Mazel, 1976).

June Noble and William Noble, *How to Live with Other People's Children* (New York: E. P. Dutton, Hawthorne Books, 1979).

Karl A. Slaikeu, J. Pearson, and N. Thoennes, "Divorce Mediation Behaviors: A Descriptive System and Analysis." In J. Folberg and A. Milne, eds., *Divorce Mediation Theory and Practice* (New York: Guilford Press, 1988).

Charles W. Stewart, *The Minister As Marriage Counselor* (Nashville: Abingdon Press, 1970).

Irving R. Stuart and Lawrence E. Abt, eds., *Children of Separation and Divorce: Management and Treatment* (New York: Van Nostrand Reinhold, 1981).

David K. Switzer, *The Minister As Crisis Counselor,* (Revised and enlarged) (Nashville: Abingdon Press, 1986).

Judith S. Wallerstein and Joan B. Kelly, *Surviving the Breakup: How Children and Parents Cope with Divorce* (New York: Basic Books, 1980).

Robert W. Weiss, *Marital Separation* (New York: Basic Books, 1975).

RECOMMENDED READING

Herbert Anderson, *The Family and Pastoral Care* (Minneapolis: Fortress Press, 1984).

W. Robert Beavers, *Successful Marriage: A Family Systems Approach to Couples Therapy* (New York: W. W. Norton, 1985).

W. Robert Beavers and Robert B. Hampson, *Successful Families: Assessment and Intervention* (New York: W. W. Norton, 1990).

J. C. Wynn, *Family Therapy in Pastoral Ministry* (San Francisco: Harper & Row, 1982).

10

MARRIAGE AND FAMILY EMERGENCIES: FAMILY VIOLENCE, PSYCHIATRIC EMERGENCIES

There are a number of different behaviors between men and women who live together, married or not, and within families, that require even more specialized understanding and attention than those described in the previous chapter. Physical violence and psychiatric disorders will receive major emphasis here. Incest is a particularly pernicious form of physical/psychological abuse and will be mentioned. Moreover, there is substantial overlap between substance abuse, especially alcohol, and all of these other behaviors, which are far more common than we used to think. But a detailed discussion of alcoholism is beyond the scope of this book. It would be important for clergy and other concerned persons in the church to read the excellent and thorough work by Clinebell (1998).

In addition, with increasing frequency, clergy and other church-related helpers are being called upon to talk with homosexual persons and/or members of their families about their relationships with one another and to assist in the varying situations of considerable stress which they often experience. This, too, is mentioned only in passing and can be found in detail in Switzer (1999).

SPOUSE AND CHILD BATTERING

Two of the increasingly reported and more and more publicized forms of family violence are those of spouse and child battering. Deschner gives a very precise definition: "Battering is a series of physically injurious attacks on an intimate or family member that form part of a repeated, habitual pattern" (1984, p. 2). Two words in her definition are important to look at.

The word *habitual* means occurring more than twice. The word *intimate* takes into account the frequent occurrence of battering in situations where couples are not married, and who may or may not be living together. For example, the battering of a child is often the child of a woman by her boyfriend or live-in lover. Deschner also suggests the use of the word *consort* to describe these relationships.

Although there are many instances of fighting within families involving other than the adult consorts and the married persons, these most usually do not fit Deschner's narrow definition. A teenage or adult child (most often a son) may attack a parent or sibling, or live-in or visiting uncles, cousins, etc. may be involved in a physical fight in a home. These don't often fit the "battering" pattern.

It should also be noted that a lesser amount of spouse or consort battering is done by women, although it does take place. Therefore, when we're talking about the battering of one adult by another, it's not out of line to assume that, with some exceptions, the reference is to battered wives or female partners. It's important to note that investigations show that one-fourth to one-third of the men who batter their mates also batter their children (Deschner, 1984, p. 11).

The attitude of clergy and all persons in the church is crucial in guiding their response to battering. Hopefully, we're beyond that attitude that whatever takes place within persons' own homes is their own business. Some things are their own business, but physical violence certainly is not one of these. We're talking about something quite different from an occasional fight between equals or occasional and quite moderate physical punishment of a child who's old enough to know family rules and who then disobeys them. Rather, battering takes place most often when a larger and stronger person repeatedly hits, often to the point of painful and serious injury, a person who's physically smaller and weaker and who either literally has no recourse (a child) or whose perspective is that she (wife or consort) has no alternative but to remain in the relationship. These persons in the weaker position need to be protected.

Also, too often the attitude toward the women has been that if they don't like it they can just leave. This unrealistic attitude fails to consider that the woman often has no income or no adequate income, has no place to go on short notice, often has children whom she needs to protect or properly wants to be with. Deeply ingrained and distorted views of male and female roles and of what loyalty in marriage means also at times severely limit the range of choices which a woman believes that she has.

There is no way that it can be shown that the intent of Eph. 5:2lff. can include the physical brutalizing of a woman by her husband, though some have erroneously used it as a justification. The expression in verse 22, "Wives, be subject to your husbands, as to the Lord," is clear enough in itself: "Subject . . . *as to the Lord*," that is, as one is subject to Christ, who "loved us and gave himself up for us" (5:2), and, in verse 21, establishing *mutuality* in spouses as the norm for Christian marriage: "Be subject to *one another* out of reverence for Christ." Then follows the "Wives, be subject to your husbands . . ." and later (v. 28), "husbands should love their wives *as their own bodies*." Both the larger context and the specific words, all based on what the love of God in Christ asks of us, cannot tolerate physical abuse. (See discussion by Martin, 1987, pp. 89–90.)

There are at least a few different considerations in regard to the battering of children.

> (Physical) child abuse can be said to have occurred when corporal punishment has caused bruises or other injury to the child, or when the child has been injured in such a severe manner that medical attention is required. (Everstine and Everstine, 1983, P. 103)

Deschner refers to D. G. Gil's finding that 65 percent of the severe and fatal injuries of children as a result of abuse by their parents or caretakers are to children *under the age of three*. Gil also reported in one study that one-half of the child abusers were mothers and one-third of these were single mothers. Many of these were quite young. Forty percent of the abusers were fathers or stepfathers (1984, p. 11).

Child abusers are usually persons of low self-esteem, feel as if they are failures, are frequently depressed, have come from chaotic and deprived families, have themselves been battered as children, have low capacity for empathy, attribute adult motives to children's behaviors, have little understanding of and skills for proper child care, and tend to be socially isolated (Deschner, 1984, pp. 11–12; Everstine and Everstine, 1983, pp. 104–7).

Child and spouse (or consort) battering are signs of extremely serious problems on the part of a man or a woman, physically and psychologically damage persons, exacerbate the overall problems of the batterer, are disruptive to the quality of family life within which people's needs, including their spiritual needs, can be relatively well met and tend to perpetuate the tendency toward battering in the future families of the children who grow up in a home where there is physical violence.

Persons within the community of faith need to have opportunity to learn the details of the nature, extent, and seriousness of this problem, and to discuss their personal and congregational responsibilities in regard to the needs of both battered and batterers. They certainly need to know their legal responsibilities as well as their moral ones. There are state laws requiring that even the suspicion of child abuse must be reported to a designated governmental agency for that agency's further investigation. People who fail to make such a report can, if discovered, be charged with a crime. Professional confidentiality does not release clergy from this obligation. The congregation needs to know the exact details of the law in its own state.

Since specialized treatment, almost always including a group setting for the best results, is necessary for both battered and batterers, clergy and other representatives of the church will rarely be the primary counselors. They may be very important to some people for caring, support, clarification of issues that may lead to the decision to take constructive action, for referral or transferral to the appropriate shelter and/or treatment agency, and for continued spiritual guidance.

The usual marriage counseling procedures alone do not seem to be effective, and, especially crucial, the minister must not (1) suggest that she or he counsel them as a couple, under the misguided notion that what they need to do is merely "resolve their marital problems," nor (2) be seduced, usually by the man, to talk with his wife, if she has left home, about coming back so they can have marriage counseling together. Adams, who has years of experience in working with battered women, is adamant on this point. An additional value of separating husbands and wives for therapeutic work is that "(both) individuals need to be able to separate their identities from one another" (Adams, 1994, p. 58). (A pastor would be well served to read the entire book by Adams.) The major issues of the men and the women differ, so they are usually treated separately and in a group setting. Absolutely critical as the first step is that the wife be protected by living somewhere the husband can't find her. Second, the battering cycle itself must be interrupted and the physical violence must stop. Even though the batterer certainly has personality deficits and is also a victim in some sense of the word, the physical abuse as such continues to make all of the problems worse. All first-order strategies must be directed toward the stopping of the hitting (and sometimes even torture), even if it means that the women and her children seek refuge away from home or a child is taken from the home by legal means. Practically all cities, even smaller ones, have havens for women and their children. These havens also usually have well-developed programs: group meetings and various training programs. Some of them have telephone hot lines.

COUPLES WHO FIGHT PHYSICALLY

The patterns of reactions between couples who frequently fight physically with one another are different from the patterns of battering that we have just discussed. The physical fighting may be by hitting, throwing objects, or sometimes attacks with more deadly means. Even when these occurrences are not frequent, the mutual fighting reaction takes place from time to time and can be predicted under certain circumstances. In battering, the primary victim usually doesn't fight back, or does so only occasionally and/or minimally. For the physically fighting couple, there may be an immediate outburst of anger followed by an attack and either vigorous physical defense or counterattack by the other. Or there may be an accumulation of anger without an awareness of each and every anger-stimulating incident and/or the intensity of the feeling involved. Finally, either in response to a relatively minor incident or when inhibitions are lowered through the drinking of alcohol or the use of other drugs, the anger can no longer be contained and there is an outburst of violence. The person who is the target of that violence doesn't understand, feels wronged, and responds violently herself or himself.

The Everstines note an interesting and potentially useful psychological ingredient in such couple interaction when they refer to "the conscious or unconscious manipulation of fear, of loneliness, or abandonment" (1983, p. 76). The parties involved, they suggest, are insecure in their sense of being "unloved or unloveable," and are therefore especially "vulnerable to real or imagined threats of abandonment" (p. 76).

It doesn't take an unusually knowledgeable person to realize that a large percentage of persons in such couples were raised in homes where they were abused as children, where they saw their parents fighting physically, and where one or both parents were abusers of alcohol. In such families of origin, children often experience themselves as "unloved and unloveable," or are sometimes abandoned, have very low self-esteem, and learn violence as a means of protection in relationships.

Ministers and other helpers need to realize that if they are called into a situation where a fight is under way, they're going into a situation of potential danger to themselves. Many people in this kind of anger are truly out of control. Unless representatives of the community of faith are very sure of having a good relationship with the persons involved, it's best that the police intervene prior to their arriving on the scene or are assured by one or both of the partners that the violence has stopped. Police themselves realize the danger since a high percentage of acts of violence committed against them takes place in these circumstances, including sometimes being attacked by *both* of the fighting partners.

If the fighting has not yet escalated to violence or if the partners have been subdued in the sense that this particular violent episode is over, persons intervening in this emergency will most often get the best results by talking with each person separately while the other is as far away as possible within the home (or is outside). Getting each person's story without interruption is helpful in diminishing the intensity of that person's feelings, the person's gaining a sense of support, and giving the helper an overall clearer picture.

Most clergy and laypeople don't have the necessary training to be the most effective primary long-term counselors for couples who fight physically with one another. Clergy can be especially important in clarifying for the persons the necessity of specialized help, the need for the physical fighting to stop in order for other approaches to be helpful, the supporting of at least temporary separation if that's necessary for the fighting to stop, in guiding the couple to the appropriate sources of counseling, and in helping arrange child care when that's necessary.

Continued pastoral visitation can be extremely useful in terms of the possible discussions of the persons' faith and relationship with God. Such discussions can support the persons' decisions to participate conscientiously in their programs of personal growth and behavior change and can contribute significantly to the increase of their sense of self-worth. Battered and batterer, fighters with one another, often feel shame and guilt and worthlessness. Their already low self-esteem is made even lower by their involvement in these relationships of violence. God *does* love even them, and it's important for them to have such love communicated to them in our helping acts and continued relationship, encouraging and supporting them in whatever openness to change they have and in the necessary procedures they may be participating in to help bring this change about.

INCEST

My impression, based on my own experience, the experience of many ministers with whom I have talked, and a couple of surveys, is that incest is the least reported to the clergy (and probably to others also) of the acts of family disturbance and disruption. This is especially true of its being reported at the time that it's actually going on in the family. It's easier than other behaviors to cover up, and the motivation not to reveal it may be the strongest. The "conspiracy of silence" is extremely difficult to break.

But incest does take place, even within families that are active in the church, and even in some clergy families. It's obviously quite difficult to estimate, much less to "know," the incidence of incest in the whole population and in various subgroupings. There are increasing numbers of women who find themselves in confusion and distress in adult life and are able to relate such disorder in their lives to the earlier sexual behavior of male family members with them, and as a result they are attending incest recovery groups. How many more have repressed the shocking picture from their early lives? How many others, recognizing the source of their difficulty, are so ashamed, guilty, and afraid that they don't take such remedial steps? Psychotherapists have, of course, been aware for a long time that such abuse of children has contributed to the development of the problems for which a number of persons much later seek help, but that fact alone hasn't adequately contributed to a picture of the frequency of occurrence. There must be many more times the number of families in which incest takes place than the number of reported instances would indicate.

Like violent behaviors, incest is a reflection of marriage/family problems which already exist, with the incest in turn exacerbating those problems. To refer to the marriage/family problems as the context in which incest takes place is not to disregard the various forms of individual psychological disturbance which can lead a teenager or an adult to engage in such sexual exploitation of a child. This behavior on the part of adults with the children in their families is extremely destructive to those children at the time that the sexual abuse is going on and in terms of those children's later lives. Almost incredibly, these adults who were so abused as children carry with them into their later lives their childhood distortions that they, rather than their parents or much older siblings, are responsible for what took place.

Most incest involves fathers or stepfathers and their daughters or stepdaughters. Uncles, older brothers, and older male cousins may also be the perpetrators. It's important not to overlook the number of male children who are also sexually abused by older males in the family. Although this is a considerably less common behavior, as far as we know, it takes place far more frequently than we realize. Situations in which children are physically sexually violated by their mothers or older sisters, to our knowledge, are much less frequent.

If and when occasions of incest are brought to the attention of clergy, other professional church staff, or laypersons in the congregation, it's best to refer the person who is revealing the behavior to a psychotherapist or to an agency which specializes in working with people who are part of such a family. That professional may then make the assessments necessary for determining the next step. Incest in the family is far too sensitive and complicated for the great majority of persons untrained in this particular area to deal with, even if they are helpful counselors in other situations.

If a pastor attempts to be the primary counselor, she or he is probably making a serious mistake. He or she has properly reported the incest to the authorities and perhaps was thus involved in the removing the child from the home. Continuing pastoral care and whatever spiritual guidance is called for may be closed off or severely complicated. But don't give up. Stay in touch, even though the perpetrator may be angry at you. Violence against you may be a possibility, and if so, use the telephone rather than a face-to-face visit.

Referrals to a psychotherapist and/or to an incest recovery agency doesn't mean the abdication of pastoral responsibility. Pastors, other church workers, and lay friends may certainly support incest victims as persons of infinite worth in the eyes of God, demonstrated by the acceptance expressed by this representative of the community of faith, and assure them that a child cannot under any circumstances be responsible for the behavior of an adult, and that the sexual abuse was the full responsibility of the adult involved. The church can also help such a person in breaking down any sense of isolation and loneliness which she or he may have. Often more difficult for pastoral caregivers is the continuing relationship with the sexual abuser in such instances. However, this person, too, is a person of infinite worth in the eyes of God, and this worth is most effectively communicated also by continuing the pastoral relationship even if you abhor the acts that were committed. Obviously, the perpetrator also needs psychotherapy, especially in a perpetrator's group. One of the ways a pastor can be helpful is to attempt to guide the abuser toward a decision to seek help. (If the situation has come to the attention of a court, the judge may have already specified psychotherapy as a requirement.)

PSYCHIATRIC EMERGENCY

A psychiatric emergency occurs within a family when one of the members is having a psychiatric disorder, at a point when the family is disrupted in some way by that person's behavior, and treatment and/or hospitalization is urgently needed. The psychiatric disorder is usually a psychotic reaction, or at least a severe depression, even if it's not technically psychotic. The disruption refers to a time when the family can no longer tolerate the person's behavior: physical aggression, suicidal threats or attempts, bizarre, unpredictable, and otherwise disturbing behavior, extreme withdrawal and inability to go to school or work, care for children, or perform usual necessary functions. Psychosis refers to a condition of radically being out of touch with reality in regard to one's own identity, the present time period, the place where one is, delusions of persecution and/or grandeur, delusions concerning one's body, severe confusion, the lack of control of one's thoughts, speech, or other behavior.

Some persons might call the minister early in the development of the disorder, their own or a family member's, when the behaviors on the part of the sufferer seem to be moderate, when the concerned persons aren't sure what to make of it. Also, at this point they may be likely to share their concern with trusted friends, a church school teacher, or another staff member. As the behavior becomes more troubled, or if it apparently begins fairly quickly in terms of its extreme forms, family members, if they don't call their doctor or take the person directly to the hospital, are especially likely to call the ordained minister or other church staff person in whom they place the most trust. Many times the representative of the community of faith may help family members clarify in their own minds the need to take immediate action and can support them in that action. Pastors may also be influential in eliciting the cooperation of the disturbed person in going to an appointment with a psychiatrist or going to a hospital.

Many times it is possible, of course, to be able to assess whether a person needs to be taken directly to a hospital emergency room where there are psychiatrists on call for evaluation, medication, and possible hospitalization or whether an appointment with a psychiatrist within two or three days would be satisfactory. All pastors are not equally trained and experienced in such evaluation, however. Factors to consider are whether a person is highly suicidal, seems to be a physical threat to someone else, is more or less in touch with reality, is capable of having a relatively reasonable conversation, and is in some control of his or her behavior. When in doubt, if it's possible, try to get an emergency appointment with a psychiatrist, but if one is unavailable, go to the emergency room.

Pastors can also be helpful to family members who themselves are often distraught, accompanying them to the doctor's office or to the emergency room, helping them think through the issues in regard to important decisions, and also often enough assisting in the control of the seriously disturbed person when that's necessary. At times, as with very depressed persons, this is not unusually difficult. But if the patient is manic, is speaking and behaving impulsively, is resisting being there, is disturbing to other persons present, it's one of the most anxiety-laden and challenging tasks family members and ministers are called upon to cope with.

The pastor, with the authority of her or his office and perhaps with a previously established relationship, can talk with the depressed or agitated person along one or both of two lines: "You seem to be very distressed, unhappy, not able to do some things you want to do," etc. (whatever is descriptive of the condition and situation); "The doctor (and/or hospital) can help you with this. Is there some reason you wouldn't want to try to do something to help yourself?" (Wait for the answer, then respond to it.) "We care for you and will be with you and will help."

Or, "You've been acting very differently from the way you had before. It's very disturbing to (name of the family member or members). Actually, they're somewhat frightened by it, so let's go ahead and see the doctor (and/or go to the hospital) and see if we can't work it out in some way. I'm concerned about your well-being and won't do anything that's not really for you."

These responses, of course, are merely "samples." The caregiver's own knowledge of the person, awareness of the present situation, and the person's behavior can give shape to the most helpful ways to try to guide the person. One can be clear and persistent, but when the person is agitated, it's important that one not push too close physically or make threats. Usually, beneath the agitation and aggressiveness is a frightened person. The pastor needs to remain outwardly calm (regardless of how he or she might really be feeling). Hopefully, the person will cooperate with the plan to see someone, and usually this is the case. If the person is perceived to be truly dangerous, especially if he or she has access to a weapon, is becoming more and more agitated and incoherent to us, then it's best for the pastor and family members to withdraw slowly. Although this last-mentioned situation does occur from time to time, I want to make it clear that the great majority of psychiatric patients are no more dangerous than are persons who are not suffering from mental illness. It's essential that we able to recognize the aggressiveness of the highly agitated person or the quieter danger of the paranoid person (one with delusions of being persecuted or hurt by someone else or of their own grandiosity) and use proper precaution (Jennings, 1986). In dealing with persons like this who seem to be dangerous, or simply with those who will not cooperate at all, the appropriate legal procedures for committing the person to the hospital need to be initiated. It's important that pastors know what these procedures are in their particular state and local community.

Ministry to the Family

Family members will usually be confused and distraught unless they've been through this painful episode several times before and are familiar with the person's behavior, methods of control, and the proper procedures to follow. Even then, the care and support of the pastor, other church staff, and members of the congregation will be meaningful and appreciated. If it's the first time for this family to deal with a severely disturbed family member, or if they've been able up to this time to keep a family member's disorder a secret, we can anticipate that some number of them will have some sense of shame. A pastor's giving them some accurate information about mental disorder in the context of a continuing caring relationship and the mobilization of support can do much to help the family's understanding and acceptance.

Ministry to the Emotionally Disturbed

If a person is placed in a psychiatric unit of a general hospital or in a psychiatric hospital, it's appropriate for the minister to call concerning the possibility of a visit. Sometimes such a visit will be possible right at the time, frequently somewhat later, occasionally not at all. We need to try to be understanding of the nature of the disturbance, the nature of the treatment program, and the possibility, for whatever reason, that the person doesn't want to see us. Some hospitals are much more open to pastoral visits than others, so we need to be prepared for such variances. We may contact the physician responsible for the hospitalized person in order to discuss these issues. Many of them will be glad to have such a conversation with us, although we can't expect an immediate return call with time for an extended discussion. Unfortunately, some psychiatrists and clinical psychologists are not willing to talk with us about a person for whom they are responsible. If the hospital has a chaplain, he or she is always willing to visit a person and to talk with us and with family members.

With the majority of persons who are in psychiatric hospitals, a conversation is going to be more or less like the conversation with anyone else, albeit focused upon their particular condition and situation. It's proper to ask how they are doing, how it's going for them in the hospital, and talk about some areas of their distress. If the person begins to grow more incoherent or more agitated, it's important to ease off of the intensity of the conversation, close the discussion, and say good-bye. It would be responsible to report this event at the nursing station. However, in my experience, the overwhelming majority of psychiatric patients visited by their pastors have not been so disturbed and have appreciated the visits very much.

One can have a "usual" conversation while paying particular attention to a number of precautions. It's useful to ask the person the specific meaning of certain things which the person has said and which may not be understandable to us. We need to avoid giving our interpretations of the statements or experiences reported and/or giving advice of any kind. As in general hospital visitation, it's always a good idea to avoid being drawn into the person's complaints about the hospital, the treatment program, the doctor, etc. A pastor may reflect that the person seems frustrated, disappointed, angry, displeased, etc., without joining the person in the criticism. Most persons have such reactions after having been admitted to the hospital, and frequently or periodically over the course of the hospitalization. In the few instances where persons may truly be delusional or having hallucinations, it's important that we continue to take them seriously, not denying what they report their experiences to be, but also not using words that sound as if we are confirming their experiences as being real for us.

In one of my local church appointments, I was making my first visit to a woman in the psychiatric unit of a hospital. We were walking and talking together in the visiting area when she suddenly stopped and asked, "Did you hear what that man said to me?"

Actually, I didn't even see a man. But I responded, "No. I didn't hear anything. What did you hear?"

The conversation continued somewhat along the following line:

"He said something bad was going to happen to me."
"Does that frighten you?"

"Well, yes, it bothers me. He has bothered me before."
"I can tell that it's disturbing to you. But you're really safe here."

Persons in a private psychiatric unit or hospital usually remain there for only a week or two. In state hospitals the stay may be as long as several months, sometimes longer. A pastoral visit in most circumstances can be meaningful and useful to the person. When there is a chaplain of the hospital, feel free to ask that person to stay in touch with the person about whom you are concerned.

Follow-up

It's also important to continue to visit the family of the psychiatric patient. Undoubtedly they are experiencing some amount of confusion and distress. Conversations with a pastoral visitor may help them with the variety of feelings which they're having and certainly can give them a sense of support by the community of faith. Often, they'll be experiencing guilt in relation to the disturbed person, sometimes realistic, but quite often unrealistic. We can either help them work their way to a realization of the irrational nature of it, or, if realistic, work with them in experiencing forgiveness and making plans to move beyond guilt to new ways of relating within the family.

It's usually helpful for the spouse or parents of a psychiatric patient or the whole family to be going to a trained professional for conjoint therapy. Some hospitals strongly recommend their beginning such a process while the family member is an inpatient. It's unfortunately not uncommon for one or more family persons to resist such a procedure. From some persons' point of view it's the designated patient who is sick. The rest of them will be fine when that person gets well. The pastor's responsibility is probably not to make a family diagnosis (or to tell the family if he or she actually does). Rather, many family members can be persuaded concerning the potential usefulness of conjoint marriage or family therapy on the basis that the other person needs their understanding and help as a part of the treatment program and that it's important to the continued well-being of all of them when the person comes back home if they can work out some new ways of relating to one another. Behind all of this, of course, is the assumption that in many instances the whole family system is in fact in need of improving its level of functioning: their attitudes, their ways of viewing themselves, their interaction patterns, their communication with one another.

When the person who has been hospitalized returns home, it's especially important that the pastor and/or other appropriate church staff, a Sunday school teacher or youth counselor, the lay pastoral representative to the geographical area where that person lives, etc. call on the person just as, hopefully, they have also been in touch with the family during the time of the hospitalization. This direct personal contact, the communication of the caring of the community of faith, and the love of God which is conveyed in the visit, can be strengthening in the person's life and the life of the family.

We, of course, do need to understand in all that has been said that some people recovering from a disturbed episode and some members of their families may be fearful of other people's response to her or him or them and are very concerned about what other people think. They may prefer not to have visits. They don't want anyone else to know, or to know any more than they already do. Obviously, it's important for us to use our sensitivity and discretion here. But the tendency to isolate themselves can itself contribute to the prolongation or reoccurrence of the disorder. The pastor can talk with them about it, be sensitive to their feelings, continue to work with them slowly and patiently to open the doors to increased receptivity to visits from others and participation in the worship and in other groups and activities of the community of faith. In some places there are also continuing support groups for parents and/or spouses and for the recovering persons themselves.

Useful to ministers and congregations is a relationship to and participation in a local mental health association, found in almost all large and small cities and often on a countywide basis in rural areas. Literature on mental illness, commitment procedures, information for families, educational programs, films, speakers for church programs, sometimes support groups for families, and other services are usually available.

FAMILY EMERGENCIES: CONCLUSION

The "Conclusion" referred to in the heading of this section refers only to the ending of these last two chapters, not to their completion and not to the ending of the total number or variety of family emergencies themselves. There are other sources of family emergencies that more and more families are experiencing: the burglary of the home; the rape, murder, or other physical assault on a family member; the decision concerning the placement of an aged parent in a retirement or nursing home; severe parent-child conflict, etc. And just when we think we have listed them all, some pastor or professional staff or member of the community of faith will be confronted with yet another one.

None of us will ever learn about it all or know clearly ahead of time how to respond in this or that situation. It is reasonable to assume that if a person understands something of the dynamics of family systems, can make a reasonably accurate assessment of the level of family functioning, is well grounded in the fundamental processes of helping (the facilitative conditions), and has learned how to guide a family through situations of crisis in general, then, with the foundation of spiritual discipline and an awareness of the presence of God, that person will be able to respond creatively and with good judgment in those new family situations with which pastoral caregivers continue to be confronted.

REFERENCES

Family Violence

Carol J. Adams, *Woman-Battering* (Minneapolis: Fortress Press, 1994).

Jeanne P. Deschner, *The Hitting Habit: Anger Control for Battering Couples* (New York: Free Press, 1984).

Joan Sullivan Everstine and Louis E. Everstine, *People in Crisis: Strategic Therapeutic Interventions* (New York: Brunner/Mazel, 1983).

Grant Martin, *Counseling for Family Violence and Abuse* (Waco, Tex.: Word Books, 1987).

Psychiatric Emergencies

Dana Charry, *Mental Health Skills for the Clergy* (Valley Forge, Pa.: Judson Press, 1981).

Floyd L. Jennings, "Ministering to the Dangerous," *Circuit Rider* (November–December 1986) (Nashville: United Methodist Publishing House): pp. 5–7.

Douglas Puryear, *Helping People in Crisis* (San Francisco: Jossey-Bass, 1979).

Addictions

Howard J. Clinebell, *Understanding and Counseling Persons with Alcohol, Drug, and Behavioral Addictions* (Revised and enlarged) (Nashville: Abingdon Press, 1998).

Homosexuality

David K. Switzer, *Pastoral Care of Gays, Lesbians, and Their Families* (Minneapolis: Fortress Press, 1999).

RECOMMENDED READING

Family Violence

Rita-Lou Clarke, *Pastoral Care of Battered Women* (Philadelphia: Westminster Press, 1986).

Paula Cooper-White, *The Cry of Tamar: Violence against Women and the Church's Response* (Minneapolis: Fortress Press, 1995).

Marie Marshall Fortune, *Sexual Violence: "The Unmentionable Sin"* (New York: Pilgrim Press, 1983).

―――. *Violence in the Family: A Workshop Curriculum for Clergy and Other Helpers* (Cleveland: Pilgrim Press, 1991).

Eliana Gil, *Outgrowing the Pain: A Book for and about Adults Abused As Children* (San Francisco: Launch Press, 1983).

Psychiatric Emergencies

Rebecca Woolis, *When Someone You Love Has a Mental Illness* (New York: Tarcher/Putnam, 1992).

Adolescents/The Elderly

Harold G. Koenig and Andrew Weaver, *Counseling Troubled Older Adults: A Handbook for Pastoral and Religious Caregivers* (Nashville: Abingdon Press, 1997).

Andrew J. Weaver, John D. Preston, and Leigh W. Jerome, *Counseling Troubled Teens and Their Families* (Nashville: Abingdon Press, 1999).

11

WHEN AND HOW TO REFER

OUR LIMITATIONS

Persons differ in their ability to help other persons in quandary and distress. Some rather obviously have higher levels of competence with a larger percentage of people with a greater variety of personalities, problems, and modes of relating. Even so, there are *no* Superhelpers (lay, clergy, psychotherapeutic professionals) who can be effective with all persons.

After all, we have different personalities ourselves, and there are simply some people who aren't going to "resonate" with us. There are those whom we're not going to like at all. There are those whose issues are going to stimulate anxiety in us, and our own defenses are going to click into place to protect us, which means, in some sense, to protect us from intimacy in relationship with this particular person. None of us have been thoroughly educated and trained to understand and function with perfection with all kinds of persons and situations. Furthermore, as stated in chapter 1, our *feelings* of love and our commitment to help are simply not going to be sufficient to overcome these barriers. Case made? I hope so.

Now, you may have the impression that I have belabored this point throughout this book. Undoubtedly, for many readers I have. Yet I still discover some number of clergy (and therefore I would assume that there would also be some lay church professionals and volunteer church visitors) who believe that they can handle everything, that because they *care* (feeling) so much, just *love* (feeling) the person(s), and are so convinced of the power of faith, all troubled people will have their problems resolved in interaction with them and with God. My impression is that the number of such clergy and lay caregivers is decreasing rather rapidly under the impact of their increased awareness of their own human limitations and the reality of the deep and persistent needs and complex behavior patterns on the part of some persons and family units.

My point is that we're only human, regardless of how self-aware and how well trained we are. Therefore, it's no sign that we're failures if, after talking with a troubled person a little while, we need to suggest that even though we can and will stay in touch, she or he really needs to be talking with someone else about this particular disturbing area of her or his life. With numerous people, it's the only responsible action that we can take.

If we truly care, that is, are willing to act for the well-being of the other, the proper caring act is to help that person be in touch with someone more competent and/or more available than ourselves for this particular person with this particular issue at this particular time.

There simply are, and always will be, some people that we cannot work with effectively *as the primary helper* in regard to their psychological and/or relational problems. We may remain a primary helper with regard to issues of their faith, their spiritual development, and the behaviors which are expressions of faith. We may continue to be pastoral guides as other professionals work with them on the more complex psychological and interpersonal issues.

In regard to emotional and relational problems people have, we all have limitations as helpers. But let me point out some of the dimensions of limitations. In terms of the interaction between my competence and time and the nature of the other person and her or his particular problem, our limits have usually been portrayed as a *warning:*

Caregiver

Don't go beyond
this point.

This is accurate. It's critical. But it's not the whole story. It's equally important to recognize that there's a certain space within that boundary mark.

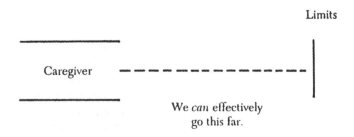

Limits

Caregiver

We *can* effectively
go this far.

There are critical human needs to which clergy and other representatives of the community of faith can effectively respond, using our own
genuine humanity, sensitivity, faith, and commitment to caring; carrying
the power of being a living symbol of the church, the faith, of God; and
utilizing what knowledge and skills we do have.

The crucial issue, then, is that each one of us be able to make a relatively accurate assessment of our own strengths and limitations, recognizing that we clergy differ from other professional groups, individually we
differ from one another, and all of us have different limitations at different
times in our lives. We also differ from one another in terms of our levels of
competence with different types of people and different types of situations.

This relatively accurate assessment is no easy task. At times we may
be very clear that we can or cannot be a primary caregiver to a person or
family. Many other times we simply are not sure. There are at least two
responsible courses of action when we are in doubt. First, we may consult with some appropriate professional person ourselves if that's possible. The process would be for us to review with the professional the characteristics and behaviors and history of the person we're working with,
what we've done and haven't done thus far with the person, and our own
feelings toward the person and within the helping relationship. This procedure, by the way, is technically not a violation of confidentiality. More
important always than secrecy is the well-being of the person. We're
seeking consultation with the well-being of the troubled person(s) as the
primary motivation, and we're doing it with a competent professional
who herself or himself is now committed to the same confidentiality as
we are with regard to the person(s).

Second, if such a professional person is not available to us, the most
useful procedure is to refer the person to the professional, agency, or
institution that has the highest probability of meeting the person's needs
most adequately. Such a move also has some likelihood of avoiding possible dangers for that person and also for ourselves.

To review and systematize:
Our limitations are defined

1. By who we are as persons.
Apart from our pastoral care and counseling skills and a knowledge
of procedures of intervention in different types of circumstances, some
of us, because of our emotional reaction, can work with alcoholic persons and other drug abusers, with homosexual persons, with child or
spouse abusers, with sexual voyeurs and exhibitionists, etc., and some
can't. Our own feelings can and do interfere with our establishing an
adequate working relationship with persons with certain categories of

problems. We need to be aware of this, candid with ourselves, and willing and capable of making the most useful referrals or transferrals.

2. By our training and our experience.

Most clergy, lay church professionals, and other members of a congregation are not prepared to do long-term counseling of *any* kind, family therapy, to be the primary helping person for the severely emotionally disturbed, or for those whose critical problems are of long standing.

3. By our time.

Most clergy are generalists. We prepare and lead worship, preach, administer the sacraments, oversee programs of Christian education and teach in several congregational settings, are responsible for the financial affairs of the congregation, direct other aspects of church programming, prepare persons for marriage and conduct weddings, represent the community in many community organizations and activities, call on the sick and dying and bereaved, lead the worship at funerals, and probably do a number of other things. Lay church professionals usually have their areas of specialty which are not pastoral care and counseling, and they are quite busy with these responsibilities. Volunteer lay caregivers very often have their own careers which call for a significant outlay of time and energy. We usually don't have time for anything but intervention in situational crises, one or two problem-solving, decision-making conversations, helping people in a marriage or a family become aware of a need for clearer and more open communication, short hospital and home visits, or limited assignments such as following one person through a long hospitalization or one family through its period of grieving.

At this point it's necessary to introduce the word *transferral*. The process has already been referred to in the discussion of the handling of a very suicidal person. In this case, as well as when a person is homicidal, or psychotic, deeply depressed, in a situational crisis where other resources are desperately needed, we're responsible for helping that person get to the professional person(s), agencies, or hospital, either by taking the person ourselves, or preferably, enlisting family members and/or other friends to assist. This action on our part is what may properly be called *transferral* instead of referral. In such instances, we're not merely making recommendations and seeking to elicit the others' cooperation in *their* taking the initiative to follow through on whatever action is appropriate. In transferral, we continue to work actively with and for a person with primary responsibility until she or he is in personal contact with the professional or agency or hospital that then assumes such responsibility (Switzer, 1986, pp. 102–4; Slaikeu, 1984, pp. 91–93).

No one of us can do it all. We all need each other, and we all need the psychotherapeutic, medical, social work, and other helping professionals. Therefore, let's take a look at when to refer, how to refer, and to whom to refer.

WHEN TO REFER

There are a number of ways of going about listing and discussing the circumstances under which it is either important or imperative that we make a referral or transferral of someone whom we're involved with as pastoral representatives of the church.

The first and most obvious statement is that we do so anytime we recognize that we're close to or beyond our own limits as these were portrayed in a general manner in the previous section.

There can be any number of more specific statements which can be guidelines for such actions, however. Such a list can never be entirely complete, because other persons with experience in caring can always think of yet another instance, and most of the ones which I shall list can usually be broken down into even greater detail. Several of them also overlap with one another. Many of the guidelines that follow are self-evident, and we can very easily be consciously aware of them. Others involve our own unconscious needs and conflicts, and therefore our perception of our strengths and weaknesses and our perceptions of the personality of the other and the meaning of that person's behavior can be hidden from us. It takes considerable perceptiveness on our part even to be aware of the clues given by certain distressed persons or by our own feelings and behaviors. Even when we become aware that there is probable cause to refer someone, we often feel our own resistance to such actions arising, and we want to keep on trying with this person.

With all of this said, here are a number of guidelines. We would be wise to refer when

1. We simply don't understand what's going on with the other person, why the person feels and behaves as she or he does, even after we've had opportunity to talk with that person about what's going on.

2. We recognize that the person is psychotic or has a tenacious depression.

3. The person is suicidal or is making serious threats against someone else.

4. We suspect that the person may have some physical disorder, may need a physical examination, and/or may need medication.

5. A person is dependent on alcohol or some other chemical substance, including prescription drugs.

6. It has seemed as if this were a person appropriate to work with, but after a while we realize that no change is taking place; we're beginning to feel frustrated and we don't know what else to do.

7. We begin to be anxious too frequently with the person, consciously anxious or feeling ourselves usually being uptight.

8. We find ourselves beginning to shut the person out emotionally.

9. We feel consciously afraid because the person appears to be dangerous to us.

10. We feel angry at the person and aren't clear as to the reason.

11. We are sexually attracted to the person to the degree that our attention to him or her as a distressed human being is consistently (or very frequently) disrupted and our disciplined helping responses (the facilitative condition) are compromised.

12. We want to take care of everything for the person and are not really helping the person to begin to be responsible for himself or herself.

13. We want to guard our relationship with the person and not let anyone else participate in significant helping with her or him.

14. The situation is primarily a family problem and the family pattern of interaction is complex.

15. We begin to see that, even if over a period of time we may be qualified to help, to do so effectively with this person or this family or in this type of situation means too much of our time and energy in the light of our other important responsibilities.

In number 2 above I used the word *psychotic*. This word refers to a variety of forms and intensities of loss of contact with reality and a severe disruption of a person's pattern of thinking and behaving which characterizes severe mental illness. Most of the time, these behaviors can be quite obvious as we observe a person or listen to the person talk about his or her experiences. There may be obvious delusions, usually of *extreme* suspicion, persecution, grandiosity, or references to the person's body: the woman speaking to me in the church office who said she was Queen Elizabeth; the man who looked me right in the eye as he told me of being so completely under the power of the devil that if the devil told him to kill me he wouldn't hesitate a second (this, by the way, was *after* my experience with the man referred to in the Introduction, so I was sitting closer to the door); the man in a hospital who told me that he was dead and didn't have a body any longer. These are obvious! Delusions, of course, may be more subtle than these, but can usually be identified in conversation with someone.

All psychotic persons do not have hallucinations, but hallucinations comprise one of the symptoms of some number of people who are psychotic. The word *hallucination* refers to seeing, hearing, smelling, feeling insects or animals crawling on one, none of which is apparent to anyone else. It does need to be noted, however, that occasionally persons may have one or a few hallucinations without being psychotic (for example, as one behavior within a transient stage of normal grief).

Other significant changes in a person's behavior may indicate psychosis: fairly extreme withdrawal, not speaking at all, an uncharacteristic hyperactivity and inability to sleep normally, saying outrageous things that are out of character with the person prior to this time, a breakdown of the person's usual rational thinking process, a loss of control leading to one impulsive act after another, talking without the usual reasonably logical connections between thoughts or with what the person has just finished saying, or with what someone else has just said, a flood of words almost without ceasing and rarely finishing sentences before going on to other ideas. An observant reader might recognize that most of us do some of these occasionally during temporary periods of distress. But what's being referred to as psychotic is a change in one's pattern of behavior which doesn't seem to be accessible to change by one's own thinking processes or by rational persuasion by another. The psychotic person usually is not able to critique his or her ideas and behaviors in the way he or she might formerly have done or the way in which most people do most of the time. Everyone who works with people in distress with any degree of frequency would do well to read a book on the sources and symptoms and treatment of mental illness.

Another disorder is clinical or psychiatric depression. Depression doesn't refer to having the blues for a couple of days or feeling down today or feeling sad for a longer period of time because of some loss. Unless covered up by other behaviors not always easily identified as being associated with depression, it is characterized by:

1. A rapid increase or decrease in appetite or weight.
2. Excessive or insufficient sleep.
3. Low energy level, tiredness, easily fatigued.
4. Psychomotor agitation and/or retardation.
5. Loss of interest and pleasure in usual activities.
6. Feelings of self-reproach and extreme guilt.
7. Decreased ability to think or concentrate.
8. Recurrent thoughts of death or suicide.

If a person has five or more of these particular symptoms, we may reasonably assume that the person is depressed (Rush). Other symptoms to look for are the appearance of sadness and the person's reporting of feeling sad, a sense of helplessness about doing anything about one's condition or situation, a sense of hopelessness about the future. Beck emphasizes that the *predominant* characteristic of psychiatric depression is a sense of hopelessness (1973, pp. 21–22). He speaks of it in terms of "negative expectations." A depressed person may or may not also be truly psychotic. If psychotic, delusions are common, and also usually accompany the manic episode of bipolar depression (formerly called manic-depressive psychosis).

We need also always keep in mind that certain moods and feelings and behaviors which are dysfunctional to a person, which are unpleasant and frightening to them, and which may often be disturbing or even dangerous to others, which seem to include symptoms of psychosis and/or depression, may not be of psychological origin, or entirely so. They may sometimes be the result of some physiological condition. So if a person's behavior has begun to change in significant ways, it's *always* imperative that the person see a physician.

Finally, we need to remember that some people can be dangerous, not only to themselves, but to others, including us. I truly believed the man who told me that if the devil were to tell him to kill me, he would try to do so. In his condition, he was capable of attempting it. After our conversation, this man remained outside of the office with a family member while his son and I talked. I then called a psychiatric hospital and arranged an admission interview for the next morning. A family member stayed awake with him all night long, and the next day he was hospitalized.

In another tragic incident, a young man entered the office of a large metropolitan church. He asked to see a particular minister. That minister was not in that afternoon. The man went down the hall, found another minister, forced him into an office, and shot and killed him. The young man had a history of psychiatric difficulties, had been in a psychiatric hospital previously, had been attending a young adults group at the church, and the minister for whom he had asked the day of the killing had been "counseling" with him off and on for a fairly long period of time. The young man's behavior that had resulted from his overdependence on the minister for whom he had asked had been, to say the least, unusual and somewhat unrealistic and, for many people, would have been frightening.

I first read of this incident in the daily paper and was stunned and saddened. I had known the young minister when he was in seminary. The event gave rise to an excellent article by Jennings, a seminary graduate and clinical psychologist, "Ministering to the Dangerous" (1986).

My point certainly is not that all psychotic people are dangerous. They are not. Only a very small percentage are (somewhat like nonpsychotic people). But there are behaviors which we need to pay attention to, and we cannot allow ourselves to believe that we can be a primary counselor to them. We can, and should, of course, be pastors and friends, with a type of caution which is appropriate under certain conditions. A major way in which this caution is exhibited is in our doing all that we possibly can to see that such a person is under immediate psychiatric care.

HOW TO REFER

Barriers to Referral

There are at least three realistic barriers to referral.

The first is when we are living in a rural area or very small town where there are very few, if any, other psychotherapeutic professionals who live right in our area. Referral becomes somewhat more difficult, though seldom impossible, especially for the elderly and the poor. Questions to be raised are:

How great is the person(s)' need? Can we contribute something significant to the person(s) or can we not?

If necessary, how skillful are we in helping the person(s) to see the degree of the need, and make some sacrifice themselves to go to the person or place where there is the greatest likelihood of the need being met? Are we willing ourselves to make the effort necessary to assist in the referral/transferral process?

I remember in my first parish a poverty-stricken, illiterate, elderly couple. The wife desperately needed a type of operation that could be done in only a few hospitals in the state (and done free in only two or three). I made arrangements by phone through the chaplain's office in one of the hospitals located three and a half hours' driving time from our rural area. These arrangements were for the surgery and hospitalization as well as for a place for the husband to stay without cost. I drove them to the hospital, helped her get settled in the hospital and him into his room, and drove back, about twelve hours for the entire trip, little enough investment for the seriousness and urgency of the need. Arrangements were made for someone else to bring them home a week or ten days later. It was all possible and it was worth it.

Counseling and psychiatric care, other than hospitalization, is often difficult to locate. But even in these cases, there are beginning to be counselors in smaller towns, and psychiatrists, clinical and counseling psychologists, psychiatric social workers, and mental health centers in very small cities. The highways are usually good, and many people are already accustomed to driving thirty minutes to a couple of hours for things of lesser importance. For the poor and elderly, we can organize car pools.

A somewhat more formidable barrier to referral is when we ourselves really don't want to do it. This resistance may be conscious or unconscious on our part. Either way, we truly believe that *we* are the *one* person the other needs, even though we are somewhat aware that one or more of the criteria for referral mentioned above are present. To put it crassly, we're saying, "I'm this person's (this family's) only hope." This is usually a delusion of somewhat grandiose proportions, and it's very rarely true. When we find ourselves beginning to feel this way, it's usually a sign that referral is *definitely* called for. We then need to find our own counselor and talk about this reaction of ours. (You had better believe that I've done this myself, although unfortunately I waited rather late in my career to begin. The psychiatrists' questions to me have always been in words more or less like the following: "What need of *yours* is so strong that it was being met in a relationship where you were supposed to be working to see that the other person's needs were being attended to?" From there, we got down to specifics.)

A third obstacle in referral is when the other person doesn't want to talk with anyone else—for examination, evaluation, or counseling. This often thrusts us back to dealing with obstacle number two, as the person tells us how much we've meant to him or her, what wonderful people and helpers we are, how understanding. They don't want to have to start all over with someone else. Often, they say they won't. We begin to feel forced into the position of beginning to think that if the person doesn't work with me, she or he won't be in touch with anyone else, so—once again, "I'm the person's only hope." We must be as rigorously honest as we can be *with ourselves first,* and then with the other person. How do we assess the person, her or his situation, and our ability to help? Can we recognize that we simply *are not* capable of assisting the type of change that needs to take place in the person's or family's life, or do we even have serious doubts about it? In these instances, we don't contribute to the person(s) involved by continuing to be the only or primary caregiver. We must then explain to the person or persons that our genuine concern for their well-being leads us to recommend that they see someone else who will really be able to help them more effectively than we can. We emphasize, if it be the case, that we shall continue to be their friend, their pastor, and that we shall stay in contact and support them. If the person or persons refuse the referral, we need to be firm in our commitment to them as friend, lay minister, or pastor, but also be clear that we can't and won't be the only one or primary one they call upon for the resolution of critical life problems.

The Process of Referring

Some people initially respond to the suggestion that they talk with someone else rather than us with the feeling of being rejected, believing that we don't want to talk with them anymore, and/or that they must be worse off than they had thought they were.

Therefore, the process of referring takes time and sensitivity and skill. It's not something we do in the last couple of minutes of a conversation, snapping off, "Oh, by the way, you need to talk with Dr. Edmonds. Here's his phone number," or "It sounds as if you need to make an appointment at Family Guidance rather than talking with me about this situation."

Clinebell (1984, pp. 316–20), Charry (1981), and Oglesby (1978, chapter 3) give very helpful and detailed guidelines for the referral process. As soon as we begin to recognize that referral or transferral may be necessary, we begin to respond in ways that might help the person(s) grasp that even though we seem to understand them and their situation, we're not the most competent person to assist with the type of problem or issue they are presenting to us. This involves our communication both of how we perceive what they are describing and of our own particular limitations. We work with them to help them clarify their own understanding of their situation and how it is that we are not really the best facilitator of its resolution. We then indicate that there are others who are specially trained and who have experience in the particular area and discuss how these persons (or agencies or institutions) function to assist in a condition or situation like theirs. If we ourselves have any doubt as to whether the person needs to be referred, or if we don't know where to suggest that the person might go, we need to seek consultation ourselves from a specialist who can help us with our decision and with the process.

We express our caring for the person or persons that we are seeking to refer and assure them that for them to see someone else doesn't mean that we quit caring or that we no longer have pastoral conversations with them. Then, at some point, we ask them how they would feel about seeing the particular professional or going to a certain agency. A few people will now respond immediately or fairly quickly that it's something that makes sense to them and that they will do it. They're grateful for the type of help that we have given them.

Others, of course, and usually for understandable reasons, will express their resistance or reluctance. We spend time with them, assisting them in expressing any feelings of rejection and hurt they have toward us, any irritation, their anxiety about themselves or about beginning over again with someone whom they don't know. This stage of the procedure cannot be rushed. If their condition or situation allows it, we might even have another conversation with them a day or two later. We need to be careful that our own anxiety doesn't lead us to abbreviate this discussion or that the others' resistance in whatever form (anger or emotional seduction) doesn't trigger our fear or our need to be needed and lead us to renege on our recommendation of referral.

Many people will complete the process by taking the next helpful step, going to the appropriate referral resource. We reassure the persons of our continued concern. We arrange follow-up steps with them by asking them to give us a call or stop by after the first appointment with someone else, or, if hospitalized, assure them that we will visit.

Some people will say that they will go to the person or place referred and not do so. Others will make it clear that they don't intend to do so. If they can't talk with us, they're not going to talk with anyone. That is their decision. We have done what we could in their best interests, and they have refused to take these steps for themselves.

WHERE TO REFER

Nothing is more helpful than a referral to a person, agency, institution, program, or the appropriate combination of these where a person or family realizes that here is the place and person(s) who know how to work with them in a way that some or many of their important needs are probably going to be met.

Few things are more frustrating for needy persons than to have been talking to someone and have this person whom they've known or gotten to know refer them on to someone else or some other place which they then discover is *not* the appropriate place to be. So they must then go on to someone else. This process only tends to increase the frustration of the person who is already anxious and distressed, probably angering them, leaving many of them with additional resistance to any other referral.

A significant part of competent referring is to know well, and as much as possible personally, as many as possible of the resources of one's own geographical area: different types of professionals and their areas of specialty and/or greatest competence; what certain agencies do and do not do and what they cost; various programs, their location and meeting times, who operates them, who's eligible for them, whether there are fees, and if so, how much they are; what hospitals specialize in what types of disorders; the details of commitment proceedings to psychiatric hospitals, etc.

The second major part of making the referral is getting to know sufficiently well the relevant details of a particular person's or family's condition and situation so that the person or family and the referral resources can be matched with confidence.

Since relatively few people know everything, we may sometimes not be certain as to the proper referral. Therefore, with any given person or family, we may have to do additional research. I've often picked up the phone while the person or persons I've been talking with are still there to make from one to three calls gathering information so that the best match may be made between them and one or more resources.

Certainly every clergy and lay pastoral caregiver needs to realize that all physicians are not psychiatrists and are not necessarily fully up-to-date on antidepressants and antipsychotic medications, that psychiatrists are physicians and that many very competent psychiatrists don't do group therapy or family therapy; that psychiatric social workers cannot hospitalize persons as psychiatrists can do, but often are the very ones to do group or family therapy; that all social workers are not therapists; that clinical psychologists are specialists in evaluation and usually do individual therapy in a competent manner, but that they may or may not do family therapy, in many states cannot prescribe medication, nor, in most states, directly hospitalize persons, although in a few states they are permitted to do so; that all psychologists are not clinical or counseling psychologists and therefore do other sorts of things entirely.

It's probably appropriate for many lay visitors to check with the ordained clergy of the congregation concerning the referral of the person the lay caregiver has been visiting. For example, the lay visitor might not have known how to handle a particular situation or question that has arisen in discussion with someone in the hospital or with the family in grief. He or she may merely consult with the clergy as to how to respond more effectively to the sick or bereaved. Sometimes it may be useful for the ordained pastor to make a visit to the person or family in question. The layperson may discover other referral sources in discussion with the minister and be the one to discuss the referral with the person he or she has been visiting. Perhaps it would be important for the sick or bereaved or the distressed person to have a conversation with the most competent person on the staff in pastoral care in order to see whether or not the staff member might become the primary helper or whether a referral needs to be made. Occasionally the minister may become the primary crisis counselor when the layperson is untrained in that area.

All of this is said in the realization that in a number of congregations there are members who know more about some aspects of these matters than do the clergy, so a layperson may recommend a particular physician or counselor or agency, or the ordained minister may often consult with members of the congregation who themselves are in the helping professions or who know about agencies and programs which the clergyperson is not aware of.

There may be times when a distressed person or family doesn't require the particular services that can be offered by a psychiatrist or clinical or counseling psychologist, but yet the nature of the problem is such that they would need a counselor with the time and specialized training beyond that of most clergy in local congregations. At the same time, there may be very good reasons for the person(s) to be working intensively with a counselor who is well educated in the various theological disciplines or even who is ordained. Parish clergy need to be aware that in many locations there are pastoral counseling centers where such specialists are performing their ministry. They are in almost every large city, many small cities, and increasingly in larger and a few smaller towns. They're usually, though not always, interdenominational. No one would really expect them all to be of the same quality, so the responsible clergy or layperson would want to check on their work before making a referral, just as we'd do with any other professional.

It's obvious that appropriate referring is a team effort. When this takes place within the congregation, the designated ordained clergy (the only one, the senior one, the one assigned to this area) is usually the coordinator of the team. The coordinator is one who knows many but not all of the referral resources and who continually draws upon the knowledge of members of the parish.

Two of the most important things any clergyperson can do upon coming to a new parish is (1) to find out what persons in the congregation are members of the helping professions, whether they are in independent practice or related to an agency, institution, or program; get to know them personally and then use their expertise in whatever ways are helpful in the total caring program of the church (I do understand that there are many congregations who have no such professional persons in their membership and constituency, the case for me in my first three appointments. In this situation, check with nearby congregations in which such professionals are found); and (2) to discover as many as possible of the other community resources; get to know personally as many helping professionals as she or he can; visit agencies; make appointments with directors of programs, halfway houses, etc. Concentrating this activity in the early weeks and months of one's ministry in a new parish will pay tremendous dividends in the long-term future. These dividends will not be confined only to the pastoral caring activities of the minister and the congregation. There will be in addition an increase of understanding and goodwill on the part of an increasing number of professionals and the agencies and programs which they represent.

REFERENCES

Aaron L. Beck, *The Diagnosis and Management of Depression* (Philadelphia: University of Pennsylvania Press, 1973).

Dana Charry, *Mental Health Skills for the Clergy* (Valley Forge, Pa.: Judsen Press, 1981), chapter 2, "Referral."

Howard Clinebell, *Basic Types of Pastoral Care and Counseling* (Revised and enlarged) (Nashville: Abingdon Press, 1984), chapter 12, "Referral Counseling."

Floyd L. Jennings, "Ministering to the Dangerous," *Circuit Rider* (November–December 1986) (Nashville: United Methodist Publishing House): pp. 5–7.

William Oglesby, *Referral in Pastoral Counseling* (Nashville: Abingdon Press, 1978).

John Rush, M.D., Lecture given at the University of Texas Southwestern Medical School, Dallas, Texas.

Karl A. Slaikeu, *Crisis Intervention: A Handbook for Practice and Research* (Boston: Allyn and Bacon, 1984), pp. 91–93.

David K. Switzer, *The Minister As Crisis Counselor* (Revised and enlarged) (Nashville: Abingdon Press, 1986), pp. 103–08.

EPILOGUE

Bringing this book to a close has been precisely like attempting to bring almost every chapter within it to an end. Each time, an additional type of situation would come to mind, as would additional illustrations and additional considerations that are important for pastoral caregivers to be aware of.

The chapters and the book as a whole can have no "conclusions," the end, there is no more. It's like pastoral work itself. At the end of each day, none of us can say, "I'm through with the work. I've done it all. There is no more." We do stop; we need rest and reflection and recreation and other relationships. But we haven't completed our caregiving. We remember those whom we didn't get to see. We replay in our minds some of the conversations we've had with persons and realize that there is something else that we need to say to the persons or another area to investigate tomorrow or the next day. And tomorrow night and the evening after, it's the same. There's no final word. Likewise, this book stops. But there's no final word here, either. There can be no adequate summary, and there certainly is no conclusion. Happily, there is the word *epilogue*. It's from the Greek: *epi*, in addition to, and *logos*, word, "an additional word." An epilogue may contain some summary statements, and it's been used traditionally as the last statement in a book of a certain kind or the final speech in a play, but it doesn't solve the mystery, wrap everything up, or nail it down. It assumes that that which has taken place will go on.

In pastoral care over the years we begin to note some similarities in people's behaviors and relationships and motives and similarities in the situations in which we find ourselves in with people. But also each time there is a uniqueness to which it's essential that we be alert and to which we respond. Then periodically there arises the startlingly different. Our ability to respond helpfully again and again in the "common" pastoral emergencies and even in the unusual and the new is always based upon our increasing understanding of the facilitative conditions of all helping relationships and their becoming increasingly a part of our lives, the natural expressions of who we are (chapter 2). Connected essentially with the growing naturalness of the expression of these conditions is our continued growth as persons, learning about ourselves, the person we bring to others in their distress and need, and learning from all of the others to whom and with whom we minister (chapters 1 and 2). Of course, our commitment to ourselves and through ourselves to others will lead us to continue our pastoral education through reading hungrily about all human situations which offer pastoral care opportunities and by attending seminars and workshops which contribute to our understanding of persons and their interactions and their situations and to our knowledge and skills in helping. Finally, and again essentially, for ourselves and for the others, we need to stay in touch with and constantly recommit ourselves to the God who calls us to care for others, who is the continuing "additional Word," and the only final Word, Alpha and Omega.